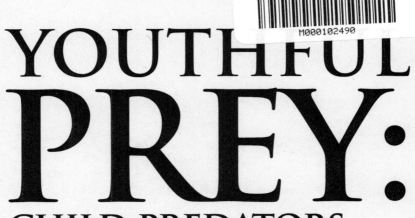

YOUTHFUL PREY:
CHILD PREDATORS WHO KILL

By Carol Anne Davis

First published in paperback 2008
by Pennant Books

Text copyright © 2008 by Carol Anne Davis

British Library Cataloguing-in-Publication Data:
A catalogue record for this book is available on request from
The British Library

ISBN 978-1-906015-17-6

Pennant Books' True Crime series is edited by Paul Woods.

Design & Typeset by Envy Design Ltd

Printed and bound in Great Britain by Creative Print & Design, Blaina, Wales

Pennant Books
A division of Pennant Publishing Ltd
PO Box 5675
London W1A 3FB

www.pennantbooks.com

YOUTHFUL PREY:
CHILD PREDATORS WHO KILL

ABOUT THE AUTHOR

Carol Anne Davis was born in Dundee, moved to Edinburgh in her twenties and now lives in south-west England. She left school at fifteen and was everything from an artist's model to an editorial assistant before going to university. Her Master of the Arts degree included criminology and was followed by a postgraduate diploma in adult and community education.

A full-time writer since graduating, her crime novels *Sob Story*, *Kiss It Away*, *Noise Abatement*, *Safe as Houses* and *Shrouded* have been described as chillingly realistic for their portrayals of sex and death.

She is also the author of the true crime books *SADISTIC KILLERS: Profiles of Pathological Predators*, *COUPLES WHO KILL: Profiles of Deviant Duos*, *CHILDREN WHO KILL: Profiles of Preteen and Teenage Killers* and *WOMEN WHO KILL: Profiles of Female Serial Killers*.

Carol's website is located at www.carolannedavis.co.uk.

For Ian

CONTENTS

Acknowledgements   ix
Introduction   xi

PART ONE: BRITISH PAEDOPHILES
1. Ian Huntley   2
2. Roy Whiting   27
3. Thomas Hamilton   41
4. Howard Hughes   54
5. Leslie Bailey   62
6. Raymond Morris   79
7. Brian Field   88
8. Relatives Who Kill   94
9. Mentally Handicapped Paedophiles   96
10. Wrongful Conviction   101
11. Yesterday's Paedophiles   112

PART TWO: AMERICAN PAEDOPHILES
12. Westley Dodd   126
13. Jeffrey Rissley   139
14. Thomas Soria   143
15. Richard Davis   151
16. Arthur Bishop   157
17. Richard Clark   163

PART THREE: WORLDWIDE PAEDOPHILES
18. Marc Dutroux   170
19. Javed Iqbal   181
20. Clifford Olson   184
21. Gordon Northcott   203
22. Female Paedophiles   208
23. Teenage Paedophiles   213

PART FOUR: NEUTRALISING PAEDOPHILES
24. Treatment Options   228
25. Protecting Children   240

Appendix: Useful Information   253
Select Bibliography   255

ACKNOWLEDGEMENTS

I'm deeply indebted to retired detective Ray Gardner for answering my questions about child molesters. Ray worked at Scotland Yard for twenty years on the Flying Squad, the Regional Crime Squad, the Serious Crime Squad, and, for the last ten years of his service, the Paedophile Unit. During his service he received eighteen commissioner's commendations. He spent many years as an undercover officer, posing as a paedophile and securing numerous convictions. He has also taught at international law enforcement courses on the subject of paedophilia.

I'm also grateful to former detective and true crime author Richard Kirby, who spent many years with the Serious Crime Squad and the Flying Squad, for his forthright views on the heinous crime of child murder.

Finally, thanks to Thomas Bell for sharing his experience of life on the Sex Offenders Register.

INTRODUCTION

What kind of childhood produces a paedophile? And why do some paedophiles seduce their young victims whilst others prefer to kill?

Many paedophiles were sexually abused as children and go on to molest children of a similar age – some authorities state that approximately one in eight abuse victims will go on to become abusers, whilst others believe that the figure is as high as fifty percent. But this isn't the full story, as numerous child-abuse victims *don't* grow up to feel an attraction to prepubescent bodies and don't pass the abuse on.

A failure to bond with other people during the first twelve years of life is another predisposing factor. Seventy percent of paedophiles have admitted that they didn't have a single close friend during these crucial personality-forming years. Most of the paedophiles profiled here endured such a lonely state, often rejected by their peers and even by their own siblings. As such, they grew up unable to empathise with children, and consequently were able to abuse them without guilt.

Some of the paedophiles within these pages initially seduced or coerced their prey, only later escalating to murder. Ian Huntley had lovers (actually statutory rape victims) who were as young as thirteen, before he murdered two of his teaching-assistant girlfriend's pupils. Raymond Morris repeatedly interfered with his three-year-old niece before raping and murdering girls that he abducted from the streets. Seduction and coercion didn't quell the increasing rage in these men, a rage which started during their unhappy and alienated childhoods, burgeoning in adulthood as their marriages or careers floundered and failed.

Some of these men, such as Dunblane's Thomas Hamilton, were *fixated* child abusers who had no sexual interest in other adults. His molestation sometimes included minor sadism but (unlike Thomas Soria, whose case is also profiled) he was not a fully fledged *mysoped* or sexual sadist. Soria's hatred for young girls was so extreme that it extended to mutilation before and after death. Thankfully, this type of molester is in the minority as is the *regressed* offender, a man or woman in an age-appropriate relationship who has no history of paedophilia, but who molests a child during a period of extreme stress.

Despite the stereotype, these paedophiles aren't dirty old men. Most are in their twenties or thirties at the height of their offending, and many have been married or have had age-appropriate relationships. Some are teenagers, only a few years older than their victims. The majority are of normal intelligence, though the ones profiled here had limited formal education, leaving school at the earliest opportunity to escape playground bullies and to become financially independent of their working-class families. (Paedophiles who seduce rather than kill have much more varied educational and social backgrounds, as delineated in the fourth part of this book.)

As ever, the information found in the profiles has come from a variety of sources – everything from court transcripts to the killers' own diaries.

British, American, Canadian, Belgian and Pakistani cases are explored here, as this is a worldwide problem. It's also a centuries-old problem, as the short chapter on historical cases illustrates. Most paedophiles are male, but the chapter on female paedophiles examines women who sexually abuse children. There is also a chilling look at wrongful convictions, specifically the murder of Lesley Molseed in October 1975 – finally solved in 2007 with the conviction of Ronald Castree – for which an innocent man, Stefan Kiszko, served sixteen years.

The penultimate chapter outlines treatment options. As most of these men and women will eventually be freed, society has a duty to prevent them preying on further victims. It also includes testimony from a detective who lived undercover for years as a paedophile, and secured numerous convictions. Finally, there is a chapter on protecting children from seductive paedophiles, which contains advice from child safety experts.

PART ONE
BRITISH PAEDOPHILES

CHAPTER ONE

IAN KEVIN HUNTLEY

After preying on teenage girls for many years, twenty-eight-year-old Huntley became a double murderer in 2002 when he lured ten-year-olds Holly Wells and Jessica Chapman into his Cambridgeshire home.

Bullied

Ian was born on 31 January 1974, at Grimsby Maternity Hospital. His father Kevin was a gas fitter, whilst his mother Lynda was employed by a printing firm. Both eighteen, the couple married when Lynda was three months pregnant. Kevin immediately moved in with Lynda and her parents as they couldn't afford their own home.

A few months later, they moved with baby Ian into a rented house in Immingham, a few miles north of Grimsby. On 16 August 1975, they had a second son, who they christened Wayne. By now, eighteen-month-old Ian was going down with numerous cold and stomach bugs and cried constantly. Later he developed asthma. The next few years were financially difficult for the family and Kevin frequently had to work overtime to support the four of them – acquaintances considered him to be a good husband, but a very strict dad.

Ian was very quiet and was bullied when he went to school. Some of the other children mocked his curly hair so he had it cut short and wore it flattened, a style that he would maintain into adulthood. Desperate to be liked, he made up grandiose stories and wept when no one believed

2

him, or when they refused to pick him for the football team. Later he began to invent stories about other pupils, inciting trouble. He was clearly becoming more disturbed. Another pupil, who he occasionally played computer games with, noted that he seemed terrified of his father but close to his timid mother. He increasingly hated sports and would get out his inhaler before each gym lesson, claiming that he was having an asthma attack.

Alleged sexual abuse

At age eleven, he went to Healing Comprehensive School where the bullying intensified. He was hit and kicked on a daily basis, and was so traumatised that his grades slipped. During this period he told various acquaintances that he was being sexually abused by an adult male – the thin, lonely child would have been the ideal victim for a paedophile.

By the time Ian was thirteen, the bullying was so bad that he was transferred to another school, Immingham Comprehensive. But bullies can always identify the child who is different, so the cruelty went on. The teenager even joined the Boy Scouts in the hope of making friends, but the curriculum was sports-based and made his asthma worse. His father persuaded him to join the Air Training Corps, hoping that this would instil a little machismo, but the sensitive young boy had little interest in the military training, though he loved the planes. He began to spend hours in his room, making model aeroplanes and painting them before hanging them from his ceiling. He also read plane-spotting magazines.

Beaten

At age thirteen, he came home unexpectedly and found his father in bed with a sixteen-year-old girl, one of the family's babysitters. His father jumped out of bed and battered him repeatedly, warning him not to tell anyone. The boy kept the knowledge to himself as long as he could, but felt that he was betraying his beloved mother and so eventually confided in her. She immediately left home, taking Ian and eleven-year-old Wayne with her, but returned after a few weeks.

By now Kevin was drinking heavily and he became more violent towards Ian. He blamed the unhappy teenager for his failing marriage and often refused to speak to him for months at a time.

First suicide attempt

At fourteen, Ian seduced a twelve-year-old and lost his virginity. Reasonably good-looking and superficially sensitive, he briefly charmed the younger girl. She doubtless thought that it was cool to have an older boyfriend, and he seemed intelligent as he was good at computer games. But she soon sensed his insecurity and need for control and backed off, whereupon the heartbroken teenager took an overdose. He swallowed an entire box of paracetamol that he found in the family's bathroom cabinet, and lay down on his bed to die. His mother discovered him there, semiconscious, and he was rushed to Grimsby Hospital to have his stomach pumped out. (If he'd been discovered much later he would have suffered liver damage, one of the side effects of a paracetamol overdose, which eventually becomes irreversible and can result in an agonisingly protracted death.)

He now took up weightlifting in the hope that he'd be able to build some muscle and start defending himself. He also bought an air rifle, something which made him feel powerful and in control. Thomas Hamilton, profiled later in this section, similarly bought an airgun as a teenager in an attempt to feel less inadequate.

Work experience

Though Ian Huntley was reasonably bright and gained five GCSEs, he understandably hated school and left at the earliest opportunity, hoping to reinvent himself. But he didn't have the qualifications or the staying power to build a career.

He was a salesman for a few weeks but hated the rejection, so he took a job filleting fish. But he immediately alienated his fellow workers by telling them that he was a trained pilot and that he'd soon be a millionaire. More realistic about their own futures, they despised him and made him feel even worse about himself.

Huntley failed at job after job, sometimes leaving before he was sacked. He'd sign on the dole for a few months and gradually rebuild his emotional resources, then apply for another manual position, only to find that he hated it as much as the last. He stacked shelves at Kwik Save for a while, and then helped assemble toilets. But he always had Friday on his mind. Every weekend he'd dress to impress, have a few drinks in the pub then make his way to the local nightspots. There, he'd chat up very young or very drunk girls, inventing a good career with future prospects. He was a reasonably accomplished liar and the naïve or inexperienced fell for his patter, often going to bed with him.

By now, he'd left home and rented an inexpensive flat, but he was never to enjoy security of tenure. Within weeks of taking up residence, he had irate parents demanding that he stop dating their underage daughters. The neighbours were also concerned at the number of girls who arrived at his flat in their school uniforms. Afraid that he'd be beaten up, he moved to another address, something he'd continue to do at least every six months – paedophiles often move house, workplace and even town, in a bid to keep one step ahead of the law.

To casual strangers he appeared successful, being well-dressed, clean and well-spoken. But his flat was filthy and he lived off crisps and takeaways. He also smoked heavily and went drinking in the evenings, so he never managed to save any money. It was difficult for him to plan for the future when he was so afraid of the present, unable to find a job that he could tolerate or a girl who could cope with his frequent mood swings and increasing propensity for violence.

The world was a frightening place for Huntley and he increasingly made it a terrifying place for the girls who crossed his path.

Statutory rape

The eighteen-year-old continued to date girls of fourteen or fifteen, quickly lowering their inhibitions by giving them large quantities of alcopops. Some of these girls willingly had sex with him, but this was statutory rape as they were below the age of consent. All went well whilst they bought into his fantasies – but if they dared to question his worldview, asking why a millionaire was living in a filthy bedsit, he turned nasty and slapped them or threw them against the wall. Aware that their parents wouldn't have approved of their drinking or consorting with an older man, most of these girls kept silent about their ordeal.

A second overdose

Huntley's relationships continued to be understandably short-lived, but he was devastated by each break-up – and equally upset when his parents split up again. He began to overeat and his normally slender frame ballooned to fourteen stone. Still only eighteen, he took another overdose and was again rushed to hospital. He believed in the supernatural and so he thought he would be reborn into a peaceful afterlife. On his release from hospital he lost weight, still getting by on junk food but keeping his calories down by not eating so much of it.

Harassing behaviour

When he was nineteen he got a job in the same Heinz factory as his parents, but remained a solitary figure, largely ignored by the other employees because of his boastful behaviour. He dressed neatly and formally, in an environment where most people wore casual clothing; from his perspective, the workplace was yet another of his not-so-happy hunting grounds and he was determined to impress. In reality, he was a nuisance to the female staff, and at least one went to the management and explained that he'd been sexually harassing her.

A new stepmother

After living alone for a while, Lynda Huntley began a lesbian relationship with Julie, aged twenty-one. Ian got on well with his new stepmother – they shared an interest in computer games – though he continued to hate his father, who was now cohabiting with a woman called Sandra. Ian's own relationships remained violent and unstable, and his mental health declined yet again.

He remained impulsive and lawless. In October 1993, he was

convicted of riding an unlicensed and uninsured motorbike and was fined £250.

A failed marriage

In late 1994, Ian's spirits revived when he met eighteen-year-old Claire Evans, who was on the rebound from another relationship. They married the following January, three days before his twenty-first birthday, opting for a low-key ceremony at the local registrar's office. Doubtless Huntley was afraid to advertise the wedding, knowing that some of his exes might try to warn Claire of his promiscuity and violence.

The couple took up residence in their new flat, where the bridegroom soon reverted to type by trying to control his teenage wife's every movement. He even refused to let her visit her parents, whom she loved. When she insisted that she had to go out he beat her up, locked the door and pocketed the key. Ironically, like most violent and controlling men, he was terrified of losing his partner – so when she said that the marriage was over he faked an epileptic fit, somehow managing to froth at the mouth. The frightened teenager phoned for an ambulance, but when the paramedics arrived they said that Huntley was fine.

Shortly after this, Claire fled and phoned for her father to come and collect her. She told Ian's brother, Wayne, about what she'd been through and he genuinely sympathised. Wayne had done well at school and now had a good job as an RAF engineer; Claire found him to be caring and supportive. They began a relationship and, when it became serious, Wayne told Ian the truth.

Devastated

Though he'd almost literally driven his wife into another man's arms, Huntley was devastated by what he saw as a joint betrayal. His already faltering self-esteem plummeting, he went to the doctor and was prescribed antidepressants. He gave up work again and refused to speak to Wayne for the next two years. His pain was intensified by the fact that Claire and Wayne had a loving relationship, which eventually resulted in marriage. Wayne had the status and stability which Ian craved.

Lay people often ask why one sibling becomes a killer and the other becomes an upstanding pillar of the community. The reason can partly be found in the fact that most families treat their children very differently. Thus, the son who is intrinsically shy may be bullied by a macho father, whilst his sports-mad brother is praised and shown respect. In other instances parents see resemblances to other relatives, and the child who looks like a hated in-law becomes a scapegoat, whilst the child who takes after the parent is the clear favourite. As psychologist Oliver James has noted, "The changes in the emotional state of each parent, and in the marriage between one child and the next, combine with the biographical bric-a-brac that each parent loads separately onto each child, creating a unique psychological environment every time." (His landmark book, *They F*** You Up*, is a must-read for any adults who don't wish to parent as they themselves were parented.)

Further suicide attempts

In June 1995, the newly separated, twenty-one-year-old Huntley began dating yet another fifteen-year-old. He continued to both turn his anger outwards, directing it at young women, and to turn it inwards, making another two attempts at ending his life. Always living on the edge of a breakdown, he wasn't resourceful enough to read up on how to successfully commit suicide, always found in time to have his stomach pumped out. That said, these weren't half-hearted attempts designed to win him sympathy – he was unconscious by the time that he was found.

His itinerant working life continued, and by 1996 he was selling scratch cards from door to door for a local charity. He perked up when he heard that one of his supervisors had a fifteen-year-old daughter, and soon managed to wrangle an invitation to her home. The supervisor liked the cleancut, polite young man and initially approved of his relationship with her daughter. When the girl turned sixteen and left school, she went to live with him.

As usual, now that he'd snared his prey, Huntley dropped the Mr Nice Guy act and began to beat her and to undermine her confidence. He stopped her from seeing her family and got her a job in a seafood factory. She hated the work but he insisted that she stay there to support them – he was deeply unhappy and, as ever, it was a case of misery liking company.

Burglary

That same year, he burgled the home of a female neighbour, stealing several hundred pounds worth of cash and jewellery. She suspected him of the robbery and, when questioned by the police, he admitted the offence. The neighbour had a feeling that he'd invaded her property out of a sense of 'badness', that his primary motive wasn't to steal. She may well have been right – Huntley, the girlfriend beater and pathological liar, had no respect for other people's boundaries and wanted to invade their lives.

Realising that her life had become both joyless and frightening, his latest teenage cohabitee left him. Almost immediately, he began an affair with a young-looking nineteen-year-old who was on the rebound from another relationship. Like many damaged people, he felt completely adrift whenever he was single – but he also couldn't bear the thought of sharing love and attention with a baby, so he ended the affair when she told him she might be pregnant, screaming at her to leave him alone. (Thankfully it was a false alarm, though he'd later impregnate a younger teenager, exiting her life before the child was born.)

Rape

In January 1998, Huntley was taken to court on the burglary charge but, for some unspecified reason, the prosecution offered no evidence and the case collapsed. A sensible man would have thanked his lucky stars and vowed to keep out of trouble, but the deeply disturbed young man wasn't capable of being sensible. Within months, he'd had sex with at least four underage girls, sometimes locking them in his bedroom, hitting and belittling them. He soon graduated to rape . . .

On Saturday 16 May 1998, he went out drinking heavily and ended up in Grimsby's Hollywood nightclub. As usual he was on the look-out for vulnerable women, zeroing in on an eighteen-year-old blonde girl

9

who'd also had a lot to drink. He danced next to her in a very outlandish way to get her attention but she ignored him, realising that he was a prat.

An ordinary man would have let her go, but Huntley needed to control someone in order to feel better about himself. Whilst forcing sex on a girl or young woman, he felt authoritative, important. Without such symbolic actions he was merely a casual labourer who no one liked.

He waited until the girl left the club at 2am, then quietly followed her to a cycle path known as Gas Alley. Grabbing her throat, he wrestled her to the ground, punched her in the face and tore off her underwear. His features were so contorted with hate that she feared she might die. She tried to scream, but he put his hand across her mouth and kept it there as he raped her. He said that he'd kill her if she told anyone.

Sadism tends to decrease for a while after orgasm, and Huntley was no exception. Within seconds of climaxing, he tried to act as if this were a consensual sex session, chatting to the traumatised teenager as if they'd just made love. Waiting until he'd rolled off of her, she jumped to her feet and raced shakily home to her parents, who promptly phoned the police.

The following day, Ian Huntley's description appeared in the *Grimsby Evening Telegraph*. For five days he waited for detectives to come and arrest him. Then, probably keen to exert control, he gave himself up. It's likely that he said the sex was consensual and that they had a few hours of shared history – his dancing next to her at Hollywood had been captured on CCTV. He was remanded in custody for several days, during which time he was a nervous wreck, and then bailed.

A fortnight later the police dropped the case for lack of evidence. Huntley wept copiously for hours, but assumed that he could now get back to normal – or whatever passed for normal in such a predatory individual. But most of his acquaintances believed that he was guilty of rape and he was convinced that he was the talk of the town, adding to his already rampant paranoia. Desperate to be part of a partnership, he began to propose to woman after woman on their second or third date. Recognising that these weren't the actions of a sane man – that he wanted *anyone* rather than a woman with their particular qualities – they backed off and he felt rejected again.

By now he hated his father so much that he didn't want to be a Huntley, so he began to use his mother's maiden name of Nixon. Doubtless this also helped him distance himself from the many statutory rapes that he'd committed under his birth name.

At some stage during this chaotic lifestyle he acquired a dog, a beautiful Alsatian-cross bitch called Sadie. Men who want to project a macho front tend to buy pit bull terriers, Rottweilers or Alsatians (although, in fairness to Huntley, the Alsatian is also the dog that genuine animal lovers tend to choose).

Younger victims

As the millennium approached, Huntley turned to ever younger girls, sexually interfering with a twelve-year-old. He began to get a reputation in Grimsby as a paedophile and enraged locals smashed his windows and kicked in his door, causing him to move house yet again. In late February 1999, he went to a nightclub on one of his weekly prowling sessions and met the girlish looking, twenty-two-year-old Maxine Carr.

Brand new girlfriend

Maxine, born 16 February 1977, was the kind of girl that abusive men like Ian Huntley can pick out of a crowd as ideal victims. She'd battled with anorexia for years, and so had the pale skin of the perpetually undernourished and the hunched posture of someone with low self-esteem. Abandoned by her father as a two-year-old, she was desperate to win the attention of every man who crossed her path.

All of her previous boyfriends had finished with her, unable to stand her daytime neediness and nightly flirting with strangers. She'd get so drunk that she'd raise her top and bra to show off the tattoo on one of her breasts. Maxine was still making a living from gutting fish – but Ian told her that he'd given up this unskilled work to become an insurance rep. The lost girl was impressed, seeing him as someone who was going up in the world. Within weeks she'd moved into his unkempt flat and become the perfect housewife, cleaning the place for hour after hour, a veritable Stepford Wife.

As soon as she was living with him, Huntley showed his true colours,

11

becoming obsessively controlling. He wanted to know where she was for every hour of every day. A healthy woman would have fled – but Maxine saw this behaviour as caring. For the first time, someone was interested in her, and she fell hopelessly in love.

In an ideal world, these two desperately lonely and inadequate people would have shored each other up, but the reality was very different. Deep down, Huntley despised himself and despised anyone who claimed to love him. So he began to phone Maxine from his work, telling her that the house wasn't clean enough, that she was a stupid cow, a lazy bitch, a slut. In turn she wept, then fled to her mother's house in Grimsby and went out clubbing. She'd get very drunk and flirt outrageously with strange men, sometimes having sex with them in the car park after the nightclub shut. After a few days, Ian would persuade her to come back and they'd have a brief honeymoon period, then he'd call her names and the whole debacle would start again.

Suicide attempts

Maxine would make two serious suicide attempts during her years with Ian, and ended up close to death on one occasion – spending several days in hospital in November 2000. Upset at the thought of losing her, he left his latest temporary girlfriend and rushed to her bedside to proclaim his undying love. When she was released, they moved to Scunthorpe, to make a new start – but within days they were fighting again and, after one beating too many, she prepared to leave.

Engaged

Huntley now suggested that they get engaged, knowing that a ring was irresistible to a conventional girl like Maxine who wanted a cosy home, marriage and children. Bizarrely, for a man on a low wage, he managed to get a loan of £4,000 and spent all of it on a diamond ring. He was trying to hide his inadequacy behind expensive symbols, and it worked for a while – Maxine, who'd grown up in a poor family, was thrilled. But he soon fell behind with the payments and had to deal with debt collectors knocking at the door.

12

Flirting with children

The couple wanted to move to another area but had outstanding debts and no contacts. Then Ian's father suggested that he apply for a caretaking job at a primary school in Soham, a small village in Cambridgeshire. Kevin himself was by now working as a caretaker and enjoyed the job.

Ian applied for the job at Soham Village College, and the authorities ran his name (both as Ian Nixon and Ian Huntley) through the computer – but, because the various charges against him for rape, statutory rape and burglary had been dropped, he had no criminal record and he got the job, starting in September 2001. He was able to rent a subsidised cottage in the school grounds, and was allowed to bring Maxine and his dog Sadie with him. At first, this was on an unpaid three-month probationary period, but he was so eager to please and so well-meaning that Soham College kept him on.

He was now given the title of senior site manager – it sounded much better than janitor or caretaker. But even this wasn't grandiose enough to gratify the would-be pilot, and he told his former neighbours that he'd won the lottery.

Most people would have been very pleased with Huntley's lot: a loving partner and a straightforward job, with a nice house in beautiful surroundings. But he was permanently in search of people to dominate and soon began to boss the primary school boys around. More alarmingly, he began to flirt with the schoolgirls who were, at most, eleven years old.

Disturbingly, one of his tasks was to supervise children in detention, which meant that he could be alone with a child for up to an hour. With a grim irony, he was the supposedly cleancut replacement for the previous caretaker, who had behaved inappropriately towards one of the girls.

The following spring Ian's parents reunited, his mother becoming a cleaner and dinner lady at the school in Ely, Cambridgeshire, where his father was caretaker. Ian began to feel closer to his father and returned to using the surname Huntley. He even made a tentative peace with his brother, Wayne. But he didn't nurture himself, having a pizza, a doughnut and a cola for his lunch every weekday, a junk food diet which must have played havoc with his blood sugar and his moods.

Unsurprisingly he remained mercurial, and he and Maxine continued to row. But Maxine's spirits picked up when she was given a part-time job as a teaching assistant at St Andrew's Church of England Primary School. However, she was turned down for a permanent post as she'd been unable to relate to the other teachers, being too shy to make good eye contact or engage them in conversation. On the plus side the pupils thought that she was brilliant, and this strengthened her hopes that one day she'd create a loving family of her own. She talked about her forthcoming wedding to some of the female pupils, and was so childlike that she completely identified with them.

The murders

Meanwhile, Ian had just about been coping with his new job – though he'd burst into tears a couple of times when reprimanded by his superiors for making errors. But now the school holidays stretched before him and he lost his daily routine. He and Maxine were at home all day and got on each other's nerves, so she often returned to her mother in Grimsby for a few days' holiday. She was doubtless aware that absence made the heart grow fonder as far as the possessive Huntley was concerned. Left to his own devices, he'd walk the dog and then lie on the settee for hour after hour, watching videos, eating sweets and smoking. But he found it impossible to relax or be alone with his thoughts. He needed someone to boss around, to be there for him sexually and emotionally – though he gave very little back.

On 2 August 2002, Maxine went on yet another trip to her mother's, given a lift there by Ian's parents. He was wildly resentful, convinced that her insecurity would cause her to flirt outrageously with every male in the pub. (He was right to worry – that evening she kissed another man passionately and asked him to take it further, her failed attempt at seduction filmed on the pub's CCTV.)

Early that evening, at 6:24pm, the couple exchanged angry texts.

14

Moments later, Huntley looked out of the window and espied two pretty ten-year-olds that Maxine had taught – Holly Wells and Jessica Chapman – walking past his house. The girls had been out to buy sweets and were now enjoying a stroll in the summer sunshine. They had no idea that the caretaker, who they knew by sight, meant them any harm.

Huntley hurried outside to greet the children, Sadie following at his heels. As he'd expected, the two children stopped to pat the dog. He invited them into the house, probably saying that Maxine wanted to see them – Holly had previously sent her a card saying that she was a brilliant teaching assistant, and that everyone would "miss you lots." He knew, of course, that Maxine was many miles away, and that he was going to have the girls to himself. He probably had some ridiculous notion that they'd respond to his flirting, or else he planned to ply them with alcopops so that they'd be too drunk to resist.

The exact sequence of events may never be known, but it's likely that Huntley took both girls into the dining room then made a pass at one of them. When she rejected him, he attacked. It's thought that he asphyxiated Holly then quickly suffocated Jessica. During the struggle, one of the children managed to scratch his jaw three times. What's likely is that he killed both girls very quickly – they had entered the house circa 6:30pm; sixteen minutes later he switched off Jessica's mobile phone. (Months after the trial he would suggest to a relative that he killed Jessica when she tried to phone for help, but this was just one of several versions of the murders which he gave.)

Destroying the evidence

He apparently took the girls' corpses into the bedroom – he'd later say that Holly sat on the bed and that a single drop of blood from her nose fell onto the duvet cover, but no one believes the nosebleed story. However, he did apparently lay the bodies on the duvet cover and remove their clothes. He carried the dead girls into the bathroom, intending to wash away any DNA evidence, but dropped one of them and cracked the side of the bath. After soaping and rinsing them thoroughly, he re-dressed them and cleaned the rest of the house, even putting the duvet into the washing machine.

Checking that there was no one in the vicinity, he concealed both bodies in his car then drove seventeen miles to a vast wooded area close to Lakenheath airbase, an area that he knew well from his teenage plane-spotting years. Parking in a secluded area, he tied carrier bags over his shoes so that they couldn't leave any telltale impressions in the mud.

Working swiftly and hoping against hope that he wouldn't be disturbed, Huntley lifted first one corpse then the other onto the grass, then knelt and used his pocket knife to cut off all their clothing. He also removed their trainers, tearing them from their feet and leaving the laces done up. He hoped that if the bodies were found in a few years, they would be unidentifiable – but, because it was dark and he was panicking, he missed the jewellery that both children wore.

Stuffing a binbag filled with the girls' clothes into his Ford Fiesta, Huntley returned to the bodies and carried them to a nearby ditch which was partly overhung by a fallen tree. Jessica's hair caught in the tree and he had to pull it loose, leaving some telltale hairs on a branch.

Surprisingly, given his keenness to get away, Huntley now laid the girls carefully on their backs and entwined their arms, creating an almost peaceful tableau. Psychiatrists would later speculate that this made him feel better about himself.

His next task was to destroy the children's clothes, which he concealed in his car for the forty-minute drive home. Returning to Soham Village College, he went straight to the school's outhouse – known as the hangar – and threw the sweatshirts, trousers, underwear and shoes into one of the large bins before setting them alight. But the blaze was so fierce that it singed the ceiling and sent clouds of choking black smoke into the atmosphere. Terrified that someone would investigate, he used a large container of water to douse the flames. Finally, he disposed of Jessica's mobile in a nearby skip.

That night Huntley was approached by Holly Wells' father, Kevin, who was out looking for the children – both girls were from loving families who immediately raised the alarm when they missed their curfew. The caretaker, freshly showered, promised to look out for the ten-year-olds. In reality he stayed up all night, cleaning the house of any traces of them. He phoned Maxine just before 7am, desperate to speak to his one ally, but she was so hungover that she quickly hung up on him.

An avid viewer of crime drama, Huntley knew that his car tyres could be matched to those found near the scene, so he drove to Ely and replaced them. He gave the mechanic £10 to falsify the records so that his number plate wasn't registered in their books. Returning home, he changed the carpet in his car and washed the vehicle thoroughly inside and out, before joining in the village-wide search for the two girls, walking through the fields for hour after hour. He worked hard to ingratiate himself with the other searchers so that the finger of suspicion wouldn't be pointed at him.

A changing story

But police were slightly suspicious of the immaculate young man, despite his superficial affability. They noticed that he was much cleaner than the other searchers and that his house was also unusually pristine, smelling strongly of disinfectant and bleach. He also sweated noticeably when asked a couple of casual questions and mumbled his replies.

He'd at first told Kevin Wells and some of the other searchers that he hadn't seen the girls, then realised that someone might have spotted him talking to them. So he now stated that he *had* seen them after all, but hadn't realised that these were the two that were missing as he didn't know them well. He said that he'd chatted to them briefly as they walked past his garden and that they'd asked after Maxine, their former teaching assistant. He added that he'd explained to the children that she was having a bath.

Huntley now had to get Maxine to partake in this lie, so he phoned her again shortly before teatime, saying that Holly and Jessica were missing and that he was one of the last people to see them. He added that he'd be framed for their disappearance, due to his being previously accused of rape. He wept copiously and warned her that he'd have

17

another nervous breakdown if he was suspected of foul play, and that she would have to give him an alibi.

We'll probably never know if Maxine Carr was simply devastated at the thought of the friendly and fun-loving ten-year-olds going missing, or if she realised that her lover had murdered them. What's known is that she started crying and was so upset that she couldn't eat the meal that her mother prepared. She agreed that Huntley could pick her up and drive her back to Soham, though she'd originally planned to stay in Grimsby until Wednesday.

On Tuesday morning, the double murderer set off for his mother-in-law's Grimsby home and, at lunchtime, collected a still-weeping Maxine. Her mother, Shirley, noticed that Ian was very anxious and refused to stay for a meal, though he accepted a bag of crisps.

By now, the fact that the two girls had gone missing had become national news and the media had descended on Soham. Keen to ingratiate himself with everyone, Huntley told one journalist after another that he was probably the last friendly face the children had seen. He claimed that he'd been washing his dog outside when they'd stopped to speak to him and asked if they could see Miss Carr, but he'd explained that she was in the bath and they moved off somewhere and disappeared.

Facing the cameras, his features dark with anxiety, he was a convincing figure. Maxine was equally believable, talking of how brilliant the girls were, and how they wanted to be her bridesmaids when she and Ian wed. It threw the general public off the scent, as they tend to believe that paedophiles are lonely old men or sinister bachelors. The reality is very different – most of the British paedophiles profiled in this section were married or divorced.

Fire

The police began to make door-to-door enquiries, and when they talked to the helpful caretaker he casually asked them how long DNA remained available for testing. He was stunned when a detective told him that traces had been found in woolly mammals buried for thousands of years. He'd hoped that Holly and Jessica's corpses would decompose quickly in their watery grave, and that no trace of his having handled them would remain.

Huntley decided that his best bet was to return to the bodies and completely immolate them. So he put a can of petrol and his cigarette lighter in the car and drove under cover of darkness to the body dump site. Throwing the flammable liquid over the corpses, he watched as the flesh burned away. It must have been a traumatising sight, yet he steeled himself to go on and visit his grandmother, who lived nearby, knowing this would give him a genuine reason for having been in the vicinity.

By now, he had lost weight, had dark circles under his eyes and was having nightmares about his victims. Every time that there was a knock on the door he feared it would be detectives with a warrant for his arrest. Maxine also found it difficult to eat, and her already low weight dropped even further, her skin breaking out in spots. She cleaned the house even more obsessively than before, whilst Ian helped out at press briefings held in the school, putting out the chairs and commiserating with the shellshocked parents and distraught community.

Ten days after he'd poured petrol over the bodies, they were found by a horrified gamekeeper. Huntley wept when he heard of the discovery. To the press it looked as if he were genuinely distraught about these two young lives being prematurely ended, but in truth he was probably weeping for his own predicament – he still hadn't been able to finish burning the children's clothes in the school's 'hangar', as there were too many journalists and police around. Moreover he'd lied to the police, saying that he didn't have the key, so it would look very suspicious if he was suddenly seen unlocking the hangar's door.

False alibi

Meanwhile, detectives had received dozens of calls from the people of Grimsby, pointing out that Maxine Carr had been in the town from Saturday until Tuesday lunchtime, so she couldn't have been having a bath in Soham on the Sunday when the girls disappeared. The police had doubtless also heard that Grimsby residents had previously broken Ian

Huntley's windows as they suspected he was a paedophile, and that he'd been accused of both statutory and actual rape.

Twelve days after the girls had disappeared, police took the caretaker in for formal questioning. But he refused to incriminate himself and they let him go. On 17 August, however, they gained access to the hangar and found the girls' partially burnt clothes. They also learned that Huntley *did* have access to this building, and that he wore the key on the keychain attached to his belt. Convinced at last that they had their man, they arrested him in the early hours of the morning at his parents' house. They also arrested Maxine.

Huntley now went to pieces, or pretended to do so – as detectives asked him question after question he became increasingly inarticulate, starting to rock back and forward and to foam at the mouth. It's possible that he was regressing, his always fragile ability to cope breaking down. Alternatively, he could have faked his distress, just as he'd faked epilepsy in the past.

Aware that it was a waste of time to question him further, but that he would remain a danger to vulnerable females, the authorities had him indefinitely detained in Rampton Special Hospital under the Mental Health Act.

Psychopath

For the next few months Huntley remained incarcerated and under close supervision at Rampton, where staff eventually diagnosed him as a psychopath. It explained his lack of remorse and his inability to identify with the pain of the murdered girls' parents. With his limited conscience, he thought only of himself. Bizarrely, many lonely and delusional females were also thinking of him and he received love letters from all over the world. But he continued to write daily to Maxine, whom he'd now reinvented in his imagination as the love of his life.

Meanwhile, Maxine was having a horrendous time in Holloway Prison as the other prisoners wrongly thought that she was a child killer. The press were to blame for this as they'd compared her to Myra Hindley, who'd been present when her lover Ian Brady murdered three children and two teenagers.

But Hindley had lured the youngsters to the psychopathic Brady, whereas Maxine Carr hadn't even been in the same town as Ian Huntley when he'd murdered Holly and Jessica. Hindley had seen the bodies of her lover's victims, whereas Carr may have been able to convince herself that Holly and Jessica had been murdered by a stranger. After all, she was able to convince herself that Huntley, a former rapist, would make a good husband and that she could become a teacher despite having no GCSEs. She had a tenuous grip on reality and was desperate for love from Ian Huntley, and for approval from almost anyone else.

Yet the public's response was to attack her and call her a 'murdering bitch'. When she appeared in court to answer the charge of perjury a baying mob threw eggs at her, and were so vicious that the children in the crowd broke down in tears.

Hanging

In May 2003, Ian Huntley was told that, as he wasn't mentally ill, he would be moved from his secure hospital environment to Woodhill Prison in Buckinghamshire. Before the move could take place, he tried to hang himself, but was quickly found and revived by hospital staff.

That same month, Maxine tried to slash her wrists but was stopped after just one non-life-threatening gash. By now, she'd stopped eating completely and her weight had dropped to six stone, yet she was still trying to exercise obsessively to take her mind off things. She eventually lost consciousness in her cell and had to be rushed to hospital and hooked up to a drip.

By the following month, her legal team had made her realise she had to emotionally distance herself from Huntley if she wanted to rebuild her life. Agreeing, she put his name on a list of people that she never wanted to hear from again. She was able to close down her feelings for him – as a hysterical personality type, she could swing from being madly in love to being completely indifferent.

A near-lethal overdose

When Ian heard that Maxine wouldn't accept his letters, he began to save up the Amitriptyline antidepressants that he was taking. He only pretended to swallow the pills each day, hiding them behind his tongue and sliding them inside empty teabags to conceal in his rectum until he'd saved a potentially lethal dose.

In June 2003 he took twenty-nine of the tablets, more than enough to kill him. By the time prison warders found him he had slipped into a coma and was close to death.

Huntley was rushed to hospital where the staff pumped out his stomach. He remained in a coma but rallied within hours of being attached to a life support machine. When his mother and brother later visited him, Wayne demanded an explanation: "How the hell did this happen? I thought that prisoners were monitored when they took medication."

Many members of the community were outraged that the double killer had survived. It costs the taxpayer £35,000 a year to keep the average prisoner in jail, and a high-profile prisoner like Huntley, who is often on suicide watch, costs even more.

The trial

In November 2003, Huntley's trial finally began at the Old Bailey. For almost four weeks, the prosecution set out the evidence against him. He'd claimed that he'd only spoken to the girls in his garden – but dozens of fibres found in his car and house matched Holly and Jessica's shirts and tracksuit bottoms. And five hairs that matched samples taken from Huntley were found in the dustbin where he'd thrown the children's clothes.

Evidence from botanist Patricia Wiltshire showed that Huntley had dumped the girls' bodies in the ditch shortly after abducting them: he'd caused the adjacent nettles to produce side-shoots, something they only do after being trampled on. Pollen specific to the area was found on his car and on two pairs of his shoes, proving that he'd visited the scene twice. Realising how strong the evidence was, he belatedly admitted that the children had been in his home and that he'd killed and disposed of them.

Taking the stand, he told the jury a preposterous story about how the girls had died by accident. He said that Holly had a nosebleed so he'd taken her into the bathroom, but accidentally knocked her into the full bath which he had been using to wash his dog. He'd allegedly frozen with fear and watched helplessly as she drowned. He added that Jessica had screamed and he'd put his hand over her mouth to stifle the sound, accidentally asphyxiating her. As it normally takes three minutes to suffocate someone, this was patently ridiculous.

Maxine took the stand and made it clear that she now despised her former boyfriend. She said that she'd originally been sure that Ian hadn't hurt the girls, which was why she'd given him an alibi – they'd previously discussed paedophiles and had both agreed that they didn't deserve to live. He was having a full sexual relationship with her and had previously dated a nineteen-year-old, so she had no reason to believe that he was attracted to little girls.

On the other hand, she'd come home to find that he'd scrubbed the house and laundered the duvet; this being a man who never did any cleaning. And she knew that he'd previously been charged with rape.

Ian gazed at her with devotion as she stood a couple of feet away, but she was determined to distance herself from him. "I am not going to be blamed for what that thing in that box has done to me or those children," she said. Huntley flinched at being called "that thing", and his perpetually sad face took on an even more wounded look.

Verdict

On 13 December 2003, the jury went out. Four days later they returned with the verdicts. Huntley was given a life sentence for each of the murders, whilst Carr was found not guilty of aiding an offender but guilty of perverting the course of justice. She was given three and a half years.

After their son was found guilty of the murders, Kevin and Lynda Huntley split up again. Kevin was assaulted in the street by yobs angry at the violence inflicted by his oldest son. (Clearly they'd never heard of irony.) Lynda was so traumatised by Ian's actions and ongoing death wish that her health deteriorated markedly.

Foolishly, given that she'd been spared a life sentence and given a comparatively lenient tariff, Maxine Carr asked to be released on licence with an electronic tag, something she was technically eligible for. Aware that the public would lynch her, the authorities immediately changed the law to exclude high-profile prisoners.

Obliterated

In April 2004, the house where the two girls were murdered was razed to the ground. The rubble was taken away so that it couldn't be collected by souvenir hunters. In September 2005 Maxine Carr was released, having served one year and nine months of her sentence. She'd naïvely hoped to return to her mother, but the authorities knew that she'd be pilloried and instead gave her a new identity, ordering the press to leave her alone.

That summer, Ian Huntley told his parents that, after he'd accidentally drowned Holly in the bath, he'd deliberately strangled Jessica as she moved towards the door. Previously he'd told the Old Bailey that her death, by suffocation, was also an accident. He has lied pathologically since childhood and doubtless will continue to do so for the rest of his life.

Attacked in prison

Huntley's life continues to be dominated by fear, as other prisoners are keen to assault him, professing to hate paedophiles more than any other type of prisoner (while the man who batters his own child to death or bludgeons a stranger is arguably just as bad). On 14 September 2005, he had boiling water poured on him by another inmate and had to be hospitalised. He later launched a compensation bid against the prison, claiming that they'd failed to protect him, and was given legal aid.

On 20 September 2005, Mr Justice Moses, the High Court judge who had presided over Huntley's murder trial, ruled that he should spend forty years in prison before becoming eligible for parole. Life would not necessarily mean life in his case because there had been no premeditation. The victims' families were understandably devastated to hear that he could be released at sixty-eight – some paedophiles, such as

Sidney Cooke (overviewed later in this section), are still sexually active at that age.

The following August he implicated Carr in his crimes, telling his mother that she had known about the murders of Holly and Jessica and had covered up for him. He also alleged that Maxine had told him to burn the bodies, saying, "If you don't do it, I will." It's not unprecedented for a spurned killer to turn against a lover in this way – every time that Myra Hindley looked likely to be offered parole, her former paramour, Ian Brady, told the press that she'd helped kill some of the victims rather than just luring them to him.

Another overdose

Ian Huntley has continued to suffer precarious mental health, sometimes feeling motivated enough to exercise in the prison gym, at other times sliding into a deep depression. In September 2006 he took yet another overdose and was found unconscious in his cell. He'd allegedly swapped a tape-recorded confession of his crimes for another prisoner's tablets, knowing that the prisoner could sell details to the tabloids once Huntley was deceased. This time he spent two days in hospital, guarded by prison officers around the clock, and later told his mother that God must want him to live.

Further allegations

In December 2006, he was again granted legal aid to refute the claims of a teenager who'd gone to a newspaper during his murder trial, alleging that he'd sexually assaulted her five years earlier when she was only eleven years old. Later he admitted assaulting various teenage girls.

In March 2007, one of his ex-girlfriends told her story to a woman's magazine, saying that she'd been fifteen and pregnant with his child when he'd made further sexual advances. She'd rebuffed him and he'd raped her, punched her in the stomach and pushed her downstairs. That same day – in February 1998 – she'd left him and never returned. The woman said that she'd recently told her eight-year-old daughter that

Huntley was her biological father because she feared that she'd find out from someone else.

The suicide attempts continue

Huntley overdosed again in September 2007, after swallowing Cocodamol pills possibly supplied by another prisoner. He was rushed to Pinderfield Hospital, where he made a quick – if reluctant – recovery within hours, and was returned to his cell. He allegedly went on to form a gay relationship in Wakefield Prison, Yorkshire. Later, Huntley was transferred to Frankland Prison in County Durham.

In January 2008, the tabloids reported that Maxine Carr was pregnant by her new boyfriend, and said that it was 'hideous' that she should be allowed to raise a baby. But Carr had been appreciated by the primary school pupils she worked with, and has never harmed a child.

In conclusion

Ian Huntley's only victims were girls, so he is presumably a low risk to other male prisoners – though he might attack a weaker man that he is sexually involved with. Given the numerous suicide attempts he has made, he will remain a danger to himself. One study of British murderers has shown that a third subsequently kill themselves, albeit often after their release into the community.

CHAPTER TWO

ROY WILLIAM WHITING

Though his initial attraction was towards women, Roy Whiting eventually fixated on prepubescent girls. At thirty-six years old, he horrifically abused a nine-year-old. Five years later, in July 2000, he assaulted and murdered eight-year-old Sarah Payne.

Formative experiences

Roy was born on 26 January 1959 in Horsham Hospital, West Sussex, to George and Pamela Whiting. He was the couple's third child, their first son having died at two days old of congenital heart disease. Their second child, Roy's older brother, was called Peter. Soon after Roy's birth, the family moved from Horsham to nearby Crawley, where they rented a three-bedroom terraced council house on the Langley Green estate.

George was a sheet metal worker whilst Pamela, a former cook, kept house and looked after their two sons. When Roy was three, his parents had a fourth child, Claire, but, like their first child, she was severely disabled and died when she was only a month old. Despite their heartache, the couple went on to produce another daughter who they named Gillian.

By the time Roy went to school he was timid and withdrawn – psychiatrists would later label his early years as "lonely and confusing". He struggled to cope with his class work and was soon put into the remedial stream. Because of his shyness he was frequently bullied and withdrew further into himself. He didn't make a single friend at primary

27

school and spent every day alone, one of the predisposing factors for becoming a paedophile. Journalists would later speculate that his life was devoid of happiness, and that his rage against other, better-adjusted children had simply grown and grown.

When the browbeaten schoolboy was eleven or twelve there was a traumatic event in his life which has not been made public. Referring to it elliptically in court decades later, his barrister said that he had "drawn down a conscious barrier . . . in respect of that incident". And a psychiatrist noted that, because of early trauma, he had closed down part of his mind and was unable to reopen it.

Family break-up

The Whitings' marriage had been unhappy for some time and, when Roy was seventeen, his mother left to live with her boyfriend, leaving George to look after the children. She later remarried, becoming Pamela Green. Roy struggled to become an autonomous adult, and remained in the family council house with his father long after his siblings left home.

Though he didn't bond with most adults, he did become friends with various teenagers and helped run a youth club from two sheds at the nearby adventure playground. The teens would play table tennis there and Roy, and another twenty-something, showed them how to fix up old cars. He even taught some of the fourteen-year-olds how to drive. Roy was well thought of by these youngsters as he was able to share his knowledge of motor mechanics. He was a helpful big brother presence to them.

Marriage

But he remained restless and frequently changed jobs during those years at home, at one stage working as a delivery man for the Co-op, at another becoming a paint sprayer at a local garage. By now he'd grown into a well-built man, though he retained the slightly sloping shoulders that tend to form during an unhappy childhood. And he smoked heavily, though (perhaps fearing what he might do if drunk) he completely avoided alcohol. He yearned for a relationship but lacked the empathy that women look for. Yet he wasn't a man's man either, and failed to bond with his male colleagues at work.

Despite this social awkwardness, Roy's life wasn't all bad. He eventually trained as a mechanic and also successfully refurbished motor boats, becoming a skilled manual worker. Later he took up stock car racing at weekends and was very good at it, driving for a team called the Gatwick Flyers at the Smallfield Raceway near Crawley.

But he still wanted to share his life with someone, so he was delighted when he stopped at a petrol station in 1984 and successfully chatted up the attendant, Linda Brooker, five years his junior. He continued to visit the station and they soon started dating. They married in June 1986, whereupon Roy left home for the first time and became his own boss, renting a garage from which he repaired cars.

Fatherhood

Unfortunately, he was unable to budget and was soon evicted from the garage for non-payment of rent. He was enraged that his wife earned more than him, seeing this as a personal slight, so the couple argued frequently. Despite being pregnant and married for less than a year, Linda left him, never to return. Roy was present at the birth of his son at Crawley Hospital in July 1987, but the couple remained estranged and within two years were divorced.

Following the break-up, Whiting rented a bedsit and took up with several other females, but none of these relationships lasted. He was often oilstained and dirty, and his bedsit was filthy, yet he bragged at length about how successful he was. Women found him immature and soon ended the romance, whereupon he became bitter and enraged. He found it impossible to examine his own failings and always blamed the other party for the breakdown of the relationship.

Whiting eventually resigned himself to solitude and took a flat above the shop where he worked as a mechanic. He continued to neglect his appearance, turning up at work with dirty clothes, unwashed hair and unbrushed teeth. Yet his dreams were grandiose and he told his colleagues about various get-rich-quick schemes that he'd planned. He lied constantly, even when the truth would have suited him better, which is one of the hallmarks of an antisocial personality. Roy would exhibit several of the other criteria which make up this disorder, namely lawbreaking (he was a dangerous driver), irresponsibility (failure to pay his debts) and a lack of remorse.

Around this time – the early to mid-1990s – Roy Whiting appears to have recognised or begun to act on his attraction to children. He started to leave work at 3:30pm for an hour every afternoon and to park outside various schools, watching the little girls leave. A colleague noticed him parked outside a playground one day, and thereafter his mid-afternoon trips were jokingly referred to as 'the school run'. His workmates saw the divorced mechanic as a slightly odd loner, and had no idea that he held deeply depraved fantasies which he was about to enact . . .

Abduction and sexual assault
In spring 1995, the thirty-six-year-old was rejected by yet another woman and decided to force himself on a young girl. Claiming sickness, he took a fortnight off work, using the time to finalise his abduction plans. This involved purchasing a second-hand red Ford Sierra and putting a rape kit – comprising a rope and knife – in the boot. He also removed the existing cartoon stickers from the car, determined that it wouldn't be identified. And, in the hope of altering his appearance, he cut all the grey out of his hair.

On 4 March 1995, he drove to the Crawley estate of Langley Green where he'd spent his lonely childhood. Driving into a cul-de-sac, he parked and watched three young girls at play. When he was sure that the coast was clear, he attempted to abduct all three, angrily ordering them into his car. Two of the girls escaped and would later identify him, but the third – aged nine – wasn't so fortunate and was bundled into the passenger seat.

The pitiless man then drove her to an isolated stretch of woodland thirty miles away, made her take off all of her clothes and threatened to tie her up. He sexually assaulted her at length, and was preparing to abuse her further when he heard other people approaching. Throwing her into the car, he drove her back to her neighbourhood, the entire abduction having lasted two terrifying hours. She later said that the assault involved his licking her and that what he'd done was "disgraceful, disgusting". Needless to say, the police and the public agreed.

For the next few weeks, Whiting relived the event in his mind and must have believed that he'd gotten away with it. But someone who knew about his tendency to hang around school playgrounds heard that the abduction vehicle had been a red Ford Sierra, and gave the police Whiting's name. They found that he exactly matched the description that the child victim and both of her friends had given, and promptly arrested him. Knowing that the game was up, the thirty-six-year-old confessed. But he denied the premeditation of the act, saying that he'd pulled into the cul-de-sac to urinate, had seen the children and "just snapped".

His ex-wife Linda was so horrified by his actions that she refused to ever see him again, and destroyed their wedding photographs. It's likely that this brought an end to his relationship with his son, though journalists would later allege that he hadn't seen much of the child over the preceding years. This may or may not be true – there is a tendency for the press to demonise every aspect of a paedophile's life, implying that everything he has ever said or done has been at best unfeeling, at worst monstrous. This makes it harder for the public to identify superficially friendly paedophiles in their vicinity.

Court
At Lewes Crown Court, Whiting pleaded guilty to the abduction and indecent assault of the child. His mother took the stand to describe him as a Walter Mitty character with grandiose fantasies. The case was adjourned for background reports which concluded that he was a "high risk" – presumably because he'd put a rape kit in the car, showing clear premeditation. But the criminal psychiatrist who'd made the report added that Whiting wasn't a paedophile, doubtless because he had been married, fathered a son and had relationships with other women, none of whom looked childlike. As such, the expert saw the abduction of a minor as a one-off regressive act. He didn't realise that Whiting had

become a fixated paedophile who made a special journey to the nearest primary school every weekday, and fantasised endlessly about undressing little girls.

Whiting's barrister said that his client was desperate to receive sex therapy in prison – this in itself is odd, as the psychiatrist had concluded that he had no paedophiliac tendencies. But, satisfied that the assault was an aberration by a man under stress who had recently been ditched by his girlfriend, the judge sentenced him to a mere four years.

Once he was behind bars, Whiting refused therapy as he didn't want the other prisoners to know that he was a sex offender. He was given an additional few months in prison as a punishment for refusing treatment, but saw this as preferable to being labelled a nonce, the type of offender who is frequently beaten up – or even murdered – in jail.

Realising that he no longer wanted to work as a mechanic, Whiting learned about the building trade in prison. He told everyone that he was inside for car ringing, served a mere two and a half years of his sentence and was released.

Amusement park

When he left jail in 1998, Whiting asked the authorities to relocate him to Littlehampton where his mother had once lived – he knew that he'd be beaten up by the locals if he returned to Crawley. He moved into a flat close to an amusement park and a children's playground and became a jobbing builder, walking his boss's dog at lunchtimes. The boss didn't find him to be particularly sociable, but he got on well with the dog.

One of his work placements took him to the village of West Kingston in West Sussex, which included an area called Kingston Gorse that contained a cornfield. After the placement ended he often drove to the area and walked through the field. It was an ideal place for him to abduct a child, as he'd be able to quickly drive the few miles home – yet it was sufficiently far enough away that he wouldn't be committing an offence on his own doorstep, and hopefully wouldn't be the first offender in the frame.

He obviously knew nothing about geographical profiling, which shows that criminals offend within a defined radius of their home but not too close to it. If asked, a geographical profiler would probably have earmarked West Kingston as one of the areas where Littlehampton-based Whiting was most likely to offend.

But throughout 1998 and 1999, there's no evidence that the builder sexually assaulted a minor. Indeed, he tried hard to make friends of his own age. He socialised with five other locals at a café close to home, always sitting at the same table and ordering the same snack meal of a cheeseburger with two mugs of tea. Unfortunately the group broke up, leaving him friendless again. Indeed, his main visitors were the police. Because he was on the Sex Offenders Register, they called unannounced every time that a sexual assault took place in the vicinity, questioning him about various offences including two Brighton rapes.

He remained a solitary man, who now ate at most lunchtimes in a local fish and chip restaurant. Neighbours found him polite but distant. He continued to haunt places beloved by children, namely the shingle beach, the park and the fair. It was reckless behaviour for a man who ought to have been trying to control his attraction to young girls – and his driving was often equally reckless. He was well-known to the local police for speeding and driving erratically.

Eventually his desire built, and he decided to abduct another little girl. During the third week of June 2000, he phoned his work and said that he was sick, just as he had before abducting the nine-year-old. He claimed that he had a twisted gut and this may well have been true – people with unhappy childhoods often suffer from stomach pains, headaches and numerous other stress-based symptoms. Indeed, Whiting often looked unwell. Unfortunately, sexual predators are most likely to assault others when they themselves are feeling stressed. It acts as a catharsis for them, albeit only briefly, until their rage-fuelled lust builds up again.

The builder now bought himself a white Fiat Ducato van, made cable-ties into makeshift handcuffs and purchased baby oil to use as a lubricant. On 1 July he drove to the beach, funfair and various other venues frequented by children, looking for a female victim. Eventually he ended up at his favourite field in Kingston Gorse.

Murder

Whiting soon espied eight-year-old Sarah Payne, who was playing in the field with her five-year-old sister and her two brothers, aged eleven and thirteen. She fell and banged her head, so she decided to return to her grandparents' house, located nearby. She ran towards Peak Lane with her thirteen-year-old brother, who was very protective, in hot pursuit. As he raced to catch up, she disappeared through a hole in the hedge.

Whiting grabbed her and bundled her into the van, returning to the driving seat seconds before Sarah's brother reached the lane. The paedophile grinned and waved at the teenager, then drove away.

Doubtless he parked somewhere private as soon as possible, but paedophiles often sexually assault a child for the first time as they drive them to a more remote location. The obsession for young flesh is so great that it overrides road safety, or the increased risk of driving dangerously and getting caught.

What Whiting did to the eight-year-old will never be known, but the authorities would later speculate that it involved indecent assault as this was a sexually motivated homicide. It's known that he stripped the child and that he probably suffocated or strangled her. Her death was possibly deliberate – the last time he'd left a living witness, he'd been sentenced to four years.

Meanwhile, Sarah's siblings continued to look for her, and when her parents returned from the local pub they joined in the search. They reported her missing within an hour and a half of her disappearance, and the police launched an intensive search. Over the next few hours they examined their records of local paedophiles and noted that Roy Whiting, now residing at St Augustine Road, Littlehampton, fitted most of the criteria. He drove a white van, had a missing front tooth and had previously abducted a child of Sarah's age. Detectives drew up a list of the five paedophiles most likely to have taken the eight-year-old and Whiting was at the top of it.

The day after Sarah's disappearance, the police interviewed Whiting at his home. Looking unconcerned, he said that he'd driven to a funfair in

Hove, and was in bed by 9pm. (It wasn't the smartest alibi, as Ian Brady and Sidney Cooke had both abducted victims from funfairs.)

After questioning Roy at length, police waited outside and soon saw him leave the house, go to his van and remove various items. He did this three times, then got into the driver's seat and began to drive away. They stopped him and found a receipt for diesel which he'd bought at 10pm on the night of Sarah's disappearance. It showed that he'd been close to Littlehampton, many miles from the fair. Whiting was shaking visibly when he was arrested, but soon calmed down and presented a composed, even indifferent front.

Scratches

At the police station, when he was examined, scratches were found on his body and arms. He refused to explain how he'd gotten them, but, as a manual worker, he could easily have hurt himself in this way at work. He looked at detectives blankly as they asked him question after question, though his stress showed in how he chainsmoked throughout three days of interviews. He eventually elected to answer, "no comment" to every question and, unable to connect him to Sarah's disappearance, the police let him go.

In the meantime they'd searched his van. He'd washed the floor and changed the doors on the weekend of Sarah's abduction, but the vehicle still contained a knife, a spade, the makeshift handcuffs and a bottle of baby oil. Presumably he hadn't had time to dispose of them. He'd also apparently run low on fuel and so had filled up on diesel at a garage close to the abduction site.

Police began to conduct forensic tests on the vehicle whilst hundreds of their colleagues, plus concerned members of the public, continued to search for Sarah Payne, though they realised that she was most likely dead. (Paedophiles who are going to kill usually do so within an hour of abducting their victim – though there are exceptions, like Marc Dutroux, profiled later, who keep their abductees alive for many months.)

Body

On 17 July, seventeen days after Sarah's disappearance, the eight-year-old's partially-buried nude body was found by a farm labourer in a field in Pulborough, fifteen miles from where she'd been abducted. She hadn't been raped but police believed she'd been sexually assaulted. Death had probably been due to strangulation or suffocation, but it was hard to tell as the body had decomposed markedly in the summer sun and the extremities had been eaten by animals. One of Sarah's shoes was also found in a lane near the village of Coolham, close to where Roy Whiting had bought diesel on the night of her abduction. The rest of her clothing has never been found.

Vigilantes

As police were still conducting forensic tests on his St Augustine Road flat, Roy Whiting went back to live with his father. But local vigilantes stormed the house and police had to remove George and Roy from the building for their own safety, smuggling them out under blankets. Now homeless, Roy took to sleeping in a tent. Terrified that the mob would find him, he stole a Vauxhall Nova in Crawley and began sleeping in it, parking in a different place each night.

On 24 July 2000, the police recognised the stolen vehicle and gave chase. When two police cars blocked his way he rammed both of them. He was consequently sent to a prison in Kent for twenty-two months.

Slowly, the authorities conducted their tests and – five months after Sarah's murder – stated that various fibres from Whiting matched some of those found on the velcro strap of Sarah's shoe. They concluded that Sarah Payne hadn't been taken to the filthy flat, with its overflowing ashtrays and scum-covered bath, but that the fibre evidence from the van was sufficient to justify arresting the known paedophile.

Murder charge

On 6 February 2001 they charged him with Sarah Payne's abduction and murder. He chose not to comment, as was his right, and seemed indifferent to the fact that a child had been murdered. He was remanded in custody until the trial.

The trial began at Lewes Crown Court on Tuesday 13 November 2001. Sarah Payne's mother took the stand and described the events surrounding her daughter's disappearance – and Sarah's oldest brother (who wrongly felt guilty at being unable to save her) described seeing the man in the white van who was unshaven and dirty, with piercing blue eyes and yellowish teeth.

The following day, the pathologist described the child's death as a "sexually motivated homicide". For the next few days, the prosecution detailed the forensic evidence against Roy Whiting: four microscopic red fibres on Sarah's shoe were identical to red fibres on one of his sweatshirts. A hair was also found on his sweatshirt, with DNA tests suggesting that there was only a one in a billion chance that it wasn't the victim's hair. A blue fibre from Sarah's shoe strap was matched to a clown-patterned curtain in Whiting's van, and two fibres from one of his socks were found in the body bag which had contained Sarah's corpse.

The defence counsel countered that the fibres on Sarah's shoe and hair were not a perfect match with those in Whiting's van, but in fact were "indistinguishable and not identical". She added that, after eighteen months of intensive police work and an investigation costing over £2,000,000, all the prosecution had found were a few fibres. Sarah's brother had failed to pick Whiting out of a police line-up and one of the supposedly telltale scratches on his body was several days old, so it couldn't have come from the victim's nails.

The jury, comprising nine men and three women, weren't allowed to hear about Whiting's previous conviction for child sexual assault as this would have made it impossible for him to have a fair trial.

Journalists reported that he looked indifferent during the proceedings, rocking back and forward in his seat and often stifling a yawn. But in fairness, like most trials it was often boring and repetitive, and doubtless confusing to someone of Whiting's educational level. Nevertheless, he opted to take the stand.

On Tuesday 4 December he gave his evidence, claiming that he'd spent the day of Sarah's abduction travelling around at random, visiting three parks, a boating lake, a beach and a funfair. The jury must have noted that these were all venues beloved by children. He said that it was simply coincidence that a man matching his description had been seen in the lane at the time that Sarah Payne disappeared. Whiting seemed relaxed when telling his side of the story – but his demeanour changed when the prosecution questioned him. He became increasingly irate and aggressive, unconsciously revealing his darker side.

Indeed, his performance was so bad that his barrister declined to re-examine him, knowing that he'd further alienate the jury. Only then did Whiting realise that the case wasn't going to end in his favour, and buried his head in his hands.

Despite her obvious distress, Roy's mother, Pamela, supported him throughout the trial, sitting as anonymously as possible in the public gallery. This must have taken courage and is comparatively unusual – criminals with sexual convictions are often ostracised by their families.

The trial lasted for over three weeks, before the jury deliberated on the verdict. They were out for three days, before deciding that the fibre evidence was compelling enough to find the defendant guilty of murder. Only then was the prosecution allowed to tell of Whiting's remarkably similar sexual assault on a nine-year-old girl.

Trial judge Mr Justice Curtis said that Whiting was evil and cunning, adding, "You are and will remain an absolute menace to any little girl." He recommended that Whiting's life sentence should actually mean life, only the twenty-fourth time in British legal history that this recommendation has been made. Whiting was sent to maximum-security Wakefield Prison.

A violent society

In June 2002, Roy Whiting was walking across the prison landing at Wakefield jail en route to the kitchen, where he planned to fill a flask with hot water. Suddenly he was slashed across the face by another prisoner in an unprovoked assault. Rickie Tregaskis, serving a life sentence for kicking a disabled man to death, was accused of using a razor on Whiting, leaving a six-inch slash running from his lip to his ear. Bleeding copiously, the forty-three-year-old was taken to Pinderfields Hospital in Wakefield where the wound was stitched.

Tregaskis said that he'd been walking alongside another prisoner when Whiting was attacked, and that it was the other prisoner who had done it. He also said that he couldn't name this prisoner, as an informant's life would be hell. But a prison officer said that Tregaskis had told her he planned to assault someone in the hope that he'd be moved to a different jail. Tregaskis, who already has one hundred and thirty convictions, was found guilty and given six years to run concurrently with his life sentence.

Blunkett's ruling

For Roy Whiting, it's likely that life will indeed mean life. On 24 November 2002, the Home Secretary, David Blunkett, ordered that he serve a minimum of fifty years in prison, ensuring that he'd be at least ninety-two when eligible for release. Lawyers immediately objected to the term, noting that Ian Huntley – who killed two girls as opposed to Whiting's one – was given the lesser tariff of forty years. In 2004 Whiting applied to the Court of Appeal for a new minimum term, but this appeal has yet to be heard.

Superstitious

In January 2007, the still unkempt killer was moved into cell 336 on Wakefield Prison's D-Wing, formerly occupied by serial killer Dr Harold Shipman. The doctor had hanged himself in that cell in January 2004.

Within days, Whiting complained to his psychiatrist, the prison warders and the governor that his new cell was haunted and that Shipman's ghost was making strange sounds every night, waking him up. Needless to say, the noises were really being made by prisoners in the neighbouring cells, who despised paedophiles. One of them later left a noose lying on his bed.

But his gullibility is shared by some other prisoners, who believe that the cell is jinxed – largely because a previous inmate, thirty-two-year-old Jashir Singh Rai, hanged himself there in April 1987.

Ill educated, isolated and loathed by his peers, it's likely that Roy

Whiting will become ever more delusional. He chainsmokes, looks older than his actual years and will almost certainly die in jail.

CHAPTER THREE

THOMAS WATT HAMILTON

Because of his status as a spree killer, Hamilton's paedophiliac actions – prior to his shooting dead sixteen children and their teacher in 1996 – have been largely overlooked.

Early confusion

Thomas was born on 10 May 1952 in Glasgow, Scotland to Agnes and Thomas Watt. Unfortunately, the couple had split up whilst Agnes was pregnant, ending a marriage which only lasted for eighteen months. By the time that Thomas junior was born, his father (who he was never to meet) was already heavily involved in an affair. Agnes found it difficult to cope with little Thomas, particularly as she only had a low-paying job as a chambermaid. She reluctantly returned to her parents' home in the Cranhill area of Glasgow when her child was two.

Agnes's parents disapproved of her divorce and insisted that they adopt the child, a process which was completed shortly before he turned four. Thereafter, he was told to start calling his grandmother 'Mummy' and his grandfather 'Daddy'. He was also told that his birth mother, who still lived with him, was now his sister and that his surname was no longer Watt but Hamilton.

The newly-named Thomas Hamilton attended the local primary school till he was twelve, after which his family – still including his birth mother – moved to Stirling. He was a good pupil academically, but very old fashioned, probably as a result of having strict, comparatively elderly

41

adoptive parents. Acquaintances noticed that he found it difficult to make eye contact and spent most of his time alone. He joined the Boys Brigade and was proficient at winning badges, excelling in solitary activities such as tying knots.

A teenage paedophile

As he moved through his teens, Hamilton became sexually attracted to many of the younger boys in the brigade. He also became interested in photography and in photographing the male children that he found most attractive, an interest he would maintain throughout his life.

He left school with several O-levels and acquired his first air gun – people who feel powerless in their everyday lives often choose to own and use weapons. He gained further qualifications at Falkirk Technical College, after which he was taken on as a draughtsman in the county architect's office. His apprenticeship was unremarkable, apart from the fact that he was excessively shy with other adults.

In 1971, aged nineteen, he became a youth club worker in nearby Dunblane, soon making it clear that the boys aged from seven to eleven were his favourites. He'd even ask each of his favourite boys to go into the staffroom with him, one at a time, to be photographed. Hamilton's behaviour was sufficiently odd for half of the parents to want rid of him. The other half wanted to retain the teenager, and the debate got so heated that Hamilton asked his MP to intervene on his behalf. The man sensibly refused, and Hamilton moved on to youth work in Stirling instead.

Camping

In 1973, aged twenty-one, he became assistant leader of a Stirling Scout troop. Later that year he became leader of another troop, at Bannockburn. But it was difficult to touch the children with other adults around, so he bided his time until early the following year, when he suggested that he take some of his favourite boys on a scouting expedition to Aviemore.

Hamilton told his superiors that he and the boys would be staying in a youth hostel. But in reality he made no such booking, sleeping instead with the children in the back of his van. He insisted that they undress before him then made them compare bodies, saying that he wanted to see which boy had the biggest chest.

When the Scouts found out about this, they warned him in no uncertain terms that he must never sleep alone with the boys again. Hamilton apologised repeatedly – then three weeks later took another group of boys hill-walking, and did the exact same thing. Insisting that he was teaching them survival skills, he made the youngsters perform exercise after exercise in the rain until they were soaked and exhausted. Most of the little boys became deeply distressed. Only when night fell did he let them change out of their wet clothes into their pyjamas, whilst he stayed with them in the back of the van and intently watched their every move.

Some of the children returned home suffering from mild hypothermia – they'd faced an even greater chill overnight when the van had frozen and had to be towed to the nearest garage. Asked to explain his conduct, Hamilton said that the youth hostel had been overbooked and that he and the boys had been turned away, but when the scout leaders checked, they found that no such booking had been made. Aware that he had manipulated the situation so that he could sleep with the boys, the district commissioner of the Scouts insisted that he resign.

But a paedophile ceaselessly looks for reasons to get close to children, so Hamilton contacted other districts, offering to become a Scout leader. Thankfully, his reputation had preceded him and he was turned down. At this stage – perhaps fearing that the local press would expose him – his supposed parents admitted that they were really his grandparents, but it's likely that he'd already figured this out.

Control

Determined to be in control of his own destiny, he quit his job with the county architect's office and opened a shop called Woodcraft in Stirling, selling fitted kitchens and DIY materials. Desperate to attract young boys to the premises, he set up a makeshift shooting range in the back. Thereafter, he often invited male children to join him in a shooting session, and a neighbouring shopkeeper was so concerned at the number of boys hanging around that he informed the police. But the police didn't tell Hamilton that he was behaving inappropriately, possibly because his grandfather, Jimmy, had been a freemason for decades and had many friends on the force at the local masonic lodge. The police were also given discounts on materials that they bought from Woodcraft by a fawning Hamilton. He could be sickeningly obsequious around adults – but his fantasies were of dominating boys, of being totally in control.

A gun freak

The twenty-five-year-old joined a local gun club in 1977, and the police issued him with a firearms certificate. Later his certificate was expanded to allow the purchase of a .22 rifle and a .22 semiautomatic pistol, and by 1979 he'd acquired a .357 revolver and a .270 rifle. He was also allowed to increase the amount of ammunition he could hold.

The overweight and bespectacled shopkeeper joined various shooting clubs and ranges, where other adults found him uncommunicative and withdrawn. Determined to exert control, he set up two boys' clubs called the Rovers, in Dunblane and Bannockburn in the early 1980s, and put the boys through rigorous exercises.

Hamilton also demanded that the boys wear black swimming trunks of his choosing and insisted that they pose for him, taking photograph after photograph which he displayed in his bedroom. (He was still living with his grandparents.) He often made the boys stretch up and take hold of a gym bar so that they looked as if they were hanging from a rack. He also made them lie in freezing water, wearing only black trunks, until they were shivering with the cold. Hamilton spent hours with the best looking of the boys, sometimes slapping their thighs for some supposed indiscretion then rubbing the pain away.

He'd take one child at a time into the club staffroom, where it's believed that he indecently assaulted many of them. One mother, noticing that her son was upset each time that he left the club, refused to take him back there – whereupon Hamilton phoned her and angrily demanded an explanation, saying that she was depriving her boy of a joyous time.

Parents began to withdraw their sons, complaining that the club reminded them of the Hitler Youth. But other parents got up a petition to support Hamilton, so he was able to continue renting council premises for his clubs. Aware that his bachelorhood looked increasingly strange, he told many of the parents that he was married, even pointing out one of the boys and claiming him as his son.

The sadistic side of Hamilton's personality continued to emerge. He took boys into the woods and encouraged them to shoot animals. He'd find a reason to punish the children, beating them with a metal ruler or wooden spoon, and then rubbing cold cream onto the weals. Afterwards he paid them to keep quiet. Many of them held their silence for years.

He bought himself a boat and suggested to various authorities that he take male children out on it, but when he failed the safety checks it wasn't allowed. The boat mysteriously burst into flames in the early 1980s and, in 1983, he collected the insurance money.

Hamilton lived off this money for a while, as by now his DIY shop was failing – unsurprisingly, given that he spent most of his time with male children. He sold the shop at a loss in 1985 and began to claim unemployment benefit, but made some money on the black economy by buying cameras and selling them on at a profit to other amateur photographers. Like many socially inept men, he was fascinated by mechanical equipment and seemed to use it as a people substitute. This was true of guns as well as cameras, and others at his shooting clubs noticed that he treated each of his weapons as if it were a child.

Sadistic games

By now his birth mother, Agnes – who was still telling acquaintances that Thomas was her younger brother – had gotten her own flat. But he remained with his grandparents, who were becoming evermore frail. He would play sadistic mind games with them, on one occasion pretending to Mrs Hamilton that he'd called an ambulance on her behalf, though she protested that she was simply feeling off-colour. For the next three hours he watched her become increasingly distressed at the thought of being taken away on a stretcher, and then admitted he'd made the whole thing up. He was equally cruel to his grandfather, frequently locking him out of the house for twenty minutes at a time and refusing to let him watch his favourite programmes on TV.

In 1987 his grandmother died, leaving him and his grandfather alone together. Thereafter, the state of cleanliness in the flat steadily declined. So did the popularity of Hamilton's boys' clubs, which often started with seventy members but quickly dwindled to a dozen or less. His dubious reputation had so preceded him in one area that, when he tried to form a new club, only one boy showed up.

But the paedophile persevered, offering gymnastic lessons to boys – though in truth he himself only held the most basic gymnastics certificate. Well-meaning parents often offered to help out but he swiftly discouraged this, suggesting that the boys would become more independent if he taught them alone. He emphasised the need for discipline and for military-style training. Sadly, this appealed to some parents and they let him inflict his training on their sons.

Needless to say, his ability to converse with other adults continued to decline. The situation worsened when his grandfather moved into sheltered accommodation, leaving Thomas alone in the flat. He rarely cleaned the cooker or did the dishes, and had no personal possessions in his home – apart from a total of five thousand photographs, negatives and slides of little boys. He would lie in his sleeping bag in his austere bedroom and stare at them, doubtless masturbating and fuelling his unhealthy fantasies.

Frightening

Increasingly lonely and embittered, he began to frighten the neighbours, sneaking up behind them before asking, "How are you?" He'd smile when he saw them jump, and then slope away again.

Hamilton continued to form clubs across central Scotland, listing a fictitious club committee on his headed notepaper. All were aimed at males under twelve. In July 1988 he took some of these boys to a summer camp at Inchmoan Island on Loch Lomond, and told them that they mustn't wear trousers as bare legs would dry more quickly. This allowed him to enjoy his fetish of young boys in black swimming trunks, but meant that the boys' calves became badly scratched by the bracken. As usual, he revelled in their suffering. He also spanked two of the boys on their bare bottoms, which for him was an erotic act, and made several of them rub suntan lotion all over his naked body whilst he writhed in ecstasy inside his tent.

Hamilton gave the children the same unappetising food each day, refused to let them phone home and generally treated them like slaves. But a couple of parents made a surprise trip to see their sons and were appalled at what they found. They complained to the police, who investigated and found that the children were underdressed, cold and, in some instances, frightened. They were removed from the camp.

The police put in a complaint to the Procurator Fiscal, who suggested that they inform the social services. Meanwhile, deciding that attack was the best form of defence, Hamilton made a formal complaint against the police, suggesting that they hadn't behaved professionally when they'd investigated his camp.

The controversy faded away, and the paedophile took another group of boys to Mullarochy Bay on Loch Lomond. Again he spanked them and ordered them around. He also photographed them in their bathing trunks in various positions, and made one youngster lie in a pool of cold water while he took photographs. He took another into his tent and insisted he wear a pair of scarlet swimming trunks, then took photograph after photograph, demanding that the frightened child change his position each time.

Again the police responded to complaints, and arrived to find Hamilton videoing the children. Indeed, a film processor in Stirling had been so concerned at all of the snapshots of half-dressed boys that he too had contacted the police. Unfortunately, the authorities decided that they couldn't prove criminality on Hamilton's part – so they gave him his photographs back.

Unstable

But in November 1991, there was a moment of sanity when a detective discovered that the suspected paedophile had a firearms licence. He wrote a memo which said, "Hamilton is an unsavoury character and unstable personality . . . who is not to be trusted," and suggested that the man's right to bear arms should be withdrawn. But his superior ignored the warning, and Thomas Hamilton continued to hold guns and grudges – a potentially lethal combination.

Further cruelty

The following summer he ran a sports training course at Dunblane High School and took some of the boys camping within the town. Three were later found by the local police, wandering the streets in their pyjamas. The Child Protection Unit was informed.

But Hamilton was allowed to continue his work with young males, and, by June 1993, was again photographing youngsters in tightly-fitting trunks, choosing them from the boys he coached in Dunblane and Stirling. The police asked the Procurator Fiscal if they could search Hamilton's flat for these photographs, fearing that some might be pornographic, but permission was refused. The following year, two men tried to kick his door down, screaming that he was a pervert and demanding that he return photographs he'd taken of their young male relative. Neighbours overheard the commotion and phoned the police. The police arrived, listened to the men's complaints and then told them to leave, and that everything was under control.

By March 1995, three more of the bachelor's clubs had ended after boys complained of ill-treatment or parents witnessed him dominating their children. He'd forced some to strip to their underpants, favouring the quietest boys as they were the most biddable, the least likely to make a fuss when he videoed them. Rumours about his weirdness continued to circulate, yet the previous month he'd had his firearms certificate extended for another three years. Six months later he added to his arsenal for the first time in almost a decade, buying a second Browning 9mm pistol and ammunition.

In retrospect it seems he'd already begun toying with the idea of killing as many people as possible, to exact revenge on those who had shut down his existing clubs. Indeed, he'd already chosen Dunblane Primary School as a possible target, asking one of its pupils about the school layout and questioning him closely about when morning assembly began. Over two hundred pupils would gather in the school hall at this time, which would allow him to cause mayhem with his guns . . .

Increasing lawlessness

He also considered massacring the children at Bannockburn Primary School, and was seen there checking out the layout. But his plans were briefly put on hold when he succeeded in starting a new boys' club at Bishopbriggs on the outskirts of Glasgow, further away from his home. The convenor of the education committee even gave him a reference. Needless to say, he soon began to behave inappropriately with the children, and concerned parents took their sons away. This club – and a couple of others – continued, but were poorly attended and comparatively muted affairs.

Hamilton's life continued to go downhill. The authorities realised that he was selling photographic equipment on the side and not declaring his earnings, so they stopped his unemployment benefit. He took out a loan but was unable to pay it back. Partially funding his lifestyle through credit cards (his boys' clubs didn't make a profit because he had alienated so many parents) he ran up debts of £8,000.

In January 1996, he purchased another Smith & Wesson revolver (and pliers which could be used to cut telephone wires), and started a letter-writing campaign to local schools and Scout leaders, complaining that he'd been wrongly branded a pervert. These missives showed his increasing paranoia, claiming that his standing in the community had suffered as a result of unfounded gossip.

He was further enraged when an acquaintance admitted that, if he had sons, he wouldn't send them to one of Hamilton's clubs. Determined to cause maximum fear, the paedophile pointed a 9mm pistol at him and pulled the trigger. The gun wasn't loaded, but this was still an aggressive and troubling act. Around this time he also apparently asked Dunblane Primary School if he could work as a volunteer, but they knew that his intentions towards children weren't honourable and turned him down.

By the following month he'd become even more troubled and wrote to the Queen, patron of the Scouts, urging her to restore his good name. He copied the letter to various local dignitaries, including the headmasters of Bannockburn Primary and Dunblane Primary.

At the start of March 1996, he bought two expensive shirts on his credit card and began wearing them on a day-to-day basis, an unusual extravagance for a man who normally lived in his anorak. He told an acquaintance that he would never have to pay for them, so it's probable that he'd already planned mass murder and suicide. Later that same week, whilst shopping in Stirling, he bumped into a retired policeman whom he knew and talked to him at length about the Hungerford massacre, which entailed loner Michael Ryan murdering sixteen people and wounding fifteen others in 1987, before committing suicide. Chillingly, Hamilton also asked the constable how quickly a firearms response unit would take to reach a murder scene.

Robotic

On 12 March, the day before his intended killing spree, Hamilton rented a white van in Stirling, the vehicle he would use to drive to the site of the massacre. The receptionist said that he spoke slowly and methodically, and sounded robotic. She looked into his eyes and felt that they were devoid of humanity. He then visited his birth mother, Agnes, for six hours, having a bath and a meal at her home. She noticed nothing unusual about his behaviour, and had no idea that she'd never see him alive again. (Many spree killers, including the aforementioned Ryan, kill their mothers during their shooting spree, but Hamilton let his live.)

The massacre

On 13 March 1996, a freezing, cloudy Wednesday, Thomas Hamilton went outside and scraped ice from the van that he'd rented. According to neighbours, he looked unusually cheerful. At last he was going to wreak his revenge on those he believed had belittled him. He knew that, by killing as many small children as possible, he'd leave utter devastation and despair in his path.

Driving to Dunblane Primary School for 9:30am, Hamilton parked in the school grounds. Fetching a pair of pliers from the vehicle, he walked to the nearest telegraph pole and cut what he thought were the school's telephone wires – in fact, he cut the wires of nearby houses in error. Walking into the assembly hall and finding it empty (he'd been misinformed about the assembly's starting time and it was already over), he angrily fired two shots from one of his Browning 9mm pistols into the stage. He also had a second Browning and another two handguns about his person, plus enough ammunition to kill hundreds of people. He'd deliberately chosen soft-nosed bullets which are designed to stay in the body and cause maximum damage.

The forty-three-year-old man then walked into the gym where three women, twenty-six five-year-olds and two six-year-olds were about to start a gym lesson. He shot first at PE teacher Eileen Harrild, bullets entering both of her arms, her hand and her breast. Badly wounded, she staggered into the open-plan storage area of the gymnasium and several of the children instinctively followed her. He also shot at her assistant, Mrs Blake, who was wounded but managed to usher some more of the children into the store.

Hamilton continued to fire indiscriminately, killing many of the children and their teacher, Gwen Mayor. During the next four minutes he fired one hundred and three times. Leaving the room for a moment, he walked towards the nearest classroom with his revolver pointing at the window. Espying him, the teacher screamed to the children to lie down on the floor. The gunman fired nine bullets in the room, but each of them missed. Returning calmly to the gym, he began to kill the wounded five-year-olds. Some of the children in the storage area started screaming but their teacher put her finger to her lips in a silent warning, and they managed to keep quiet. Soon the badly injured went into shock.

With fifteen children and their teacher dead – and a dozen children and two women wounded – Hamilton put the Smith & Wesson in his mouth and fired once, blowing part of his skull away.

By 9:40am, a teacher had managed to alert the headmaster that there was carnage in the gym and that the gunman had shot himself, and the police were called. The headmaster and another teacher then rushed to the gym to find it awash with blood. Teacher Gwen Mayor, aged forty-five, and fifteen of her pupils lay dead. A sixteenth was dying. Most had been shot four times. The janitor arrived and thought that Hamilton moved slightly, so he kicked the gun from his hand. Thomas Hamilton was dead by the time he was removed from the gym.

Instant profiling

That night, I was in Glasgow to hear former FBI agent John Douglas give a talk about serial killers. The story had just broken in the evening press, though the identity of the spree killer hadn't yet been made public. We only knew that a gunman had killed seventeen people and wounded a similar number at Dunblane Primary School before committing suicide.

The moment John Douglas entered the room, a local journalist asked him to speculate about the killer. Douglas said that he'd be a loner who probably lived on his own and that he'd have a prior connection to the school. This turned out to be completely accurate.

(I spoke to Douglas afterwards and he told me that he was most often approached by female abuse survivors who wanted to be profilers, as they saw this as a way of overcoming their victimhood and giving something back to society.)

Aftermath

All of Scotland – and indeed the world – was horrified by the carnage that Thomas Hamilton had wreaked, and the parents of the murdered children later founded the Dunblane Snowdrops Campaign to lobby against recreational shooters keeping handguns. Bereaved parent Mick North wrote eloquently about the subject for the *Times Higher Education Supplement*, noting that "there are alternative pastimes which can provide the pleasure that they seek. There are no alternative lives for our children." He later wrote an equally moving book, *Dunblane: Never Forget*.

Physically normal

Thomas Hamilton's autopsy revealed no physical abnormalities and showed that there was no alcohol or drugs in his system. Two psychiatrists at the subsequent Dunblane enquiry dismissed the notion that he was mentally ill. (Most paedophiles are clinically sane.) He was, they noted, exhibiting signs of a paranoid personality in that he imagined people were plotting against him and he harboured grudges. They believe that he had wanted to commit suicide for some time but lacked the courage. But by killing the children he had backed himself into a corner, and had little option but to take his own life.

CHAPTER FOUR

HOWARD HUGHES

A violent troublemaker for many years, Hughes was convicted of the
1995 rape–murder of a seven-year-old girl.

Early problems

Howard was born in 1965, the fourth child of Renee and Gerald
Hughes. The couple already had three daughters and the family lived in
Llandudno, North Wales.

Unfortunately, Howard was born with a rare chromosomal
abnormality called XYY syndrome, which caused him to grow at an
accelerated rate. He didn't learn to speak until he was five and was
developmentally backwards. At school, he was violent towards his
classmates and was so unstable that he was sent to a child psychiatrist at
the age of six.

His wealthy parents (his father owned a construction company) tried
sending him to a private school, but his instability increased and he was
expelled. They moved him to another school but he played truant
constantly. At ten he was diagnosed as dyslexic, and his parents sent him
to a school for pupils with special needs in Derbyshire, which he hated,
regarding it as punitive rather than therapeutic. He remained angry and
desperately immature.

By age eleven he'd grown to six feet and terrorised his fellow pupils.
But he was also self-destructive, biting his fingernails until they bled. His
father said that he had to discipline him as if he were a much younger

child, and their relationship was incredibly volatile. He was much closer to his mother, who indulged him both emotionally and financially. His parents' relationship became increasingly unstable and they underwent an acrimonious divorce.

Sexually abused

In his early teens Howard was sent to the Bryn Estyn care home in Wrexham, an establishment where he was allegedly sexually abused – as, it's been substantiated, were many of his fellow pupils. Recognising that he was deeply unhappy, his mother brought him back to live with her and resorted to home schooling. But he began stalking some of the local schoolgirls, spying on them as they sunbathed in their bikinis, and telling them that he knew what they looked like without their clothes. He would lurk behind garden bushes in the neighbourhood for hours, hoping to get a glimpse of female flesh.

He spent the rest of his free time hanging around younger boys, stealing bikes to impress them and showing them his extensive collection of toy cars.

Attempted murder

At age fifteen, he persuaded a seven-year-old boy, Graham Lloyd, to explore a derelict house in Colwyn Bay with him. Suddenly Hughes pounced on the child and sat astride him, holding him down. He squeezed the boy's neck until he started to lose consciousness. Believing that he was dead, Howard left the scene.

When Graham revived, he ran home and told his father. He was taken to hospital where he remained for the next two days, the doctors noting that he'd been lucky to survive. Hughes was taken to juvenile court, and then committed to a mental hospital in Northampton where he failed to respond to therapy. After his committal period expired, he was transferred to another hospital before leaving to live on the streets, becoming a peeping tom. Later still, he moved back with his endlessly supportive mother, who was still living in Colwyn Bay.

Unemployable

Despite his parents' best efforts to educate him, Howard Hughes finished his schooling without gaining a single qualification. Gerald Hughes tried to employ his son in the family construction company, but Howard often vandalised equipment. Resultantly becoming one of the long-term unemployed (though he optimistically described himself as an unemployed gardener), he spent many hours cycling around Colwyn Bay and Llandudno on his beloved mountain bike. He shouted and swore at residents as he cycled past them, and even threatened some of them with a gun.

Over the next few years, he appeared in court fifteen times on charges ranging from illegal possession of a gun to car theft and burglary, and served two jail sentences. Police became used to arresting the huge man with the rotting teeth and staring eyes. They would often see Hughes wandering about at night, picking up pieces of discarded junk to bring home.

He enjoyed terrorising the neighbours, playing his music loudly to upset them, and stealing women's underwear from nearby clothing lines. He also had a fetish for hairlessness and would shave off every inch of his body hair. The locals referred to him as 'Mad Howard'. But there was method in his madness for, rather than getting caught with incriminating paedophilic photographs in his house, he hid them in a hole in an outside wall.

Rape

Soon the indecent photographs that he took of his young relatives weren't enough to sustain him. At age twenty-two, he raped a fourteen-year-old girl. He would sexually assault her thirty times over the next two years, but she was too afraid to tell her family, though she confided in her best friend about his cruelty. The abuse would only come to light after he was charged with murder, when the best friend told her mother, who went to the police.

At twenty-five, he sexually assaulted a three-year-old girl and a five-year-old girl. These 1990 assaults were reported, but the authorities decided that the girls were too young to testify and the cases were dropped. That same year, he indecently assaulted a nine-year-old girl but her parents didn't want her to go to court.

Howard Hughes' unhealthy libido continued to rise, and in 1993 he made indecent suggestions to a four-year-old girl and sexually attacked a girl of fifteen. The latter assault wasn't reported at the time, and the former was dropped through a lack of corroborating evidence.

That same year, Hughes terrorised two eleven-year-old girls who were having a sleepover in a summerhouse at the bottom of their garden. He battered on the summerhouse walls, then fired a starting pistol as they fled. Fortunately, the children stayed indoors with their parents for the rest of the evening, escaping the paedophile's lust and his increasingly murderous rage.

By now, Hughes was taking indecent photographs of another pre-school girl which he hid in his room. He also bought a rottweiler and taught it to snarl and bark at everyone, sometimes urging it to attack small children.

On 29 July 1995, he asked a seven-year-old girl to come for a ride on his bicycle — he'd done this in the past, and then sexually assaulted his young passenger. Thankfully, the seven-year-old refused and ran away.

On 30 July, he spied on children who were playing in the local paddling pool at Craig-y-Don. Later, he cycled past a house where a seven-year-old girl called Sophie Hook was playing in a garden pool with her brother, sister and cousin. The house belonged to Sophie's aunt and uncle, and that evening they set up a tent so that the youngsters could have fun camping outside. It seemed safe, as there would be three children sleeping in the bush-encircled garden and the tent had a security light trained on it.

Hughes cycled home and spent the evening with his mother, then left the house after she went to bed. He cycled back to Llandudno and took a seat near the promenade, a couple of minutes' walk away from the garden where the children slept.

Murder
At 2:30am, Sophie's twelve-year-old cousin briefly woke up and saw her

asleep in the tent. At 2:55am police spoke to Howard Hughes, who was sitting on a bench and smoking a cigarette. He answered them civilly and seemed relaxed.

When the children woke at 7:15am, Sophie was gone. Some time in between – probably before 4am – the seven-year-old was lured from the tent then taken to a quiet location where she was stripped, violently raped and sodomised before being strangled. Her naked body was thrown into the sea, possibly from the cliff head, a steep walk away from the abduction site. It was found that morning, washed up on Craig-y-Don beach near Llandudno, by a man walking his dog.

Hughes was arrested that afternoon. He seemed the ideal suspect. After all, he'd been in the vicinity at the time of the murder, had a history of sexually assaulting children and had previously strangled a seven-year-old boy.

The police questioned Hughes for the next three days, but he continued to protest his innocence. They knew they'd have to charge him or let him go by 3pm on 3 August.

That lunchtime, he received a welfare visit from his father. When his sister Heather entered the room a short time later, she found Howard crying and saying that he was sorry. At the interview's end, Gerald Hughes told the police where to find Sophie's nightdress, information that his son had provided. Howard had tossed it over a hedge.

At 3pm the police released the suspect but immediately re-arrested him for possessing indecent photographs of one of his prepubescent relatives. Less than an hour later, they found Sophie's nightdress in the area that Hughes had told his father about.

That night, Gerald Hughes talked to his daughters and his brother-in-law; then he contacted the police to say that Howard had confessed to Sophie's murder during their welfare visit that lunchtime. Just before 10pm, the paedophile was charged.

Howard Hughes continued to deny murdering Sophie Hook. He said that, when his sister entered the interview room, he'd been saying sorry for taking indecent photographs his father had discovered a fortnight before. He added that his father had invented the murder confession in order to get rid of him, as their relationship had always been acrimonious. He maintained that he'd found Sophie's nightdress whilst on one of his nocturnal jaunts and had picked it up, planning to use it as toilet paper. Then he'd changed his mind and dropped it in the area in which it was found.

A miscarriage of justice?

A human rights organisation, South Wales Liberty, soon took up Hughes' case as a possible miscarriage of justice, claiming that his proximity to the abduction site meant nothing as he wandered around Llandudno all the time. He was also in the habit of picking things up, so he could have legitimately found Sophie Hook's discarded nightwear.

Hughes had also been wearing insect repellent that night, and repellent had been found on the nightdress – but not on the tent flap or sleeping bag. South Wales Liberty argued that this meant Sophie had exited the tent of her own volition, possibly because she knew and trusted her assailant. They said that she would have screamed if six-foot-eight Hughes had entered the tent and tried to lift her out. (An alternative explanation, of course, is that she left the tent to urinate, Hughes grabbed her and put his hand over her mouth.)

South Wales Liberty noted that the police had originally said that they had forensic evidence, and that they continued to take samples from local men after Hughes was in custody. This suggested that they had forensic material which could rule a suspect in or out, yet police later stated that all forensic material had been washed away in the sea. Moreover, though the rape and sodomy were violent, there were no marks on Hughes' genitalia, yet rapists often have reddened and even torn penises after such a forceful act.

The prosecution's pathologist said that the numerous marks on Sophie had probably been made by her attacker's nails – but when it was pointed out that Hughes' nails were bitten to the quick, they decided that the scratches had been caused by rocks when she'd been thrown over the cliff.

Liberty found that a soldier suffering from Gulf War Syndrome had left a local psychiatric hospital on the night of the murder and returned the next morning, soaking wet, as if he'd been immersed in water. Shortly afterwards he committed suicide.

Surprisingly, the group also said that Howard Hughes had no history of sexual offences. The reality was that he hadn't been found *guilty* of any sexual offences – he'd committed numerous acts of indecency but had never gone to trial. They also said that he had no history of extreme violence, whereas in truth he'd tried to murder a seven-year-old boy.

South Wales Liberty pointed out that Hughes had continued to protest his innocence. But this is meaningless, as few sexual offenders admit to their criminal acts.

Court

Howard Hughes' trial began at Chester Crown Court on 24 June 1996. Gerald Hughes told the jury that Howard had admitted the murder to him during his welfare visit at the local police station, and told him where he'd thrown the child's nightdress.

Another witness – a thief who was in jail by the time he testified – said that he'd seen Hughes carrying a body in a sack on the night of Sophie's disappearance. (Statements such as this from other convicted criminals are often self-serving, as cooperating with the authorities may bring them early release.) Howard's friend, paedophile Michael Guidi, also took the stand and said that Howard had previously boasted of wanting to rape a girl aged four or five.

The prosecution's case relied on the alleged confession made to his father plus the testimony of the two convicted criminals. The fact that insect repellent had been transferred from Hughes to the nightdress of Sophie Hook was also considered damning. The defence countered that there was no forensic evidence linking Hughes to the rape-murder, and that – given that he admitted picking up the nightdress from the street – the case was purely circumstantial.

On 18 July 1996, the jury returned with a guilty verdict on the charges of abduction, rape and murder. Only then did they hear that

Hughes had recently been charged with the rape of a fourteen-year-old girl which had taken place almost a decade earlier, in 1987.

The paedophile was given three life sentences by the judge, who called him a 'fiend' and recommended that he never be released. He was sent to Full Sutton Prison in York.

Appeals

In 1998, Howard Hughes appealed against his conviction but his petition was unsuccessful. He did so again in 2001, but his conviction was again upheld. The Court of Appeal said that he couldn't appeal again in future unless new evidence came to light. The following year, the Home Secretary, David Blunkett, ruled that Hughes and three other convicted child killers would each serve a fifty-year sentence before becoming eligible for parole. But within forty-eight hours the European Court of Human Rights had removed the Home Secretary's power to set minimum terms.

In March 2002, Hughes lodged a claim for compensation against the Bryn Estyn care home, alleging that he'd been sexually abused there as a child in the late 1970's. A paedophile ring had targeted children at the home and at other homes throughout North Wales in the seventies and eighties, the offences only being made public after the turn of the millennium.

CHAPTER FIVE

LESLIE PATRICK BAILEY

M ost paedophiles act alone, but Bailey joined forces with several other child killers – primarily Sidney Cooke, Robert Oliver and Lennie Smith – in the mid-1980's to commit some of the most brutal murders in British history.

Early hell

Leslie was born on 21 June 1953 to Lilian Bailey. The single mother would also give birth to a daughter and, for a brief period, all three lived together in a council house in Hackney, east London. (She would later have a second son.) Neglected, Leslie soon developed a speech impediment, could barely articulate his needs and would never learn to read or write. Both children were soon taken into care for their own protection – ironically, as Leslie was repeatedly buggered from the age of eleven by an older boy in the council-run care home.

He was eventually sent to a boarding school in Ongar, Essex for the educationally subnormal. One of his equally ill-treated relatives ended up in a similar establishment and would only ever attain a mental age of eight.

Leslie escaped into the surrounding forest whenever possible, fantasising about exacting revenge. He left school at sixteen and drifted from job to job, working as a bin man or as a casual labourer. Sometimes he spent his rent money on drugs and drink, resorting to living on the streets. A mate taught him to drive, though his driving would always be erratic. His thin body and bulging eyes made him look slightly comical, and his slow, halting speech made him sound harmless, but deep down he was filled with rage. And the lengthy sexual abuse that he'd suffered meant that his rage often manifested itself in a sexual form . . .

Two attempted murders

When he was twenty, he sodomised and attempted to murder a seven-year-old girl. The child was left badly traumatised. But lawyers deemed some of the evidence against him was inadmissible, and he was only sentenced for possessing a knife. Aware that he was in the throes of a nervous breakdown (abuse survivors often suffer from episodic mental illness), the authorities sent him to a psychiatric facility in Kent for three months.

For the next six years, he seemed to keep his violence under control – or maybe he just terrorised his victims into keeping quiet. But in 1979 his rage exploded again.

Following a young woman into the elevator of a housing block, he battered her repeatedly then took the elevator to the basement, where he dragged her out and viciously sodomised her. This time he served a prison sentence, other inmates giving him the nickname 'Catweazle', after the scarecrow-like magician in the eponymous children's TV series of the 1970's.

Bad influences

By the early eighties, Leslie was living on a Hackney council estate and having sex with various men, though boys were now his preference. One of the men he was acquainted with was an itinerant fairground worker and notorious paedophile called Sidney Cooke.

Sidney Charles Cooke

Sidney was born on 18 April 1927 to Elizabeth Cooke in Stroud, Gloucestershire. His father remains unknown. His mother lived a rough and ready life working on a farm, and Sidney was so unsocialised that he wasn't shown how to bathe or clean his clothes. As a result, he often stank and was ostracised by the other boys. Lonely and unloved, he was a magnet for equally dirty and brutalised paedophiles.

At seven, he was sexually abused by his uncle and would later claim that he enjoyed it, as it was the closest thing to love he'd ever known. His surname meant that he was unimaginatively nicknamed Cookie, but there was nothing sweet natured about a boy capable of incredible mood swings who was fast becoming a sociopath.

Sidney left school at fourteen and became a farm labourer like his mother. By adulthood he'd grown to a mere five foot six and was slight of build, with a stoop and a slight limp. Illiterate and inarticulate, he knew nothing of the world but was possessed by an almost animalistic sexual drive.

Conscripted into the army during the Second World War, he was sent to the Middle East but was considered a poor soldier, detained several times for going AWOL. Eventually discharged in 1952, Cooke then began to work at fairgrounds, travelling around Britain and sexually assaulting young boys. He often worked on the dodgems and would join a lone youngster in one of the little cars, putting his coat over both their laps in order to fondle his victim. On other occasions he ran a ring-the-bell-and-test-your-strength machine for children, and would offer attractive youngsters extra prizes if they'd accompany him to his van ...

Marriage

But though children, ideally boys, were his preferred sexual partners, he was happy to have sex with grown men and women. He eventually began an affair with a young woman called Ivy. They married when he was twenty-eight and remained together for the next six years – though he continued to corrupt prepubescent children, including some of his own relatives.

In the spring of 1961, aged thirty-four, he sat next to a little boy in a cinema and attempted to fondle him. He was arrested and fined £20 for indecent assault.

Undeterred, Cooke continued to molest vulnerable children throughout the sixties, seventies and eighties, often persuading homeless or neglected youngsters to become rent boys, living with him and handing over part of their earnings. Many of these boys would later admit to police that the sex was brutal, and that Cooke enjoyed inflicting pain. In 1984 he was seen to lure two boys, aged six and seven, into a lorry cab at a London fairground. He molested them, and then gave them £1 each. Another fairground worker, realising belatedly what had happened, hit Cooke so hard that he almost knocked him out.

But nothing would stop Cooke – whose nickname had now changed to the more aggressive 'Hissing Sid' – from sexually abusing children. His youngest female victim was six years old, whilst his youngest male victim was only four. He also liked to club together with other paedophiles to 'buy' a boy for the evening, setting up a gang bang in some dingy fairground caravan or filthy flat. One of Cooke's many male lovers – who would later boast of helping to kill over a dozen boys – was Robert Oliver.

Robert Francis Oliver

Robert's early life had been as brutalising as Sidney's. He'd been born in 1954 to a mother who was full of violence and rage. She already had four daughters and wanted another girl. Rather than accept Robert's gender, she dressed him up in skirts and dresses, put his hair into pigtails with pretty ribbons, and called him by a girl's name. She continued to do so when he went to school. Needless to say, he was bullied mercilessly and his perturbed teachers begged her to buy him some boy's clothing, but she repeatedly refused. Terrified of her violence and wounded by her constant taunting, Robert turned to food for comfort and soon began to gain weight.

At age six, still dressed as a girl, he was lured into a van by a man asking for directions. The man brutally sodomised him. Robert, who was terrified, screamed in pain, but the man told him to shut up and enjoy it, then gave him £2.

The teachers and some of the parents at his school eventually clubbed together and bought him an appropriate school uniform. But it was too little, too late, and he remained effeminate. A magnet for paedophiles, he was picked up by various men over the next few years and eventually sent to a school for children with learning difficulties. He would remain unable to read or write.

By age fourteen he'd left school and started to sell sexual favours to older men, telling police that he felt safer with the punters than he did with his own increasingly vindictive mother. Though his spiralling weight problem limited his appeal to many men, some were attracted by his high, feminine voice.

At seventeen, his mother threw him out because she realised that he was gay and he supported himself by burglary, later convicted of five separate charges and spending several short spells in jail. By his very late teens he resorted to unskilled factory work, at one stage working for a confectionary firm.

But his main focus was always on sex, and he became more interested in very young boys. He began to hang around public toilets and proposition pre-teens, and was sent to prison for buggering a nine-year-old. He served another sentence for committing the same act with a thirteen-year-old.

But sex wasn't enough to block out the memories of his appalling childhood, and Robert Oliver turned to prescription tranquilisers, spending most of his days in a vallium-induced haze. Reverting to his formative experiences, he began to dress as a woman and called himself Susan Ward. He lived with Leslie Bailey for a while and the men were lovers. He also had sex with Sidney Cooke, who dominated him to an unhealthy degree and treated him like a slave. Robert also kept in touch with another damaged man whom he'd known since his mid-teens, a vicious but businesslike paedophile called Lennie Smith.

Lennie Gilchrist Smith

Lennie was born on 23 August 1954 to Eileen Smith. He was illegitimate, her fifth child after two sons and two daughters from various relationships. The family, plus Eileen's long-term boyfriend Jack, lived together in Montgomeryshire, Wales.

Little is known of Lennie's formative years, but he was sufficiently desperate for cash by the age of thirteen to become a rent boy. His dark hair, his small frame and, in particular, his boyish appearance ensured that he was always in demand. By turns emotional and aggressive, he left school at fourteen. That same year, his mother broke up with Jack and Lennie was taken into care.

He soon ran away from the care home, supporting himself through burglary and by selling his body. Brought back to the home, he ran away again and again. He worked as a rent boy at Victoria station in London, but was later given lodgings in upmarket Belgravia by the wealthy son of an MP. The man liked to be bound and whipped, and this suited the rage-filled Lennie just fine.

But by his late teens he could no longer attract wealthy paedophiles, and moved on to Southend, Essex, where he got a job at an amusement arcade, sleeping with the elderly gay owner. There Lennie targeted younger boys for rough sex. He liked to inflict maximum pain during these sessions, pulling the boys' hair and tightening his hands around their necks to restrict their breathing as he sodomised them. During this period, he was convicted of trying to obtain goods by deception and also of theft.

At twenty-three, he was caught whilst committing an act of gross indecency in a public place and sentenced to a year in prison. He later moved to Birmingham, where he was convicted of burglary and served another year. On his release he returned to London and became a pimp, finding prepubescent boys for a group of paedophiles. He would sometimes keep a boy for himself and tell him that he loved him, but familiarity soon bred contempt and he'd sell the child on to another man. If a boy didn't want to have sex with him, Lennie would simply crush muscle relaxants into the child's glass of cola, then taking advantage of the situation when the boy went limp. He was still reasonably good looking, but some of his teenage partners walked out on him when they realised that he was sodomising children as young as six.

A marriage of convenience

In 1984, Lennie Smith married a Bolivian student so that she could gain British residency, a scam for which he was paid £500. But his only genuine sexual interest was in young boys, including a shy teenager called Jason Swift who he sometimes pimped. But, before the group ensnared Jason for a final time, they'd kill an even younger boy called Mark Tildesley . . .

Mark Tildesley's murder

On Friday 1 June 1984, Sidney Cooke hitched a lift to Wokingham, Surrey, where he knew there was a fair and that he'd have access to a caravan. He soon started talking to a local child, seven-year-old Mark Tildesley, taking him on the dodgems and buying him sweets. Cooke then phoned Lennie Smith and Leslie Bailey, telling them that he'd found a suitable victim. Leslie immediately drove himself and Lennie from Hackney to Wokingham.

As Cooke walked him towards Bailey's car, Mark realised that he was in trouble and began to struggle. But Cooke simply picked him up and threw him into the white Triumph 2000. Bailey then drove to a caravan owned by his equally dissolute relative, a man who had the nickname 'Oddbod'. The latter had been unsocialised as a child to the degree that he hadn't been shown how to wipe himself after evacuating his bowels. As a result he stank and his clothes were filthy. But that was of little consequence to the other men, who were equally dirty and unkempt.

The men gave Mark a glass of milk that had been heavily laced with the tranquiliser Diazepam, leading the still struggling child into the bedroom where Bailey held his head, Smith held his hands and Oddbod held his feet whilst Cooke sexually assaulted him.

Mark screamed repeatedly, but the members of the paedophile ring were indifferent – they were doing to him what had previously been done to them. Leslie Bailey would later tell police that Mark had been sodomised by all of the men present, that Cooke went first and Smith last. Bailey would also later say that Lennie strangled Mark to death – but another of Sidney Cooke's acquaintances said that Cooke had killed him. What's certain is that, immediately afterwards, the four men enjoyed a coffee and Cooke said he would dispose of the corpse. (It has never been found.)

Leslie drove Lennie home, then drove towards the council house he was sharing with a couple. But the police stopped him for driving erratically and, when they found a stolen blank certificate of insurance in the glove compartment, he was arrested and later fined £30. By then Mark Tildesley's mother had reported that he hadn't returned from the fair, so he was an official missing person. But the police had no reason to connect the seven-year-old's disappearance with this thin, stuttering man.

A bisexual fairground worker later made a false confession to Mark's murder, claiming that he'd stripped, buggered and bludgeoned the child and thrown darts at him. But he had a history of psychiatric problems, and police were eventually able to eliminate him from their enquiries. Sadly, such false confessions are common, as retarded, mentally ill and guilt-ridden men can temporarily feel better by claiming responsibility for some reprehensible criminal act.

Barry Lewis's murder

Months passed after Mark's death. There may have been other murders that were never discovered – Leslie Bailey would later tell fellow prisoners that the gang had killed sixteen to twenty children and teenagers. Most had been operating as rent boys, having run away from desperately unhappy homes. As their parents hadn't reported them missing, no searches were underway.

What's certain is that, on 9 October 1985, the gang went out in search of another victim. Driving through a council estate in south London, they saw six-year-old Barry Lewis playing football. A beautiful mixed-race child, he was being cared for by one of his mother's friends, as his mother was living in a hostel. But she visited him regularly, had got herself a flat and was about to reclaim custody.

The group drove Barry to the flat of another of their acquaintances, paedophile Donald Smith, who lived in Ashmead House on the Kingsmead estate in Hackney. Smith – who'd become bisexual during his years as a merchant seaman – was present during the horrendous acts which followed. Barry was crying and saying that he wanted to go home as he was led into the filthy flat. But the seven or eight men there (some of whom have never been identified) were indifferent to – or in some cases excited by – his distress. They gave him three powerful tranquilisers hidden inside a glass of cola to relax his muscles, and then took turns raping him. Thankfully, he soon lost consciousness. At the end of the orgy, with Barry covered in blood, the men went on to have oral sex and mutual masturbation with each other.

When the boy was apparently dead, Leslie Bailey wrapped him in a blue blanket and carried him out to a car that belonged to a friend of a friend. He drove past Waltham Abbey, Essex, travelling towards an area he knew well, the Crooked Mile. He planned to conceal the body there, hoping that it would never be found.

But to his horror, Barry suddenly sat up in the back seat – he'd been deeply unconscious rather than dead, and was now mumbling incoherently. Before Bailey could react, the Ford Granada spluttered to a halt. It had run out of fuel.

Too much of a sociopath to truly panic, Bailey put a petrol can under one arm and Barry under the other, and began to traipse towards the nearest garage. He managed to hitch a lift from a kindly couple who asked him what was wrong with the child. Bailey explained that the little boy was ill and was on medication, that he'd feel better after he'd had a sleep. Reassured, they dropped the man and boy off at the nearby petrol station and Bailey filled up his can. The petrol station attendant also commented on how drowsy Barry looked, and Bailey said that he wasn't very well but that he'd soon be fine. A schools inspector gave them a lift back to the Ford Granada, with Barry sitting on Bailey's lap. He opened his eyes once and mumbled something unintelligible. Bailey said that he needed a nap.

Back at the car, alone at last, Bailey hid Barry under the blue blanket then covered the child's nose and mouth with one hand, pressing so hard on the back of the boy's head with his other hand that he left fingertip bruises in the scalp. After a minute's suffocation, he took the corpse into a field at Monkhams Park and dug a hole about a foot deep. Stripping the child, he put him into the makeshift grave and filled it in.

Jason Swift's murder

Less than two months later, the paedophile ring killed again. On 26 November 1985, Leslie Bailey, Sidney Cooke, Robert Oliver and Lennie

Smith, plus two other men, clubbed together to buy themselves a rent boy for the evening. (They contributed £5 each, but the money didn't ever change hands.) Leslie told his landlord, twenty-six-year-old fishmonger Steven Barrell, that "something exciting" was going to happen, so Barrell accompanied him. Adopted at age four, Barrell was a bisexual sadomasochistic transvestite, with two biological children and three stepchildren, who also indulged in paedophilia from time to time. Bailey shared a house with Steven, his common-law wife Janet and all five children.

The men congregated in their friend Donald Smith's flat. Smith himself was also present. A notorious paedophile, he had the nickname 'Uncle', though he was far from avuncular. (Smith would repeatedly lie to the police, saying that he'd been absent from the flat that night. But, when he became seriously ill with cancer and wanted to clear his conscience, he finally admitted being present at the homicidal orgy and at Barry's murder, though he said that Lennie Smith was the ringleader.)

One of the men briefly left the flat and returned with fourteen-year-old Jason Swift. He was an exceptionally attractive boy who had been taken into care when he was a year old, as his mother couldn't afford to feed him and his four siblings. She'd taken them back briefly but they had to be taken into care again, as they were hungry and affected by the rows she had with her various boyfriends. Jason liked his Dr Barnardo's care home so much that he wanted to stay, but was returned home and sent to a day school for children with learning disabilities. There, a psychologist asked him to name three wishes and he replied, heartbreakingly, "Money, a house and food."

At fourteen he moved in with his half-sister in London, but remained restless. That same July he ran away, taking her savings and his beloved Monopoly game. He moved around the country, doing odd jobs and sometimes staying at homeless shelters. At one stage he sent his mother a postcard from Crawley in West Sussex, saying not to worry about him.

The teenager eventually returned to London and survived by offering sexual services to gay men. Like most rent boys, he tried to avoid painful penetration, preferring to masturbate or fellate his clients. But the men in Donald Smith's flat wanted to cause as much pain as possible . . .

The paedophiles gave Jason two powerful tranquilisers hidden in a drink before the sexual assault began. What happened, police would later state, was an orgy of violence as the men abused Jason over a number of hours. They hated his weakness, as it reminded them of their childhood vulnerability. They wanted to be powerful, in control, and took their rage out on the defenceless boy. They tore off his clothes and some of them held him down over the kitchen table whilst others assaulted him, at various times inserting a brush, a knife and a vibrator into his anus. One paedophile ran a knife blade over his buttocks to cause additional distress. They covered the boy's own body with their own, piling on top of him in an animalistic frenzy. Already weakened through drugs and shock, Jason's face and neck were now pressed into the table as he suffocated and died. His killers, aware that their semen was smeared across his body, then dumped him in a bath of water and left him there overnight.

Steven Barrell was genuinely shocked by the fourteen-year-old's death, returning to his wife covered in the boy's blood and shaking visibly. Leslie Bailey, accompanying him, also looked disquieted. Barrell had enjoyed other young boys, and the police suspected him of incest, but murder had never figured in his plans.

The following day, Cooke and Bailey carried Jason's corpse, hidden in a carpet, to Leslie's car, and drove to a spinney at Stapleford Tawney near Ongar, twenty miles from London. This was close to Bailey's former boarding school, so he was very familiar with the area. The men had planned to bury the body but the ground was frozen, so they dumped it under some bramble bushes, putting twigs and gorse on top.

Jason's body found

On 30 November 1985, a farmer out looking for pheasants found Jason's naked body, which showed clear signs of abuse. By then, Lennie Smith was in jail for other offences against young boys, but he denied ever knowing Jason Swift. After he was released and further questioned by police, he took an overdose of Robert Oliver's tranquilisers. But he made sure that Robert, who he was living with, saw the dramatic gesture. Oliver took him to hospital where he was detained overnight.

Later, Sidney Cooke went to jail for molesting boys and allegedly told a cellmate that he'd murdered Jason. But he denied this when questioned by the police. Cooke ultimately served two years for buggering a thirteen-year-old boy, whilst Smith served two and a half years for sexually assaulting the same teenager.

Barry's body found

Two days after Jason's body was found, Barry's decomposing corpse was discovered in a field close to Waltham Abbey, when a farmer saw a limb sticking out of the soil.

Bailey confesses

The police knew that Leslie Bailey was familiar with the area where Jason's body had been discovered, and their enquiries suggested that Jason had sometimes stayed with Lennie Smith. But Smith always answered, "No comment," whereas Bailey, keener to please the authorities, was potentially the weak link. He had a lower IQ than the others and was dominated by Cooke and Smith. Separated from their influence, he began to crack and told police that he had seen Jason Swift.

Still lying to cover up his own part in the sex murder, he said that he'd met Robert Oliver, gone to his flat and seen a boy lying, still and pale, on a bed. He added that Robert had told him that this was Jason, and that Sidney Cooke had killed him during rough sex. Later, Bailey got closer to the truth, admitting that he'd seen the murder. "I saw his face go white. His eyes bulged and went purple at the bottom. A tear ran down his face . . . and then he went unconscious." Later still, chainsmoking in between tea breaks, he said that his involvement had gone further and that he'd helped hold Jason down, clutching one of the fourteen-year-old's wrists whilst he was sexually abused.

The police patiently asked for further details, as it could take the inarticulate Bailey some time to form a single sentence. Bailey said that they'd held Jason in a star pattern, and that he was screaming. The teenager had begged them to stop, said that he was frightened, but the paedophiles had carried on. Then, after the boy had died they'd thrown him in the bath, dumping the body the following day.

Leslie admitted that his landlord, Steven Barrell, had been at the flat during Jason's fatal abuse. Arrested, Barrell at first denied everything, then admitted that he'd been in the kitchen at the flat, making tea, when he heard Jason screaming. He'd looked out and seen the boy go limp.

Leslie Bailey had now implicated his friends in Jason's murder, and the police interviewed them at length. Sidney Cooke, already in Brixton prison on other charges, eventually broke down and said that all of the men present at the flat, except for himself, had buggered Jason. He sobbed, "It wasn't meant to be like this." Holding onto his belief in a forgiving God, he was comforted by a Salvation Army officer. All of the others separately admitted raping the boy, though they tried to pin the actual death on each other. Robert Oliver lied and said that Jason had died of hypothermia in Sidney Cooke's car, after Cooke had sex with him.

Charges

Leslie Bailey, Steven Barrell, Sidney Cooke and Robert Oliver were all charged with Jason's murder. Only Lennie Smith refused to make a confession and, though the others implicated him, the charges against him were dismissed. But the police knew that he remained a danger to children, keeping him under surveillance and arresting him when he entered public toilets in Stoke Newington, and grabbed the penis of a thirteen-year-old boy. The judge, taking his previous convictions into account, sentenced him to three years in jail.

Court

Meanwhile, the other men went on trial together for murder. In a Manchester courtroom – chosen because it was a neutral venue, where the defendants could get a fair trial – the jury got to hear Sidney Cooke's taped confession in which he emulated Jason Swift's death rattle. Many people were visibly shocked and sickened, but Sidney just smiled.

Robert Oliver also seemed to be enjoying the attention and showed no remorse for the teenager's untimely death. Leslie Bailey looked blankly ahead as usual, whilst Steven Barrell's demeanour wasn't commented upon by anyone present.

The jury were out overnight, then returned with their verdict: all four defendants guilty on all counts. Three days later, on 16 May 1989, the sentences were handed out. Leslie Bailey and Robert Oliver were both given fifteen years for manslaughter and conspiracy to bugger, whilst sixty-two-year-old Sidney Cooke was sentenced to nineteen years for the first two crimes and also for disposing of the fourteen-year-old's body unlawfully. Steven Barrell received thirteen-and-a-half years for manslaughter and conspiracy to bugger.

Aftermath

The world remained a violent place for all four defendants, who were now on the receiving end. Lennie Smith was beaten up by a stranger who had read of his paedophilia in the tabloids. His injuries were so severe that he had to be hospitalised. Sidney Cooke, Robert Oliver and Leslie Bailey were all kicked and punched when they arrived at Wandsworth Prison, and had to live under Rule 43 (segregation) for their own protection. Even in segregation, Cooke was attacked and had his jaw broken by another prisoner.

In Wandsworth, Bailey allegedly told his cellmate that he and his friends – including Cooke and Oliver – had committed up to twenty child murders. He talked about Jason Swift and Barry Lewis, but also said that he'd contributed to the deaths of a nine-year-old called Paul and a thirteen-year-old called Steven, both of whom were buried in the West End. He mentioned four others whose names he didn't know, including an eleven-year-old buried in Walthamstow, east London.

Another life sentence

Police were told of Bailey's latest jailhouse confession and went to question him there. He eventually admitted that he'd suffocated Barry, and demonstrated how he'd done so on a detective. The demonstration left them in no doubt that he was the six-year-old's killer as he sank his fingers into the back of the detective's head, leaving the same type of marks that had been found on the little boy. This was information which had been withheld from the public; it was something only the killer, or someone watching the murder, could know. Bailey was returned to court and given a life sentence. He remained indifferent.

A final confession

After Leslie Bailey belatedly confessed to Barry's murder and was charged, police began to question him about the Mark Tildesley homicide. He admitted that too, naming several of the other paedophiles who had contributed to Mark's demise.

Bailey said that he and his fellow paedophiles had thought up the codeword 'Showtime', and that, when one of them uttered that word, it was a signal for them to murder Mark.

A police team worked tirelessly to put together the evidence against the men Bailey had named, but the Crown Prosecution Service declined to prosecute (probably because the men were already serving sentences for other child murders), leaving some of the officers deeply distressed.

Bailey went on to confess to yet another sex murder, telling police that he'd helped to kill a thirteen-year-old Pakistani boy at a sex party attended by sixteen men. The child had been raped and strangled, and Leslie had buried him near to his old boarding school. But police were unable to locate the body – unsurprisingly, as Bailey later heard that it had been moved by a friend. He told them of another young teenager who had been multiply sodomised and strangled, then buried by one of the gang at an unknown location near Chingford, on the London-Essex borders. Though they had no way of verifying this, police were convinced that his account was genuine.

Bailey was given a new identity as Leslie Hawkins, told to keep quiet about his paedophilia, and moved to Winson Green prison near Birmingham. Like the others, he was so damaged that he remained untouched by the enormity of his crimes.

Meanwhile, Sidney Cooke was proving to be an even more repellent cellmate for other prisoners, as he'd masturbate openly in front of them whilst talking of the abuse and murder of little boys. Robert Oliver remained equally unrepentant, changing his name to Robert Cooke and telling anyone who would listen that he was Sidney Cooke's wife. Unsurprisingly, his only visitors were police officers questioning him about other child molestation complaints.

Lennie Smith sentenced again

Lennie Smith served his three-year sentence, and continued his relentlessly predatory behaviour upon release. In December 1992, he was sentenced to ten years for buggering a six-year-old boy. He had offered to babysit, then taken the child to a gay club and made him watch men having anal intercourse on stage. Smith had told the boy that he loved him, but had sexually assaulted him on numerous occasions. He was unconcerned by his latest sentence, which gave him the opportunity to corrupt younger prisoners.

Murdered by murderers

It's not known if Leslie Bailey also interfered with younger prisoners or if his true identity became known. But, in October 1993, two other convicted killers crept into his cell at Whitemoor Prison and hung him by the neck until he was dead.

Freed

The years passed, and the men began to reach the end of their sentences. Steven Barrell was released in 1995 and moved to a flat near a Nottingham school. When his identity was discovered, he went underground.

Robert Oliver served ten years of his fifteen-year sentence for the manslaughter of Jason Swift, and was released in 1997, moving to a probation hostel in Brighton. He immediately changed his name to Francis Lee for his own protection. (The probation service, keeping him under close supervision, knew about his change of name.) He remained anonymous until December 2006, when the *News of the World* newspaper revealed that he was living on a council estate in a village in

Somerset. A mob of fifty gathered outside his home and began to chant, "Paedophile out!"

Avon & Somerset police took fifty-two-year-old Oliver to their headquarters and kept him in a visitor's room until they could find him alternative accommodation. He then spent four months in voluntary police custody in Milton Keynes. When interviewed, he continued to play down his part in many molestation charges, claiming, "The boy got into bed with me." Police feared that, left to his own devices, he would offend again.

Though initially given nineteen years, Sidney Cooke was paroled after only a decade, when the appeal court ruled that one of his accomplices was the ringleader in April 1999. In the same timeframe, an accomplice said that Cooke had murdered Mark Tildesley but he was never investigated for this. (Only Leslie Bailey was ever convicted of Mark's homicide.) Cooke was immediately taken to a safe house at a Yeovil police station and given a round-the-clock chaperone, as the authorities knew how dangerous he was to young boys.

In October 1999, after a few months of freedom, Cooke was rearrested when some of his earlier molestation crimes came to light. In court, he admitted repeatedly buggering and indecently assaulting two brothers in 1972 and 1973. He was sentenced at Manchester Crown Court to life imprisonment, with the mandate that he should serve at least five years.

Whilst serving this sentence in Whitemoor Prison, Cooke raped a much younger prisoner. He was released at the end of this sentence, but returned to a unit adjacent to a prison for his own safety. He volunteered to live there permanently, terrified of what vigilantes would do if he stepped outside.

In 1999, his friend Lennie Smith was released from a Nottingham prison, but immediately volunteered to live in a bedsit in a unit that formed part of that same prison. For the next seven years he remained there, dying of AIDS, aged fifty-one, in 2006.

CHAPTER SIX

RAYMOND LESLIE MORRIS

Dubbed the 'Cannock Chase Murderer', Raymond Morris is serving a life sentence for some of the cruellest sex murders of the 1960's.

Early sociopathy

Raymond was born on 13 August 1929, in Walsall, to a middleclass couple who had two other sons and a daughter. Unfortunately, little is known about his formative experiences, but he was a cruel child who didn't bond with his younger brother, with whom he shared a room.

Raymond was a bright child with an IQ of one hundred and twenty – the level needed to succeed at university – yet he left school at fourteen and took a factory job, a strange choice for a young man who made it clear to his family that he was desperate for approval and attention. But he found an outlet for his creativity by writing poetry and playing the piano, and would later excel at photography.

Sexually insatiable

When Raymond was sixteen he met fourteen-year-old Muriel, who worked at the same factory, and immediately fell in love with her. Within a week he'd promised to marry her one day.

At eighteen, he was called up to do his National Service with the RAF, but he still found time to send his girlfriend a daily love letter. He seemed like the perfect beau.

In June 1949, aged almost twenty, he was demobbed. It was not until 28 July 1951, however, before he was able to marry Muriel. Even then they had to live with her mother for a while, but Raymond remained a considerate husband, bringing his new wife huge boxes of chocolates and helping her with the housework when she was ill.

In turn, however, he expected sex constantly. Every morning he wanted intercourse and, when they got their own house, he wanted it every evening as well, throwing himself upon her whilst they were watching television. She noted that, during these sex sessions, he emulated some of the macho actors of the time. It was a form of posturing that he increasingly adopted during the day. He would suddenly turn to her and demand that she strip, and if she didn't he would become incredibly angry. Once, Raymond put his hands around her throat, before she broke free and fled to his parents' house for the night.

Family estrangement
Raymond fell out with his father, but he would sneak around to see his mother when the rest of the family were out, occasionally bringing her gifts. It was obvious that control was central to his existence: he didn't smoke, didn't drink, and was exceptionally neat and clean.

He fathered two sons with Muriel and was very good to them, but remained dissatisfied and tried to shore himself up by buying expensive goods. He installed a piano in the house and acquired a tape recorder and a car, but soon started saving for a bigger and better model.

Raymond would go to work in a suit, change at the factory, then wash and change back into his suit for going home. He also began demanding that his wife wear stylish clothing and put on airs and graces. Uncomfortable with this, she refused.

He must have brooded silently about his relationship, realising that his wife was not controllable and no longer an asset. As a result, he turned on her one day in 1960, said that the marriage was over and that she had one week to find somewhere else to live.

Sex and the single life

Perhaps to his surprise, she succeeded. Anxious to retain control, he said that he'd pay her £5 maintenance a week, but only if she continued to have sex with him. She did so twice a week for several months. Later, she had a baby girl by another man and Raymond came round to make a fuss of the child. He was always so good with children that it never occurred to anyone he was a paedophile.

The couple were finally divorced in July 1964 – and the following month Raymond married again.

A second marriage

This time his wife, Carol Dianne Pearse, at only twenty-one was fourteen years his junior. She was an attractive brunette who worked as a wages clerk in a Walsall office. Her parents lived next door to his.

But Raymond rarely took his wife home to meet his parents as he'd told her that his job was better than it actually was, and he was concerned that they'd ask about his factory work. He felt an overwhelming need to be seen as superior to everyone.

In the same year as his second marriage he left Healey Mouldings Ltd, where he'd worked for twelve years, and took a job selling washing machines. But after seven months he switched to working with the Gas Board as a salesman, a job which allowed him to travel and prey on little girls. When it came to his ambitions he was all talk, however, for though he told everyone he was about to set up a photographic studio with another man, all he ever did was get the business cards printed.

Yearning for more excitement, he began to read horror novels and collect pornography, but his second wife objected to this – though she let him take some glamour shots of her. He tried taking her to strip shows but she was obviously uncomfortable, so he settled for making sketches of nude women, using photographs from magazines as a guide.

He remained as sexually insatiable as he had been with his first wife; perhaps sex used up the energy which a man of his intellect and talent would normally have expended through his career.

A vicious rape

In December of that year, he drove up to a nine-year-old girl in Bloxwich and told her that he was her Uncle Len, and that her mother had sent him. She trustingly entered the vehicle, whereupon he drove to a remote road and raped her, viciously lacerating her vagina. She screamed throughout the fifty-minute ordeal, at the end of which he strangled her.

Believing that she was dead, Morris threw her into a ditch in Bentley, where a passing cyclist heard her moans. The police later said that, when discovered, she was twenty minutes away from death. (Though Raymond Morris was never charged with this crime, the child pointed him out in court four years later, when he was facing a murder charge, and exclaimed, "That's him!")

The following June he left the Gas Board and began sales work for a Sheffield firm, which took him through Shropshire, Worcestershire, Staffordshire and Birmingham. It was an ideal job for a man who liked to molest little girls and be home in time for tea.

Three unsolved Cannock Chase murders

It's likely that he remained an active predator throughout the mid-1960's, for a man matching his description tried on several occasions to lure local girls into his vehicle, offering them sweets and telling them that he was their Uncle Len. Most fled – but on 8 September 1965, six-year-old Margaret Reynolds was lured into a car, sexually assaulted and murdered, possibly strangled with a ligature.

On 20 December 1965, five-year-old Diane Tift was similarly raped and suffocated, her pixie hood pulled over her face at the same time as the drawcord was tightened around her neck. Semen was found in her anus but it was believed to have drained from her vagina, which was badly torn. Both corpses were found in a ditch in Cannock Chase on 12 January 1966.

On 14 August 1966, ten-year-old Jane Taylor also disappeared from the same area – near the A34 – but her body has never been found. The police were later convinced that Morris killed all three of them. Indeed, his younger brother Peter had the courage to phone the police and suggest that Raymond was the killer as he knew he'd been very familiar with the area, owned the same make of car as the killer, and had acted sadistically while they were growing up.

Indecency

Only two months after this third murder, Raymond Morris took a ten-year-old and an eleven-year-old girl to his house and gave them two shillings to photograph them in their panties. He also got one girl to photograph him with his hand on her friend's private parts, and then asked the other girl to take a photograph of him touching her friend.

Unfortunately, the girls didn't tell their parents for some time – and when the police investigated they couldn't find the photographs, so they dropped the charges. (It was wrongly reported that the girls had been sexually assaulted in separate rooms, and so couldn't corroborate each other's stories.)

Sexual molestation

In April 1967, having previously been sacked from his Sheffield job for falsifying his hours, Raymond Morris found work as the foreman of an engineering firm, where some colleagues found him cold but others considered him a real gentleman. His wife also considered him gentlemanly in his liking for children, knowing that he wanted some more of his own in due course, and so trusted him with their four-year-old niece who came to stay in August for two weeks. Raymond soon suggested he take the child into the spare room and photograph her in her prettiest dress.

Whilst Carol washed up in the kitchen, the predatory paedophile took off the little girl's panties and fingered her, before taking numerous indecent photographs of the child lying on her back with her knees raised. When she got home, her mother noticed that her genitals were sore but assumed it was some sort of urinary infection. She remained naïve even when she noticed that the four-year-old's vagina was slightly torn.

Christine Darby's murder

That same month, on 19 August 1967, Raymond Morris struck again. He parked beside a group of children and asked one of them, seven-year-old Christine Ann Darby, to hop into the passenger seat and give him directions. One of her friends noticed that the car was heading the wrong way and ran for help, but by the time the police set up roadblocks it was too late. Morris sexually assaulted the child in his car, throwing her knickers out of the window. She'd presumably lost control of her bowels during the abduction, as the panties were soiled. Then he drove her to Cannock Chase, and either attempted to rape her or digitally entered her so brutally that her vulva was badly torn. She had bled heavily from this wound, but the cause of death was suffocation, caused as he stifled her screams with his hand.

That night, he took his wife and her parents out for a meal in a restaurant and behaved normally. His in-laws didn't really like him – and noticed that he constantly eyed up younger women – but would have been amazed to find that he'd just torn a little girl's genitals and crushed the breath from her.

A false alibi

Determined to find Christine's killer, the police visited thirty-nine thousand Walsall houses and interviewed twenty-eight thousand local men, including Raymond Morris. They were suspicious of him as his name had come up several times in relation to unsavoury incidents with children, but his doting wife Carol gave him an alibi, saying that he'd been shopping with her all day.

Further child pornography

In August 1968, Carol and Raymond again collected Carol's niece for a fortnight's holiday at their flat. This time the five-year-old began to scream when Raymond Morris picked her up to put her in his car, but her mother simply assumed that she was unhappy about leaving home for two weeks.

Once again, he took the little girl into the spare room, digitally entered her and took photographs of her naked below the waist, manhandling her so that her legs were spread wide apart.

Another attempted abduction

By 4 November 1968, the factory foreman was prowling the streets again, this time offering fireworks to a ten-year-old girl. At the last moment she hesitated and refused to get into his car, noticing that he had spread newspaper on the passenger seat (doubtless to avoid the transference of fibres). He reached for her arm and she raced off. A passerby saw the incident, attempted to memorise the car registration number and phoned the police. She'd remembered the number as being 429 LOP, whereas it was actually 492 LOP but, given a good description of the vehicle model, the police worked it out.

The car belonged to Raymond Morris – and they found that his previous car matched the vehicle seen in the area just before other little girls disappeared.

Arrest and trial

This time a detective spoke to Carol Morris at much greater length, explaining to her that paedophiles didn't look like monsters, that indeed, they were often superficially very kind to children and made a fuss of them. He asked her if she wanted to be another Myra Hindley. He then asked her again what time her husband had come home on the day of Christine's murder. "4:30pm," she whispered, adding that he'd said his work had kept him late.

Arrested, Morris was awash with self-pity, making statements to the police such as, "I'm finished," and, "It's all over." He refused to appear in an identity parade and accused the police of beating him up.

Later, Carol Morris visited her husband in prison, and said that she'd put her wedding ring back on if he could give her an innocent explanation of where he'd been when Christine was murdered. He couldn't, and she left the prison in tears.

The police now searched Morris's house and found the pornographic photographs of his niece, hidden in a box under the floorboards beside the toilet, where he'd obviously been using them for masturbatory purposes. Morris's penis was in one of the shots and his wrist, with its distinctive wristwatch, was in another. The child was posed in some of the shots in the same way as Christine Darby's body had been found, the pose that Morris fantasised about. He had labelled the box "only to be opened in a dark room", knowing that his wife wouldn't disturb the contents in these circumstances.

He wrote eloquently to her from prison, saying, "It is like some kind of nightmare, but we must both have enough courage to see it through. I need terribly to be reminded of your love. That is all that keeps me within the bounds of sanity . . ." Later he wrote again, stating, "I cannot stop loving you, even though you have deserted me when I need you most." Remembering the ways in which he'd violated her four-year-old niece, she didn't write back.

Trial

The trial was held at Staffordshire Assizes on 10 February 1969. Raymond Leslie Morris admitted taking the indecent photos, but said that the child had entered the room in a state of partial undress and that he'd reluctantly taken the semi-nude portraits, then encouraged her to put her clothes on. But the prosecution were able to produce the numbered negatives which showed that the little girl had started off wearing clothes, which had been progressively removed. He could give no explanation for the photos, except to say that he felt disgusted with himself.

Carol Morris reluctantly appeared for the prosecution, though she wept after giving evidence. Numerous witnesses (seventy-eight of them called by the prosecution) had seen a vehicle matching his in the area before the various abductions and murders – and he perfectly matched the police identikit.

It took the jury only an hour to find him guilty. He shook his head in disbelief at the verdict then glared at his wife. He was sentenced to life imprisonment and sent to Durham maximum security prison. Psychiatrists subsequently classified him as a dangerous psychopath.

Appeal

A year later he appealed on the grounds that the pornographic photos of his niece shouldn't have been admissible at his trial. His appeal was unsuccessful, and for the next thirty-five years he kept a low profile in prison; then in 2004, he appealed again, claiming that new information was available. The seventy-five-year-old's appeal failed for a second time.

CHAPTER SEVEN

BRIAN FIELD

Though he murdered in the same period as the aforementioned Raymond Morris, Field preferred boys to girls.

Early hell

Brian Lunn was born on 7 June 1936 in Bourne, Lincolnshire, to a prostitute who abandoned him when he was one day old. He was taken into care and sent to an innovative local foster home run by Paul and Ruby Field, who gave him their surname. The foster home was so successful that it featured in a series of news broadcasts.

Unfortunately, Brian was repeatedly abused by an older boy and later sought out victims of his own. He would at first befriend someone he liked at the foster home, offering friendship and protection, then sneak into the younger child's bed and force the boy to masturbate him. Later he graduated to sodomy, threatening to kill his traumatised victims if they told of their ordeal. Many of the younger boys were terrified of the sly and violent bully, by daytime an angelic choirboy, by night a vicious predator.

Though he preferred boys, the teenage Brian was opportunistic when it came to inflicting pain on younger victims. In 1951, he was walking in a quiet forest near his foster home when he saw an eleven-year-old girl skipping alone. The fifteen-year-old grabbed her, threw her to the ground and used her skipping rope to strangle her. When she was unconscious he sexually assaulted her and left her for dead, but she eventually revived. It's unclear if she was able to identify him at the time, but he was never charged with this serious sexual crime.

In 1957 Brian did his National Service, joining the Royal Marines. Good looking, well dressed and outwardly affable, he got on well with his peers, who had no idea that he had a penchant for boys and fantasised about violently sodomising them.

Marriage and fatherhood

Physically strong and good at sports, Field was an attractive figure. He married a girl named Celia, but she died in a road crash in 1966. The following year he married his second wife, Mary, and they had a child – he would eventually father three children. By now he was employed as an engineer by the Milk Marketing Board in Thames Ditton, Surrey, and was considered to be an exceptionally good worker. But his deviant tendencies remained, and police were later convinced that he continued to molest young boys.

The following year, on 12 April 1968, another child was born. An endlessly crying baby can test any parent's patience – but it was doubtless worse for Brian Field, as it reminded him of his own unmet childhood needs. He'd allowed himself to become trapped in a nurturing role that he really wasn't capable of fulfilling. The stress built and built . . .

Roy Tutill's murder

On the eleventh day after his baby was born, Brian returned to work where he drank heavily. Late that afternoon, he drove home looking for a vulnerable victim. Eventually he espied a small boy in school uniform, standing by a bus stop and attempting to hitch a lift. The child was fourteen-year-old Roy Tutill, who was saving up to buy a new bicycle and so planned to save his bus fare by hitching a lift home from Kingston Grammar School. Roy looked younger than his fourteen years, and Field was immediately attracted to him.

Roy doubtless felt safe with the friendly, avuncular man driving the white Mini, though he panicked when Brian turned off the main road and drove to an isolated lane. There, the married man stopped the car;

he stripped and raped Roy over its front seat. Afterwards, he strangled the boy from behind with his school tie, lying on top of him and feeling his body convulse. He continued to strangle the child until his gasping and writhing stopped and he went limp. Field would later say that he killed the boy so that he couldn't be identified, but, given his sadistic side, strangulation doubtless figured in his sexual fantasies.

Putting the body and school uniform in the boot, Field drove home to his unsuspecting family, leaving the car with its grisly cargo in the garage for the next two days.

Later he drove to the Beaverbrook Estate near Dorking and dumped Roy's body, putting his school blazer over it. The corpse was found by a shocked forestry worker on 26 April. The police were so determined to catch the killer that they organised the first ever television reconstruction, appealing for the relatives of likely suspects to come forward. But no one connected the sex murder with the doting family man.

Shortly afterwards he left the area and began to move around Britain, repairing farmyard machinery. It gave him the opportunity to assault victims then move on before he could be caught. Brian would talk about his wife and children to everyone he met, so they had no reason to think that he was a paedophile. These were comparatively innocent times and the public thought that paedophiles were unwashed, elderly bachelors or mentally deficient men.

Another victim

In the same timeframe, Brian was becoming friendly with his young brother-in-law and, when the boy turned fourteen in 1970, he sexually assaulted him for the first time. He continued these assaults over many months, telling the teenager that he would kill him if he told anyone.

Abduction

But he wanted to kill rather than merely commit assault, and saw his chance when he was working in Aberdeenshire in 1971. Grabbing a fourteen-year-old boy, he began to strangle him whilst dragging him towards his car – but, when a dog began to bark hysterically, Field fled.

Fortunately, the boy was able to give a good description of the car and the paedophile was arrested three days later. He served two years in prison, during which he was questioned by detectives from Surrey about the unsolved murder of Roy Tutill, but he denied everything. On release from prison, Field returned to his wife. The marriage eventually broke down and, in 1981, the couple were divorced.

Single again, Field continued to trawl for youthful prey. One probable victim was Mark Billington, a fifteen-year-old schoolboy, who disappeared on 1 September 1984 and was found a few days later, hanging from a tree, seven miles from his home in Meriden near Solihull. His parents were convinced that it wasn't suicide, that someone had murdered him.

On 1 January 1986, Brian saw what he thought were two twelve-year-old boys walking towards Stafford, en route for home after visiting friends. Hitchhiking was common in the area, so they weren't surprised when he stopped and offered them a lift. He was well dressed and quietly spoken, so they accepted and got into the back seat, but Field drove in the opposite direction from their home and, when they challenged him, he produced a tyre wrench, brandished it at them and ordered them to strip.

Fortunately, the boys were both teenagers rather than pre-teens, and had the presence of mind to jump from the car when Field slowed down to take a corner. They gave police a good description and the paedophile was arrested later that day. At Stafford Crown Court he was sentenced to four years, of which he eventually served two.

Another move

After his release from prison in 1988, Brian Field moved to Solihull and soon became a regular at his local pub. Everyone liked him. He played chess, ran the quiz night, and was a quietly charismatic man. No one knew much about his past except that he was divorced and, as he occasionally made appreciative comments about various women, it didn't occur to anyone for a second that he was a murderous paedophile.

Field also kept his name out of the system during these years by only working for cash, never filing tax returns or claiming benefits.

Further victims?

As the years passed, Brian remained popular in the community. When he turned sixty on 7 June 1996, his fellow drinkers had a collection for him and raised so much money that they were able to present him with a watch, a silver tankard, a cake and £60.

But serial offenders rarely stop assaulting victims until they are imprisoned, so it's possible that Field struck again on 27 December that year, when eleven-year-old Patrick Warren and thirteen-year-old David Spencer disappeared from the Chelmsley Wood area of Birmingham, close to where Field was working as a farm labourer. The two friends were seen at a petrol station shortly after midnight, and Patrick's bicycle was later found hidden behind the building. Originally believed by the police to be runaways, the children were never seen again.

Drink driving

If Brian Field had continued to keep a low profile, he would literally have got away with murder – but, one night in 1999, he had too much to drink then attempted to drive home. He was stopped by police, breathalysed, and had his saliva sample placed on the DNA database. It matched the DNA of a tiny speck of semen found on Roy Tutill's trousers. Field's thirty-odd years of freedom were about to end . . .

Police quietly investigated his background – by now he was working as a self-employed gardener, and was still a very hard worker – finding that he had prior arrests for the sexual assault and abduction of teenage boys. Field's brother-in-law also told them that he'd been sexually abused by the paedophile when he was fourteen. The police arrested a visibly shocked Brian Field in January 2001.

The sixty-four-year-old was taken to Staines Police Station and questioned, with requisite breaks, for the next three days. At first he stressed his conventionality, explaining that he was a divorced father of three and a gardener-cum-handyman. He said that he'd never driven past the bus stop where Roy had been abducted, had never seen the child.

But Detective Sergeant Graham Hill proved to be a masterful interviewer, gently explaining that the DNA evidence was irrefutable.

He made it clear that, though Field had done monstrous things, he didn't regard him as a monster. Eventually, sensing that Field was ready to confess, DS Hill said, "It's time for the truth, Brian."

Moments later, Field said, "I tried to bugger him . . . across the front seat."

"How did you strangle him?" the detective asked.

"I put the tie around his neck and just tightened it . . . he just sort of convulsed a bit . . . gasping for air. I just carried on." He said that he'd left the body in the boot of the car for two days.

Life

In November 2001, Brian Field pleaded guilty at the Old Bailey and was sentenced to life imprisonment. The judge told him, "Advances in modern science techniques should stand as a warning that there is no hiding place for sexual and violent criminals."

Afterwards, DS Graham Hill – who admitted that he'd found the interviews with Field to be exhausting – said, "What we really want to do is understand why people commit these offences so that we can protect children in the future." Sadly, no one cared enough to protect Brian Field during his formative years.

Subsequently, police reopened the case on Mark Billington, the boy found hanging from a tree. They also dug up secluded pieces of land that Field had access to in 1996, in the hope of finding the bodies of David Spencer and Patrick Warren, or some of their belongings. They stressed that they were doing this at their own behest, that their actions weren't a result of new information from Field.

Brian Field is currently imprisoned at Full Sutton Prison in York, home to many violent offenders. He will probably die in jail.

CHAPTER EIGHT

RELATIVES WHO KILL

Though eighty percent of child sex victims are molested by someone they know, comparatively few of these friends or relatives kill. They have no need to abduct children as they have ongoing access whilst babysitting or staying in the child's home, and may engineer greater access by taking the child on holiday or on camping trips. One religious leader was convicted in 2007 of abusing his young relatives for fifteen years, the abuse beginning when the children were eighteen months old.

But occasionally, a relative both abuses and kills, as in the following harrowing British case.

MICHAEL MULLEN

Part-time barman Michael Mullen was a heavy drinker and regular cocaine user. In 2003, when he was seventeen, he was charged with raping a twelve-year-old girl. But on the day that he was due to stand trial, the CPS said that new evidence had come to light which cast doubt on the alleged victim's story, and the case collapsed.

By 2005, Mullen had become an uncle. He pretended to adore his brother's baby daughter, Casey, but secretly had a photo of her naked from the waist down, on his mobile phone. He was turned on by images of sadistic paedophilia, and often downloaded internet images of children being sexually abused and hurt.

On 11 February 2007, twenty-one-year-old Michael went out

drinking for the afternoon with his brother David, the baby's nineteen-year-old father. By the time that they returned to David's council house in Gipton, Leeds, Mullen was two and a half times over the drink-driving limit. He went upstairs to Casey's room and lay down beside her on the bed.

David later went upstairs and asked Michael if he'd like to go out and get some cocaine and beer. Michael replied, "Fuck off." Casey, his little niece, awoke and sat up during this exchange.

David left the room and Michael later came rushing down, looking dishevelled, and phoned a taxi to take him to his mother's house. David went with him. Shortly afterwards, at around 9:15pm, another family member went upstairs and saw the child under the covers in a foetal position. They called to Casey's mother, Samantha Canham, who went upstairs and found the two-year-old motionless in bed. She pulled the covers off and realised that the child was lying in a pool of blood.

Samantha began screaming that her baby was dead, and a neighbour rushed in to give the child mouth to mouth resuscitation. Paramedics raced to the scene but were unable to revive her. She had been viciously raped then strangled, possibly with a mobile phone charging wire. This compression to the neck was the cause of death.

Less than four hours later, detectives arrested Michael Mullen who was shaking uncontrollably. They also arrested a nineteen-year-old man and a twenty-year-old man, but both were later released without charge. Mullen claimed to have no memory of the rape or murder, but said that he must have done it. In July 2007 he was sentenced to thirty-five years for murder and seventeen years for rape, the sentences to run concurrently. A court psychiatrist said that he was an untreatable psychopath, and the judge said he would pose an ongoing danger to children. In addition to his thirty-five-year sentence, he was banned for life from consorting with under-sixteens.

CHAPTER NINE

MENTALLY HANDICAPPED PAEDOPHILES

Most paedophiles aren't mentally ill, though seductive paedophiles are guilty of repeated wrong-thinking, convincing themselves they are teaching their victims about sex and are not harming them. A seductive paedophile will misinterpret a moan of pain as one of pleasure, and will decide that the child who protests is simply following convention rather than being true to themselves.

But a tiny percentage of paedophiles are mentally handicapped, though most still know the difference between right and wrong. Autistic children, for example, may struggle to distinguish sincerity from deceit, lack empathy and have poor self-control. They sometimes react violently to teasing and need protection from abusive peers.

PAUL SMITH

After several acts of sexual violence towards young girls, this autistic teenager was found guilty of the murder of a ten-year-old girl.

Prior assaults

Paul Smith, born in 1985, had Asperger's Syndrome, a form of high-functioning autism. He lived with his parents, sister and younger brother in Sedgebrook, Lincolnshire. His stilted speech patterns and learning difficulties marked him out as different, and he was bullied at school. He suffered from emotional problems and was unable to control his temper or, in time, his sadistic sexual fantasies.

In 1999, he grabbed hold of a twelve-year-old girl at his family home, pushed her onto a bed and touched her between the legs. The family knew about this incident but it was not reported to the police.

In January 2002, the teenager struck again, forcing a twelve-year-old female cousin onto his bed during a party at his house, tying her hands together and gagging her. Then he came to his senses and let her go. The child told her mother about the assault two days later, but again the matter wasn't reported to the authorities.

Abduction

The third assault, in June of that same year, was on a sixteen-year-old female childhood friend who he pinned down on a bed, tied up and gagged, then threatened with an air rifle before forcing her into the boot of his parents' car. He drove her from his home to a neighbouring village then dumped her in the countryside. This time the police became involved, but, due to confusion between lawyers and the police, the charges were dropped. By now the police, mental health and education authorities all knew of Paul's dangerous sexuality, but none of them were aware of all three assaults, and didn't realise that the teenager's urges were escalating.

He got a job as a trainee electrician and continued to live at home with his parents. On 28 December they took him and his seventeen-year-old brother to a party at his uncle's house, though he hated crowds.

There were about fifty guests at the party, including ten-year-old Rosie May Storrie and her parents. Rosie, a talented ballerina, had taken part in a professional pantomime just two days before and had a bright future on the stage.

Watching her playing a computer game, Paul remarked aloud, "I feel like a sexual being." Later he went upstairs. At 9pm, Rosie, who was used to teasing her older brothers, also went upstairs and playfully grabbed a can of Guinness from his hand. He chased her along the corridor and the other guests lost sight of them.

A few minutes later, both families went in search of their children. A ten-year-old boy went into one of the bedrooms and found Rosie lying face down on the bed. She was half-naked, her catsuit pulled down to expose her buttocks. The boy fetched Rosie's father, who turned her over and saw that the area around her eyes was blueish-purple and that she was unconscious. Other guests tried to keep her breathing until paramedics arrived. Paul's mother, a nurse, was also called to the scene.

Rosie was taken to Sheffield Children's Hospital, where tests showed that she was brain dead. Her life support system was switched off on 30 December.

Denial

Suspicion quickly fell on Paul Smith, as he'd been missing at the same time as Rosie. His Guinness can, bearing his fingerprints and hers, was found beside the bed where she'd been held down until she lost consciousness, before being partially stripped.

Smith said that he'd been in the toilet during the attack, and that he'd left the can of Guinness in the bedroom earlier that evening, but several witnesses contradicted this.

Court

Paul Smith was tried at Nottingham Crown Court in October 2004. The court heard that Rosie had been held down by someone strong, that she hadn't had the opportunity to struggle. Her face had been forced into the pillow so that she was starved of oxygen. Her attacker had then pulled down her catsuit, but had presumably stopped when he heard her parents calling her name. The jury was also told of Smith's previous attacks on young girls.

He was found guilty, and the judge said that he should serve at least fourteen years. He stated, "I have no doubt that your reason was sexual," and added, "I am sure that you are, and have been for some time now, a considerable danger to young girls." Smith shook his head but otherwise betrayed no emotion. His parents subsequently said that they were convinced of his innocence.

A later independent report on Rosie's murder criticised the police and prosecutors, noting that, if Smith had been prosecuted for abducting the sixteen-year-old, the community would have been aware of his offending and the Storries could have protected their daughter. The couple criticised Smith's parents for keeping quiet about the earlier incidents. "We feel they are quite clearly in denial about these previous incidents and about the murder," said Mary Storrie. "The stark reality is that they raised a killer."

The bereaved family subsequently set up a website in tribute to their daughter (www.rosie-may.com) and have raised a substantial amount of money for children's charities.

Paul Smith's defence team launched an appeal in March 2005, but abandoned it in July prior to a hearing. His father said, "We were unable to present the information we wished due to technical reasons."

ALEXANDER MILLER
A convicted paedophile from the age of thirteen, mentally handicapped Miller went on to commit an appalling double murder in Glasgow.

A poor start
Alexander Miller had a dismal early life, being born into a gypsy family in 1948 who barely made a living as scrap dealers. He was put into care for his own protection – though, as care homes in the 1950s and onwards were targeted by paedophiles, it may have been a case of out of the frying pan and into the fire. At thirteen, he sexually assaulted a little girl and was sent to an approved school. Two years later he was moved to an educational establishment for the mentally handicapped, and then transferred to a mental hospital.

In 1968 he was released and went to live with his father, who was living in a rundown flat in Golspie Street, Govan, Glasgow. But he soon left and wandered around the country, burgling houses, getting caught and serving various jail sentences. By 1975, he'd returned to Glasgow and was making a modest living as a hawker, someone who goes about offering goods for sale. His mode of transport was a pony and trap. Most of the goods that he sold came from theft, as he was still burgling on a regular basis, and his customers were equally impoverished.

Miller got to know his father's neighbours, a divorced man and his three children who were living in a block of flats due for demolition. In January 1976, he burgled their home whilst the family was out. He returned on the seventeenth of the month, planning to steal further goods from them, but found thirteen-year-old John and twelve-year-old Irene at home with their mongrel dog. (Their father had gone to look at a new flat for the family and had taken his youngest daughter, Elizabeth, aged six, with him, the only reason she wasn't murdered too.)

Miller immediately grabbed John, gagged him with a sock and bound his hands and feet, before beating him to death with a hammer. He tied Irene's hands behind her back and sexually assaulted her, before battering her to death with the same implement. Passersby heard screams coming from the flat, but no one investigated, assuming that it was a domestic incident – parents were legally allowed to beat their children at the time. The children's father and sister returned home at 4:15pm to find the youngsters dead on the settee, their faces battered to a pulp.

It was 19 March of the following year before police arrested Alexander Miller, following a tip-off from the Glasgow underworld. He pled guilty to culpable homicide (known as a manslaughter charge in England) on the grounds of diminished responsibility. The judge said that only Miller's mental condition had prevented a murder charge.

The twenty-eight-year-old was ordered to be detained indefinitely at Carstairs Mental Hospital. He remained there throughout the seventies, eighties and nineties, but in January 2004 there were plans to transfer him to a mental hospital in Pollock. However, John and Irene's surviving sister, Elizabeth, was living in the area and publicly opposed the move. She'd spent years fearing that the killer of her siblings would come back to get her, and was able to persuade the authorities to keep him at Carstairs.

CHAPTER TEN

WRONGFUL CONVICTION

T o ruin a man's reputation, all you have to do is accuse him of being a paedophile. Sadly, this happens in some acrimonious divorces, when embittered women falsely tell the courts that their ex-husbands molested their children.

To be suspected of such seductive paedophilia must be terrifying – but, in the following case, a man was imprisoned for sixteen years after wrongly being convicted of the sex murder of a little girl, a case which was only successfully resolved in 2007.

STEFAN IVAN KISZKO

Though he'd never committed a single act of violence, Kiszko was bullied into a false confession by detectives who were convinced that they had their man.

A sheltered childhood

Stefan was born on 24 March 1952 to Charlotte and Ivan Kiszko, from Austria and the Ukraine respectively. They had emigrated to England after their marriage and settled in Rochdale, where the local mills offered steady work. At six months old Stefan developed asthma, whereupon his parents took him back to Austria whenever possible, believing that the purer air was better for his health. This meant that he didn't get to play with other schoolchildren during the holidays and felt increasingly alienated from them, especially as his illness prevented him from joining in at sports. His mother dressed him in traditional Austrian clothes so that he looked different to his classmates, and he was considered old beyond his years.

Stefan grew to an imposing six foot two, but his voice didn't break and he was considered to be a gentle giant. His addiction to confectionary – and an undiagnosed hormonal problem – meant that he ballooned to seventeen stone, but he was generous with his sweets and gladly gave them to the other kids.

On leaving school, Stefan attended commercial college and evening classes, before obtaining a post as office clerk with the Inland Revenue. Shortly afterwards, his father died and the eighteen-year-old became totally dependent on his mother and her sister for companionship. He would drive them to the shops or to the garden centre, and share a bottle of fortified wine with them at the weekend. On other occasions they went to the moors and dug up peat for their numerous houseplants. In the evenings he often played the accordion for his mother, and they'd frequently make a pilgrimage to the cemetery to visit his father's grave.

In August 1975, Stefan, who had poor spatial awareness, fell and broke his ankle. Doctors set the bone but carried out further tests because he looked unwell, and found that he was severely anaemic and hypogonadal – that is, he had an exceptionally small penis and no testicles in his scrotum. He was immediately started on testosterone injections, administered every three weeks.

A sexual murder

At lunchtime on 5 October 1975, eleven-year-old Lesley Molseed (who had a mental age of six) went to a corner shop in Rochdale to fetch a loaf for her mother. She was a small, thin girl with a heart defect which often left her breathless. But on that particular day she was in good spirits, and was proudly wearing her favourite raincoat and prized Bay City Rollers tartan socks.

Lesley reached the shop within minutes, but it was closed and she headed along a narrow dirt pathway to buy bread at the nearby Spar. En route, she was intercepted by her killer – who drove her to Rishworth

Moor in the Pennines, parked, and carried her up forty feet of moorside to a heather-covered area, where he stabbed her in the back, causing her to fall to the ground. As she lay on her stomach, he stabbed her a total of twelve times, several of the wounds penetrating her heart and lungs. Raising her raincoat and skirt, he masturbated over her body, leaving semen on her underwear. At some time during the assault, the child bled to death. The paedophile then returned to his wife and family. He would not be detected for another thirty years . . .

Forensics

Three days later, Lesley's body was found and scientists were able to determine that her killer had a low sperm count. Unfortunately, there wasn't enough semen for them to establish the killer's blood group. A woman thought that she'd seen Lesley in a car about the time that she disappeared but, with no definite witnesses to the abduction, the trail went cold.

Then two teenage girls said that a man had indecently exposed himself to them on Saturday 4 October, the day before Lesley had been abducted. The following month, one of them pointed out the alleged culprit to her mother in the street. It was Stefan Kiszko, well known in the area as a mother's boy.

Questioned

On 5 November 1975, police came to Stefan's house and questioned him over the allegation that he'd flashed at the girls outside a youth club. He denied doing this and his mother backed him up, telling the constables that this was a ridiculous claim.

They left but returned later, asking him what he'd been doing at the time of Lesley Molseed's disappearance, on 5 October. Stefan said that he thought he'd been in hospital. Police would later find out that this was wrong, and that he'd been discharged several days before.

They returned again and searched his home, finding some girlie magazines and sperm-encrusted tissues under his bed. Detectives now took him down to the station and questioned him relentlessly.

Out of his depth, Stefan said that he might have gone out on 5 October after all. He added that the testosterone injections that he was being given at the hospital made him feel strange. They asked him for further details, and he admitted that he'd never fancied girls until earlier that year, when the hormonal medication had stimulated him sexually. He'd begun to masturbate in his car whilst looking at girls who were walking along the road.

Convinced that he'd turned into a sex maniac because of the hormone treatment, they continued to question him for fifteen hours, during which time he refused anything to eat and constantly asked to see his mother. After a night's sleep at the station, the questioning began again. Kiszko then said that he'd exposed himself to the girls and that he'd stabbed Lesley. After giving a formal statement, he asked if he could go home to his mum.

Given a solicitor, he told the man that he'd made up the confession so that police would let him return home. Police charged him with murder and he was remanded to Armley Prison in Leeds. Interestingly, he wasn't beaten up by the other prisoners because they were convinced that he'd been fitted up by the police. They didn't believe that this shambling, knock-kneed mother's boy was capable of carrying or dragging an eleven-year-old girl over the Pennines, far less stabbing her to death.

Trial

Stefan Kiszko's trial began at Leeds Crown Court on 7 July 1976. Jurors heard about Stefan's confession to the murder and his immediate retraction. Two yellow fibres found on Lesley's clothes were similar to those from the rug in his car.

He'd been given a testosterone injection on 3 October, two days before Lesley's sexually motivated murder. His mother couldn't remember exactly what he had been doing on the day of the murder, but was convinced that he hadn't been out of her sight for more than half an hour.

Taking the stand, Kiszko denied killing the eleven-year-old but said that he must have inadvertently exposed himself to the girls on 4 October, whilst carrying a roll of carpet into his mother's new house. He said that the carpet must have caught on his zip and pulled it down, though he could not remember there being any girls in the vicinity at the time.

He said that the police had given him full details of how Lesley was stabbed, and he'd repeated those details in his confession after an enraged detective had terrorised him by threatening to beat him up, screaming, "I know you did it and I'm going to make you fucking admit it."

A doctor for the prosecution (albeit not Stefan's doctor) testified that the anti-anaemia medication that Stefan had been given had restored his energy. This medic also testified that the hormone medication, in the form of Primoteston injections, would have increased his aggression and aggravated any underlying abnormal sexual urges.

Unsurprisingly, the jury returned with a guilty verdict and the judge sentenced Stefan Kiszko to life imprisonment. He was now a category-A prisoner, housed in Armley's top security wing.

The following month he was transferred to Wakefield Prison, where he was attacked by five prisoners. Though not badly hurt, he was deeply shocked − his loving parents had never administered corporal punishment, and this was the first time in his twenty-four years that he'd been hit. He was immediately placed on Rule 43 with other convicted sex offenders, segregated from the general prison population for his own protection.

A living hell

Stefan Kiszko was now written-off by the local immigrant community, who were convinced that he was guilty. His mother was shunned by former acquaintances, something she found especially hard to deal with as she was suffering from a serious lung disease. But she wrote cheerful letters to her son twice a week and made the permitted twice-monthly visits to the prison by bus, despite the eight-hour round trip. She also wrote to everyone from her MP to the Council for Civil Liberties, begging them to help free her son.

On 11 May 1977, Stefan was assaulted again and had to have several stitches in his head. He sank into a deep depression. The prison doctor prescribed tranquilisers, but he remained disturbed. He threw a bucket of water over another Rule 43 prisoner, and the authorities feared that he was becoming schizophrenic.

After two years of imprisonment, Kiszko began to soil himself rather than use the toilet. He also stopped bathing, a common sign of clinical depression.

When his appeal was turned down, he became paranoid and thought that doctors were deliberately failing to treat his mother's lung disease. He also decided that the government had locked him up in order to observe how an innocent man coped with jail. The prison psychiatrist increased his tranquiliser dose, but the wrongfully convicted man remained disturbed and told everyone that his mother was also part of the government plot. He attacked another prisoner, and was later found with a pair of scissors hidden in his cell.

On 11 November 1981, he was moved to Gloucester Prison, two hundrerd miles away from his mother, but the elderly woman still made the twice-monthly journeys. By now, Stefan had regressed and was speaking in Ukrainian, his father's tongue.

In April 1983, he attempted to stab another prisoner. By April of the following year, he was so unwell that he swore incessantly and often foamed at the mouth. The following month he was transferred to Bristol Prison and diagnosed as schizophrenic with the recommendation that he be moved to a mental health establishment, but seven months later he was sent back to Wakefield and housed with the general prison population.

Kiszko's mental health continued to decline and he was increasingly tranquilised. In August 1987 he was moved to Grendon Underwood Prison in Aylesbury, which specialised in the treatment of the mentally ill. There, he was treated for paranoid psychosis and rallied slightly. But by May 1989 he was back in Wakefield, where he had visions of ghosts trying to sexually abuse him.

In March 1991 he was transferred to Ashworth Mental Hospital in

Merseyside, where he remained delusional, telling his mother that he would soon be paroled.

Meanwhile, his mother, whose lung disease (byssinosis) had been caused by inhaling cotton dust throughout her years working in the mills, was given compensation of £40,000. She went to her solicitor to collect the cheque, and told him that she was going to use the money to prove her son's innocence. Aware that many unscrupulous lawyers would take the money and do very little, he recommended a solicitor who he knew and trusted: Campbell Malone.

Malone spoke to an investigative journalist, and they tried to find a house in Rochdale which had a rug or carpet with similar fibres to the ones found on Lesley Molseed's clothes. But the search yielded nothing. He hired a private eye, Peter Jackson, who spoke to Stefan's GP and took him to the murder scene. The medic concluded that it would have been practically impossible for Stefan, with his broken ankle and poor spatial abilities, to drag Lesley up the steep bank. He had not been called to give evidence at the trial.

Further investigation showed that Stefan was sterile, yet the semen found on Lesley's underwear had a sperm count, albeit a low one. And the hospital endocrologist who had prescribed the hormone injections to Stefan said that they could not have made him aggressive – all that they could do was increase already-present aggressive tendencies. But Stefan was a mild, passive man. The endocrologist had come to court and told this to the prosecution and to the defence, but neither had called him as a witness so his expert opinion hadn't been heard by judge or jury.

The private eye also discovered that a witness had seen Lesley in a car which didn't match the description of Kiszko's, but that this information had been suppressed by detectives.

Police re-interviewed the girls – now aged thirty-one and thirty-three – who had alleged that Stefan had exposed himself to them, and they admitted that they'd made it up. This meant that Kiszko had pleaded guilty to an offence which hadn't occurred, giving details which must have been fed to him by detectives determined to get their man.

They visited Stefan and asked for a semen sample, but the poor man was so physically and emotionally drained that it took him three days to produce one. When he did, tests showed that it was free of sperm, just as his endocrologist had predicted, and that it couldn't have been his semen on Lesley Molseed. All of this information was sent to the Home Office and, on 18 February 1992, Stefan Ivan Kiszko was allowed to appeal. His conviction was quashed and, after sixteen years in prison, he spent nine months' rehabilitation in hospital before being released.

He returned home to his mother's house, still on medication for his mental health. Within weeks he was given some of the half a million pounds compensation that he was due – not that anything could compensate for the loss of freedom and the beatings that he'd endured, or for the complete breakdown of his mental and physical health.

Though unfit to work the former clerk attempted to return to his old life, driving his mother to the garden centre and the shops. (His beloved aunt had died while he was in jail.) But he often lapsed into silence and would stare out of the lounge window for hours, only speaking when spoken to. By the start of 1993, he was having vomiting fits which doctors believed were brought on by anxiety when he remembered his prison ordeal. But he was immensely proud of his mother when her dedication to his cause was formally recognised, and she was named Rochdale Woman of the Year.

That autumn, he was diagnosed with angina and prescribed heart medication. But on 23 December he collapsed en route to bed and died of a massive heart attack. He was forty-one years old. Four months later his mother died. She left most of her estate to the solicitor who had fought so valiantly to get her son freed.

The police admitted that investigating detectives had suppressed information, but much of the paperwork had strangely disappeared and it was decided that they wouldn't be prosecuted.

Killer's DNA identified

For the next nine years, the police considered various likely suspects for Lesley's murder. Then, in 2003, improved technology meant that scientists were able to obtain a DNA profile from the semen stains on the child's clothes. The profile was kept on file.

On 1 October 2005, a fifty-one-year-old comic shop owner named Ronald Castree was arrested when an allegation – which had nothing to do with the Molseed case, but is believed to involve the rape of a prostitute – was made against him. Unfortunately the woman wasn't considered a reliable witness, so the case was dropped. But his DNA had been taken as a matter of course, and was found to be a match . . .

RONALD CASTREE

Detectives began to research Castree's life, finding that he was the son of an export clerk and had been born on 18 October 1953 in Littleborough, the place where the Molseeds were living at the time when Leslie was abducted. He had gone to school in neighbouring Rochdale.

In 1973, whilst living in Oldham, the nineteen-year-old – who vaguely resembled George Harrison of the Beatles, with his long hair and moustache – married eighteen-year-old Beverley. They had a white wedding. But the honeymoon period ended quickly and she rarely saw him, as he worked as a clerk in a cotton mill by day and as a taxi driver at nights and weekends. She soon realised that he was an inveterate womaniser, having numerous affairs. Beverley also had an affair, which resulted in a son, Jason. The child was born a fortnight before Ronald Castree murdered Lesley Molseed.

Beverley was still in hospital with complications following the birth, when Castree spotted eleven-year-old Lesley out on an errand. He abducted her in his yellow van and drove her to Rishworth Moor. He parked and forced her up a steep, grassy path until they were out of sight of the road, whereupon he produced his knife and stabbed her to death.

Another victim

Less than a year later he abducted a nine-year-old girl with special needs, drove her to a derelict house in Rochdale and violently sexually assaulted her. But she ran away before he could kill her, and told her parents, who reported the sex crime to the police. Castree was caught and pleaded guilty to gross indecency at Rochdale Crown Court. Beverley, who he was abusing both physically and emotionally, stood by him and he was let off with a fine. Because Stefan Kiszko was already in prison awaiting trial for Lesley Molseed's murder, no one considered Castree as a suspect. Yet both girls, similar in age and vulnerability, had attended a special needs school a mile from where Castree both lived and worked.

The Castrees went on to have two sons together. Later, he worked as an administration manager, and later still ran a second-hand book stall at the local market. By the 1990s, he was specialising in selling collectible American superhero comics and opened shops in Ashton-under-Lyne and Rochdale, making over £50,000 a year. He told the *Daily Mail* in a 1994 interview, "The timeless appeal of the comic is escapism. As people increasingly need a break from real life, it can only mean increasing popularity for comics of all kinds."

His own love of escapism resulted in him picking up numerous drunken young women from nightclubs in his taxi, and offering to let them off of the fare if they'd have sex with him in the backseat. He told acquaintances that he "got lucky" most weekends. A disillusioned Beverley described him as a vile monster who would never change.

Castree even used family vacations to target young prey, taking his children to a holiday park where he lounged by the pool, staring at little girls in swimming costumes. He would even befriend their fathers in the hope of getting access to them.

In the mid-1990s his marriage failed and he went on to marry a divorcee called Karen, who had five children by two previous relationships. Her three youngest, aged seven, nine and eleven, lived with her and with Castree in a terraced house in Shaw, near Oldham, Greater Manchester.

Castree eventually gave up the shops and took to selling his comics on eBay. He remained superficially smarmy with a violent underside, once getting into a fight with another resident in the street. Now the police knew that the balding, overweight fifty-something was something more than a sexual predator, that he'd committed a murder thirty years before . . .

Early in the morning of 6 November 2006, he was arrested at the family home by a team of officers from West Yorkshire police. They would later claim that he said, "I've been expecting this for years," a statement which Castree subsequently denied. The following day he was remanded in custody. On 19 April 2007 he pleaded not guilty at a court hearing; on 23 April he was refused bail.

A guilty verdict

Castree was tried at Bradford Crown Court in the autumn of 2007. He denied killing Lesley, and had previously told detectives that he'd been set up, or that the DNA evidence against him was due to cross-contamination. His defence team named another convicted paedophile as the killer.

The prosecution said that Castree had abducted Lesley from Rochdale in 1975, and that his semen was a perfect match, which linked him inextricably to her murder. They were also told about his 1976 sexual assault on a nine-year-old girl.

On 12 November 2007, the jury found Ronald Castree guilty and he was jailed for life, with a recommendation that he serve at least thirty years before becoming eligible for parole. He is likely to die in jail.

CHAPTER ELEVEN

YESTERDAY'S PAEDOPHILES

Sentimentalists like to suggest that children were safer in the past, that the extended family or the absence of freely available porn protected them from predators. But, as the following British cases from the nineteenth to mid–twentieth centuries delineate, this simply wasn't the case.

ALBERT EDWARD BURROWS

Albert was born in 1861 in Derbyshire. Few details have survived about his parentage, but it's clear that his childhood was unhappy – one of his brothers ended up in a lunatic asylum, and Albert himself showed psychopathic traits from an early age.

His first marriage was punctuated by violent outbursts and heavy drinking, but in those days marriage was for life and his spouse put up with his cruelty. But, after twenty years of marriage, he got wartime work in a munitions factory in Nantwich where he met a small, slim woman almost thirty years his junior called Hannah Calladine. Albert was clearly attracted to child-like women, and soon got her pregnant. He bigamously married her in 1918, but the bigamy was soon discovered and he served six months in jail. Hannah then pursued him for child maintenance, but he refused to pay it and served another three weeks in prison. By now he was unemployed and had several months rent arrears on his Glossop house.

A multiple murder

Hannah, her six-year-old daughter Elsie, from a previous relationship, and her fifteen-month-son with Albert eventually arrived on his doorstep, demanding sustenance. Whereupon Burrows' wife moved out and immediately claimed maintenance from him under the Married Woman's Act. At this stage he decided to murder Hannah and the two children, and get back with his wife.

On a Sunday evening in January 1920, he persuaded Hannah to accompany him to the pub with their baby, a trip which involved a walk across the moors. He told her to leave six-year-old Elsie in the house.

When they reached the moors he murdered both Hannah and his own son, and threw them down a deep shaft. It would be three years before parts of their broken skeletons were found.

Paedophilia

Burrows now returned to the house and spent the night with six-year-old Elsie. It's inevitable that her last hours were not pleasant. The following day he walked her to the moors and murdered her, before throwing her into the shaft where her mother and half-brother's corpses already lay.

Another child murder

Three years later, on Sunday 4 March 1923, Albert Burrows struck again, luring three-year-old Tommy Wood away from the neighbourhood. His uncle thought that he'd gone to his grandparents' house for lunch, so it was teatime before the family realised that he'd been abducted, and contacted the police.

Sixty-two-year-old Burrows – who lived across the road from Tommy – had given the child an apple and then taken him to the moors. There he viciously raped the three-year-old before throwing him into a pit filled with filthy water, where he ultimately drowned.

Bizarrely, Burrows now went to the police and told them he'd seen Tommy near a stream. He also involved himself in the police search, just as modern paedophiles such as Ian Huntley have done. But when his story didn't tally with other eyewitness accounts, an inspector questioned him further and Burrows admitted taking the boy rabbit-hunting on the moors, then losing him. He took the search team back to the general vicinity and, when they found the violated little body, the civilian searchers began to lynch him and he had to be rescued by the police.

The authorities now realised that Hannah, Elsie and baby Albert were missing, and that Albert Burrows senior had a motive for wanting them dead. They searched the moors and found parts of all three skeletons.

Hanged

On 8 July 1923, Burrows was tried at Derbyshire Assizes for the murders of thirty-two-year-old Hannah Calladine and his fifteen-month-old namesake, Albert Edward Burrows. It took the jury only fifteen minutes to deliver a guilty verdict, whereupon it was deemed pointless to try him for the murders of Elsie Calladine and Tommy Wood. Having previously boasted that he wouldn't tremble on the scaffold, he was sentenced to death and hanged at Bagthorpe Gaol on 8 August that same year.

STEPHEN MURPHY

A farm worker with a low IQ, Murphy raped and murdered an eight-year-old boy in Ireland in 1945.

Relative lunacy

Stephen was born into a mentally disordered family in County Mayo, Ireland in 1916. One of his brothers was retarded and died in 1935, and an uncle, who died aged twenty-seven, was so limited in intelligence that he was unable to dress himself. Two of his cousins were sent to the lunatic asylum whilst another had an exceptionally low IQ.

Stephen had deformed ears and a deformed breastbone. He grew up to be a loner who, unsurprisingly, never had a girlfriend. He remained at home on the family farm near Crossmolina with his father and his brother, only capable of manual work as he was unable to read or write.

Murder

By the spring of 1945, Murphy had begun to take his eight-year-old neighbour, Michael Joseph Loftus, out ferreting. He groomed the child, then repeatedly sodomised him for the next three months. On Sunday 17 June he waited for the boy to leave church, where he'd been attending mass with his family, and took him to a field near his home. Murphy then attempted to sodomise the eight-year-old again, but by now Michael's anus was badly damaged through repeated penetration and he refused to let his neighbour enter him.

Enraged, Murphy raped the boy, then picked up a spade and began to batter him. Michael put up his arms to defend himself and received wounds to his hands and wrists. The twenty-nine-year-old kept swinging the heavy implement, fracturing the back of the boy's skull. Some bone fragments even penetrated his brain. He hid the body in an outhouse for a day or two before burying it, late at night, in a nearby field.

For the next week, the police and hundreds of volunteers searched the fields, until, on the eighth day, Michael's father noticed that some bushes had been disturbed on a neighbouring farm. He informed the Garda, who investigated and found that the bushes had been uprooted and replanted. After a few minutes digging they unearthed the child's violated corpse.

The following day they discovered a pair of men's boots, which had been recently cleaned, in the neighbouring farm's hedge. Suspecting that they were tied in with the murder, the police put them back where they found them and kept watch.

Shortly after midnight, Stephen Murphy strode across the field and reached into the hedge. Arrested, he said that he was searching for a stray cow, but his edgy demeanour made police suspicious. They put him under twenty-four-hour surveillance and arrested him the following day, when he retrieved a pair of trousers from a local outhouse. They were covered in what appeared to be semen stains.

Two days later, Murphy admitted the murder, saying that he'd killed the boy with a spade and thrown it into the river. The spade was subsequently found there with clay on it – and underneath the clay, the police found human blood.

Trial

The trial was held at the Central Criminal Court, Dublin, in November 1945. Murphy pleaded not guilty. He told fellow prisoners that the murder hadn't been premeditated, and that he expected to be freed.

Two doctors appeared as witnesses for the defence, both claiming that Stephen Murphy was a schizophrenic and of limited intelligence. As such, they said, he didn't fully comprehend the gravity of his murderous act.

The jury were out for three hours on 23 November before returning with a guilty verdict. Asked if he wished to make a statement, the defendant replied firmly, "I have nothing to say." He was immediately sentenced to death, but the appeal court ordered a retrial, ruling that the judge should have given the doctors' opinions equal weight to his own during his summing up.

The following year, at his retrial Stephen Murphy was found guilty but insane, and sent to Dundrum Criminal Lunatic Asylum for life.

PETER GRIFFITHS

This soldier raped and murdered a three-year-old girl in 1948, and is widely believed to have murdered an eleven-year-old boy two months previously.

Family madness

Peter was born in 1926, to Elizabeth and Peter Griffiths senior. The latter was a schizophrenic who, eight years previously, had spent nine months in a mental hospital where he had been diagnosed as suffering from delusional insanity.

Peter lived with his parents and his stepbrother James in Blackburn, Lancashire. At six, he fell from a milk float, battering his head, but his family couldn't afford to consult a doctor. At ten years old he began to wet the bed, and spent the next two years as a full-time patient at

Queen's Park Hospital, where his enuresis was believed to have a neurotic cause.

After leaving school, he gave up one menial job after another and retreated to his room, where he played with make-believe trains. His mother told him that he was 'mental'. He joined the army and became a guardsman, but his attitude was poor and he deserted twice.

After the war, he returned to his parents' house and found manual work at a flour mill. He began to date a deeply religious girl, but she disapproved of his drinking and ended the relationship in April 1948. On 10 May he asked her to marry him, but she repeated that their relationship was over.

The murder

Four days later, on 14 May 1948, Griffiths went out alone for a drink, something he did with increasing frequency. He had five pints of bitter in one pub, then walked to another where he drank two glasses of Guinness and two double rums. Returning to the first pub, he had another six pints of bitter, leaving at closing time.

According to Griffiths' later statement, a stranger then offered him a ride and dropped him off outside Queen's Park Hospital shortly after midnight on 15 May. He took his shoes off and entered the quiet building via the veranda, then made his way to the toddler's ward and saw little June Anne Devaney sleeping in her cot. June was a month shy of her fourth birthday, had been cured of pneumonia and was due to go home the following day.

For some unknown reason, Griffiths left his fingerprints on a Winchester bottle that had been stored under June's bed. He'd later remember picking it up and almost dropping it. He heard the nurse approaching and so slipped out into the grounds again, re-entering the ward after she left – his muddy, sock-based footprints were visible on the polished floor. The former guardsman lifted the sleeping child over the side of the cot rather than lowering it, and hurried into the hospital grounds.

He took the little girl to the furthest corner of the yard, lay her down and savagely raped her. June screamed and he picked her up by both feet, his fingers leaving indents in her ankles, and swung her against the wall. Returning to the veranda, he put on his shoes then retraced his steps to have a final look at the dead or dying child. He then walked home and fell asleep on the settee.

A nurse raised the alarm at 1:15am, and two hours later they found June's despoiled body, her face bruised, her skull fractured. Police immediately feared that the man who had stabbed eleven-year-old schoolboy Jack Quentin Smith to death two months earlier, in nearby Farnworth, had struck again. Jack's friend, who had also been attacked but survived, had given police the description of the killer – a tall, thin man with an acne-ridden face. They knew that June's killer must have been equally tall, as he'd been able to bend over and remove her from her cot without opening the side.

Griffiths – who was over six feet tall, slender and had a poor complexion – got up the next day and pawned his suit in order to raise some more money. He went to the cinema and, by the time he was walking home, the evening papers were full of June's sexually motivated murder. He read the reports but felt nothing, and went home to have his evening meal.

Police now took the fingerprints of every man who had been treated at the hospital during the past two years, but drew a blank, so they extended the fingerprinting to every male over the age of sixteen in Blackburn – forty-six thousand prints were taken. They found a match to Peter Griffiths and were able to ascertain that blood on his suit matched that of the dead child.

Trial

Griffiths quickly confessed, giving full details of the abduction and murder but omitting to mention the rape. At his trial, the defence said that he had no memory of the sexual aspect, and that he'd been in the grip of a schizophrenic mania. The prosecution countered that it was odd for a man to be sane both when he took the child and some minutes after, when he made his getaway, but suffering from lunacy during the rape.

The jury, consisting of nine men and three women, retired for twenty-five minutes, then returned with a guilty verdict. Mr Justice Oliver then passed a death sentence. Later that year, on 19 November 1948 in Walton Prison, Liverpool, Peter Griffiths was hanged.

In those days too, the public were given the impression that killers were simply born bad. Griffiths' parents were described as honest and colourless, his background as unremarkable. In truth, his father suffered from clinical levels of depression and his schizophrenia was considered incurable.

No one was ever convicted of Jack Quentin Smith's murder, but the local police remained convinced that Griffiths – who fitted the killer's description and lived thirteen miles from the murder site – was responsible.

ALBERT GEORGE HALL

After murdering a six-year-old girl in August 1953, this paedophile hid her body so well that it wasn't discovered for more than two weeks.

The caretaker

Albert, who was always known by his middle name of George, was a married man and caretaker of the Park Congregational Church in Halifax. With his grey hair and slightly gaunt features, he looked older than his actual years.

On 12 August 1953, he was working as usual when he espied six-year-old Mary Hackett playing in the street. A quiet, well-behaved child, she lived across the road from the church.

Hall lured Mary into the church's crypt – an enormous underground vault that had accommodated up to a thousand people during the war, when it was used as an air-raid shelter – and either touched her or said something inappropriate. Terrified, she tried to run away from him, losing one of her shoes. The forty-eight-year-old caught up with her and smashed in the back of her head, either by using a blunt instrument or by beating her head against the floor. He then dug a grave inside the crypt, put the corpse in it face down and covered it with earth, before piling surplus chairs and pews on top.

119

Mary had been sent out to play for ten minutes before her lunch, so when she was five minutes late her parents went looking for her. The police were informed of her disappearance within the hour and immediately started door-to-door enquiries.

As the days passed, they searched derelict buildings and even drained the reservoir, but there was no sign of the little child. An appeal via the BBC also failed to unearth any clues.

On 29 August, Scotland Yard were called in and two of their detectives decided to re-examine previously searched buildings. When they went to investigate the Congregational Church, they met its caretaker for the first time. (He had previously been interviewed by the local police.) George was clearly fascinated by the detective's work, and insisted on giving them cups of tea and cakes that his wife had baked.

An unlikely story

He said that he'd seen a strange man in the church cemetery on the day that Mary had vanished, and that he'd heard voices coming from the crypt. The detectives were immediately suspicious, as he hadn't mentioned this potential suspect to the local police, but they decided to win the caretaker's trust and continued to call in on him every few days for tea and cakes. Soon he was calling them "my friends".

On 21 September, they decided to dig up every inch of the crypt and brought in a large crew of workers and equipment. George froze when he saw them, and physically barred their path, but they showed him their search warrant and he reluctantly let them through. They started in a corner which Hall had recently painted and, by lunchtime, had unearthed the little girl's remains. Her face was unrecognisable but she was identified by her green dress.

Surprisingly, the police didn't arrest him at this stage. Instead, the detectives, who he thought of as friends, asked him to help with their enquiries down at the station. There they asked him who would commit such a crime, and he said that he had no idea, that it was a terrible thing to bash in the back of a child's skull.

Hall hadn't seen the body being unearthed, and the cause of death hadn't been made public, so detectives now charged him with the girl's murder. He continued to protest his innocence and said that he'd be found not guilty at his trial. This took place at Leeds Assizes and lasted for four days.

The jury took just six and a half hours to reach a unanimous verdict, and George Hall was hanged at Leeds Prison on 22 April 1954.

JOHN LYNCH

This blacksmith murdered a three-year-old and a four-year-old girl within an hour in Edinburgh, in December 1953.

A failed marriage

Nothing is known of John Lynch's formative years, but by age forty-five he had left his wife in Ireland and moved to Edinburgh in Scotland, where he set up home with a married forty-two-year-old kitchen maid called Annie. John was a heavy drinker who looked fifteen years older than his actual age. Because all of his money went on drink, the couple lived in a tenement slum on Edinburgh's Greenside district.

A double murder

On 11 December 1953, he spent the morning drinking. In the afternoon, he saw three-year-old Margaret Johnston and four-year-old Lesley Sinclair playing on the communal stairway. They, and all of the other local children, knew him as kindly Uncle Paddy. He invited them into his flat – his common-law wife Annie was out working – and immediately grabbed both children and tore off their clothes. He also raped the four-year-old.

Lynch beat both girls about the face and, when they put their hands up to protect themselves, he continued beating their hands. Soon both children were heavily bloodstained. They were screaming – a passerby overheard their cries, but was unable to ascertain where they were coming from – so Lynch grabbed a stocking that was hanging from the fireplace and strangled Lesley. He tore a piece of cloth from an apron that was also drying by the fire and used it to strangle Margaret, who promptly vomited. Taking both girls to the communal toilet on the stair, he locked them inside.

A huge search was mounted for the missing children, and later that same day a neighbour forced open the toilet door and discovered them. Margaret was dead whilst Lesley was unconscious. She died in hospital within the hour.

John Lynch was louder than anyone else in his denouncement of the murderous paedophile, but when police searched his house they found that a torn apron matched the piece of cloth used to strangle Margaret. And Annie nervously admitted that she'd left two stockings hanging up to dry, and returned home to find that one of them had disappeared. Equally damning, the safety pin from little Margaret's skirt was found on Lynch's mantelpiece, yet he claimed that he hadn't seen the girls for two days. Arrested, he swore that the police were trying to set him up.

At the station, blood and traces of vomit was found on his clothes, yet he continued to protest his innocence – though he declined to take the stand in his own defence. His common-law wife said that he'd admitted to her that he'd committed both murders. He was found guilty and his appeal for a reprieve was turned down.

On 23 April 1954, he was hanged by executioner Albert Pierrepoint at Edinburgh's Saughton Prison, still protesting his innocence.

TOM LIONEL BURNS

This seventy-one-year-old pensioner raped and murdered two five-year-old girls on the same day.

Senility

Nothing is known of Tom Burns' childhood, but in adulthood he worked as a butcher. In 1956 his elderly wife was permanently hospitalised, after which Burns became increasingly confused. His physical health also deteriorated, his body becoming hunched, and he had to employ a home-help to clean his modest, terraced Barrow-in-Furness home.

A double murder

On Wednesday 11 June 1958, he was playing the piano in his lounge when two neighbourhood girls – Lavinia Murray and Sheila Barnes, both five – asked if they could also learn to play the instrument. He showed them the scales, after which they all went into the kitchen. Burns then felt overwhelmed by sexual desire and kissed the children, whereupon, he later said, the room started to swirl before his eyes. Grabbing a sharp butcher's knife, he cut Sheila's throat.

Lavinia struggled desperately to escape his clutches, and the kitchen was soon littered with broken crockery. She may have run into the living room; leastways, there was so much blood on the carpet there that the seventy-one-year-old later destroyed it. He cut her throat before violently raping both corpses. Afterwards, he lifted the floorboards in his shed and dug a hole that was three feet long and one foot deep.

Cannibalism

But he reconsidered and decided to eat the girls instead – psychiatrists would later speculate that he thought he'd be able to absorb their youth and their energy. He cut the foot off one of the girls and put it on a plate, planning to roast it the following day.

Meanwhile, the girls' parents had reported them missing and the police started combing the area, with frogmen searching a nearby reservoir. The following day they were approached by Tom Burns' home-help, who said that he'd surprisingly told her not to clean his house. But she insisted on making his living quarters habitable, and was disconcerted to find smashed crockery all over the kitchen. Even more worrying, the living room carpet had been removed. She had not gone upstairs, at Burns' insistence, but told police that there were two bedrooms up there.

Detectives went to Burns' property, where they found the hole that he'd dug inside his shed and asked him what he planned to do with it. He said that he was going to plant hyacinth bulbs. Unconvinced, they asked to have a look around his house but he barred their way to one of the bedrooms, saying that he wanted to keep it as a shrine to his wife.

Entering despite his protestations, they found the mutilated corpse of one girl on the bed. Another was lying in a laundry basket. Burns had used his butcher's skills to the full, with one child being almost decapitated whilst both had been completely drained of blood.

"Sex made me do them in," he admitted, as detectives stared aghast at the violated corpses. "I suppose this will mean a rope round my neck."

Trial

He appeared at Lancaster Assizes on 21 October 1958, where both a prison doctor and a psychiatrist said that he was unfit to plead, being unable to understand the charges or follow the evidence against him. He was sentenced to be detained indefinitely in a psychiatric hospital.

Mostly sane

Though many of these latter-day paedophiles were found to be suffering from schizophrenia or senility, most modern paedophiles are sane and know exactly what they are doing, as the following cases from America show.

PART TWO
AMERICAN PAEDOPHILES

CHAPTER TWELVE

WESTLEY ALLAN DODD

An active paedophile from the age of thirteen, Dodd went on to commit three appalling murders in 1989, including that of a four-year-old.

Lonely years

Westley was born on 3 July 1961, to Carol and Jim Dodd in Toppenish, Washington. He was their first child but, eleven months later, they had a second son. When Westley was three, the family moved to Kennewick, also in Washington State, where, the following year, Carol gave birth to a baby girl. It was a busy household, as Jim was a delivery driver for various dairy firms whilst Carol occasionally temped as a cook in local restaurants.

Westley was a quiet child who would later say that his mother was always cold towards him and that he was terrified of his father, who frequently played mind games and would punish him for things that he hadn't done. He said that his parents' marriage was argumentative and vicious, and that the family wasn't close. At primary school he kept to himself, but was bullied by some of the older children as he was introverted and very poor at sports. He was an exceptionally slender child, so the other boys laughed at his inability to cope with the rougher playground games, and he was much too shy to talk to girls.

Guilt

Though he was never given any formal sexual education, Westley assuaged his curiosity at age nine by looking at the genitals of his male cousins of the same age. It was the kind of inquisitiveness experienced by most young children, yet he felt incredibly guilty about it. By now the family had moved to Yakima, so he'd had to change schools; this was an ordeal for the shy boy, and once again he failed to make friends. The following year the Dodds moved to Umatilla, Oregon, despite Westley's protestations that he only had a month left in the academic year.

Shortly after the move, he talked to two neighbourhood girls of around eight and four, and they looked at each other's genitals in the girls' garage. (He claimed that this was at their suggestion.) Again, such child-to-child experimentation is a normal part of many youngsters' development. But, for a brutalised and lonely boy like Westley, it was the final life-altering moment, for he became fixated on looking at, and touching, prepubescent genitalia. Later, he would show no sexual interest in any child who had developed pubic hair.

By the time he went to high school in Richland, Washington, he was being mocked by both boys and girls as he didn't have the occasional cigarette or beer like most of his peer group, didn't wear fashionable clothes, or ever play truant. He still hadn't been told about sex and contraception, so he used the slang words for genitals that he'd once heard an eight-year-old girl use. The other teenagers laughed at him, and his only date took place when a girl asked him out. But he had such low self-esteem that he thought that she'd done so for a dare.

The well-groomed, quiet young man went to school each day then stayed behind for band practice, playing clarinet in the school orchestra. By fourteen he also had an after-school job. His peers thought of him as a goody two-shoes, an adult trapped inside a young body; yet deep down he was seething with hostility and was emotionally immature.

Exhibitionism

The increasingly disturbed fourteen-year-old began to hide away in his room, stabbing a pin repeatedly into his penis and inserting a stick into his anus. At this stage he was turning the anger inwards and exhibiting masochistic behaviour, but later he would turn the anger outwards to torture and kill young boys.

Over time, this self-mutilation no longer satisfied Westley – he wanted a reaction from another person, preferably a little boy. Getting home before his parents and siblings every night, he began to expose himself, standing naked at his bedroom window and masturbating. He'd shout down to younger boys, they'd look up and see his erection and would hurry home. Dodd did this on nine or ten occasions over the next three months, then upped the ante by going into the street and asking a younger boy to touch him intimately. The boy did so, and Dodd enjoyed the experience so much that he determined to repeat the act.

He chased a six-year-old girl down the street, straddled her and unzipped her trousers. An adult intervened and the girl ran off. But her father heard of the incident and beat up the fourteen-year-old paedophile, leaving him further traumatised. Fortunately, one of the children who had been flashed at eventually told a parent, whereupon Dodd was arrested and given counselling.

The Dodds' marriage had been poor for many years and, just before Westley's fifteenth birthday, he and his siblings overheard them discussing their impending divorce. Westley was relieved that the endless bickering would at last be over, but his brother and sister were in tears. He felt guilty that he couldn't share their distress, but was glad that he was going to escape his father's wrath.

Moving in with his mother didn't make him any less disturbed. At age fifteen, he molested an eight-year-old in a public toilet. He asked the boy to sodomise him, but, unsurprisingly, the child was unable to do this and unintentionally urinated on the paedophile instead. The following year he molested a five-year-old boy and a six-year-old girl, and was placed in a therapeutic group with other teenage sex offenders. But he found it impossible to discuss his paedophilia on anything other than a one-to-one basis, so the therapy was not a success.

After graduating from school in 1979, Westley got a job in a supermarket, working as a stock boy. He did this for two years whilst continuing his sexual offending. By now he was walking naked through cycle trails in the local woods, masturbating openly whenever children cycled past. He molested other boys, but ultimately none of them pressed charges. The police questioned the teenager about various incidents, but decided that they weren't serious enough to warrant prison time. Dodd was given further psychiatric help, his psychiatrist admitting that the urge to molest would never go away, but that Dodd could learn to control it by avoidance, just as a recovering alcoholic avoids alcohol.

In the navy

In 1981, fearing that one of his victims was going to tell an adult about repeated acts of molestation, Dodd joined the navy. For a short time he concentrated on his career, which included submarine training in Connecticut. But when he was stationed at Bangor in Washington, Dodd began to hang out at amusement arcades, propositioning a seven-year-old boy in the toilets and performing oral sex on him. On another occasion, he similarly molested an eight-year-old boy. Dodd wasn't as yet aware of his own inherent sadism, but his masochism continued to grow, and he inserted an ink-pen filler into his own penis in a public toilet whilst a young child watched.

The paedophile was eventually caught fondling a five-year-old boy in another public lavatory and fled the scene. He was soon arrested by the military police, as a result of which the navy gave him a general discharge for disciplinary reasons.

By now it was 1983, and the twenty-one-year-old moved back to Richland to stay with his mother, taking a job as a dishwasher. But within a fortnight he'd molested a five-year-old boy. He was sentenced to further therapy but failed to show up for all of his appointments, as a result spending three weeks in jail. In prison, Dodd spent his non-working hours masturbating to the thought of past victims and imagining future ones. Like most paraphiliacs (people with deviant desires) he had a very high sex drive. Sex was everything to him as he had no friends, hobbies, life goals or meaningful work.

When Dodd left prison, he moved to Idaho and lived with his father. For the next few months he worked in a grocery store, then quit and became a waiter in a fast food restaurant. The restaurant was frequented by families with small children, so when the manager heard of Dodd's previous offences against minors he fired him.

Shortly afterwards, he moved in with a woman who had a nine-year-old boy. It was classic paedophile behaviour, pretending to care for the mother whilst his only true interest was in her son. One night when she was out, Dodd molested the boy, performing oral sex on him. The child, who had already been unhappy at home and was in therapy, found the courage to tell his psychiatrist. Dodd was initially sentenced to ten years in jail, but, for reasons unknown, it was commuted to one year and he served a mere four months. When he was let out on probation he had to attend counselling sessions, but he quit these as soon as his probationary period was over as he still hated talking about his sexual offending in a group.

After his probation ended, Dodd moved back to the Tri-Cities where he'd gone to high school. For a while he lived there alone, repeatedly molesting a four-year-old neighbourhood boy. He had sex once with the child's mother (who had no idea that he was a paedophile), but was unable to maintain an erection when he tried again at a later date. Dodd remained desperately lonely and rootless, so his sister urged him to move to Renton, Washington, to be close to her and her husband. He did so and got a job as a security guard.

An infant victim

But a few months later the couple moved, and Dodd became friendly with a man who had an eighteen-month-old son. He offered to babysit and ended up fellating the infant. Over the next few weeks he repeatedly molested the child and often tied him up. He now had the ultimate victim – a baby who was too young to speak and couldn't tell on him.

On the morning of 13 June 1987, the remorseless paedophile was patrolling a construction site when he espied a seven-year-old boy and tried to take him into the woods, where he planned to torture and kill him. But the child ran away, and Dodd was soon arrested for attempted kidnapping.

His lawyer bargained the charge down to unlawful detainment, and Dodd served a mere ninety days followed by one year's probation. He again went into counselling, where a psychiatrist noted that his offending pattern (by now involving the molestation of over two hundred children) was one of the most extensive that he'd seen in a twenty-six-year-old male. He found Westley Dodd had a limited understanding of normal human emotion and incredibly low self-esteem, was emotionally immature and hadn't had a meaningful friendship in his life. As a result, he sought out young children who were unable to reject him and expected them to meet all of his adult needs. (He also used them for his sadistic needs, but it's unlikely that he admitted this to the psychiatrist.)

Dodd could have benefited from therapy, but he didn't want to change and quit as soon as his probationary period ended, taking a job as a petrol pump attendant in Renton. But the following year he moved to Buckley, east of Tacoma, to take up another gas station job. It's likely that he'd molested boys in Renton and wanted to move on before the past caught up with him.

At this stage, a girl with whom he'd had a very brief relationship came back into his life, and he quit his job and moved to Yakima with her. But after a week she ran out on him, and he moved to Vancouver, Washington, staying with his dad. A temping agency found him a month's work at a stationery company, and he was such a good employee that the firm decided to keep him on as a shipping clerk.

The first and second murders

As soon as he got his first pay check, at the end of August 1989, Westley quit his father's apartment and rented a room in a Vancouver boarding house, one of only two lodgers there. The landlady liked the cleancut young man, who alternately spent his time at work and sitting quietly alone in his room. She had no idea that he spent hours writing down his sexual fantasies in what he thought of as his 'death diary', a journal filled with graphic essays and drawings depicting what he'd like to do to young boys. He also placed many cuttings of religious art in the journal, and wrote "Satan lives" and "Satan is a Love-God" in his bible.

As soon as he was settled in, Dodd scouted out the local terrain, finding that nearby David Douglas Park had some comparatively secluded areas. That Labor Day weekend, he returned to the park again and again, hiding in the bushes and looking out for likely victims, only going home to rest and for meals. He saw numerous children that he was attracted to during these hours, but they were all in groups or were with adults. It was early evening on Monday 4 September before he saw two unaccompanied boys.

Cole Neer, aged eleven, and his brother Billy, ten, rode past on their bikes, heading home for their evening meal. They felt safe as it was still broad daylight and they were a mere half a mile away from their father's house. Dodd stepped out in front of the children, who obediently stopped for the unthreatening-looking adult. He ordered them off the cycle trail and into the adjacent wooded area. Puzzled, they did as they were told. The threesome even passed two teenage boys as they climbed up the hill to a more secluded area – but, at this stage, it seems that the children didn't know that they were in danger as they didn't ask for help.

Once he was sure that no one was around, Dodd tied the wrist of one boy to that of the other, using a shoelace that he'd brought with him. He told the children to remove their trousers, whereupon Billy became upset. Dodd then removed Cole's shorts and underpants and fellated him.

The child, not understanding, asked, "Why are you doing this?"

"Because I have to," the twenty-nine-year-old replied.

Cutting the shoelace from the children's wrists, he forced them to the ground and turned Cole over onto his stomach, rubbing himself between the boy's buttocks. But he was unable to get an erection – after all, he was a sadist, and it was pain rather than sex which most turned him on.

Pulling out his six-inch knife, he threatened the boys with it, exulting in their terror. As they begged for their lives, he stabbed Billy in the stomach then did the exact same thing to Cole. He continued to stab the older boy as he writhed on the ground, until Cole at last lay still.

Westley Dodd then turned his attention back to Billy, only to find that the boy had run away, clutching the wound in his abdomen. Dodd raced after him, stabbing him in the side and shoulder. Leaving the child motionless on the ground, he went back to Cole to make sure that he was dead.

Reassured by the fact that the older boy wasn't breathing, the guiltless sociopath then strolled down the cycle track, speaking to another walker and even throwing a ball back to two baseball players. Getting into his car, he drove home and relived the event. Billy was found, barely alive, by a teenage boy, but died of his injuries within minutes of reaching hospital. Cole was dead at the scene.

Dodd masturbated again and again at the memory, writing in his journal, "I got more of a high out of killing than out of molesting." A typical sadist, he mainly became aroused by others' fear and pain.

A witness

Dodd hid his blood-covered knife in a dumpster (it would never be found) and returned to work, exuberant at getting away with the double murder. But another park goer had seen him lurking in the bushes, and gave police a good description of the slender, moustached young man. As a result, a fairly close sketch of him appeared in the local paper and he spent an anxious few days indoors, then kept a particularly low profile when he was at work. But no one who knew him connected the hard-working, quietly-spoken employee with the homicidal maniac that the police were looking for.

Further sadism

Within days he was planning further torture murders, writing that he might experiment with "starvation or bleeding to death or suffocation", if he could get a child back to his room. He added that he wanted his next victim to die by a method other than stabbing, which was too quick.

Dodd believed that Satan existed, and he asked the mythical demon to provide him with a six- to ten-year-old boy. Fortunately, he was given lots of overtime for the rest of the month and for much of the following month, and this kept him from scouting for future victims. Then, on Sunday 29 October, he had the day off . . .

A third murder victim

He drove to Richmond School in Portland, where he'd previously seen children playing alone on the climbing frame, and found a four-year-old boy there named Lee Joseph Iseli. Lee had arrived at the playground with his nine-year-old brother, who was now playing football nearby.

Dodd spoke to the little blonde boy for a few moments, then took his hand and led him to the car, driving him to Dodd's room at the boarding house. The other lodger saw the child there but just assumed that it was Dodd's son, or one of his other relatives.

Locking the door, the paedophile stripped the child and tied him spreadeagled to the bed, then took photographs with his instamatic camera. Untying the child, he performed oral sex on him for the next hour. Lee became upset and, doubtless fearing that others in the house would overhear, Dodd promised him a Robocop toy if he'd stop crying. Dodd then took the child to the nearest K-mart and bought him the toy, but Lee again became upset. A kindly employee intervened, but Dodd said that he was Lee's uncle and that Lee was missing his mother. (In reality, Lee lived with his father and brother, and hadn't seen his mother for a long time.)

By now the little boy was hungry, so Dodd took him to McDonald's for a hamburger. Back home, he got into bed with the sleeping child and molested him again and again, at one stage inserting an ink-pen filler into the child's penis. Early in the morning, he choked the boy manually then revived him with mouth-to-mouth resuscitation. When Lee regained consciousness, the sadist choked him again. But the boy was still alive, so Dodd wrapped a rope around his neck and hanged him from the wardrobe rail, leaving him there until he died.

Cutting the corpse down, he performed oral sex on it, then concealed it behind some pillows and went to work. That night, he had anal sex with the child's mottled body, wearing a condom to prevent leaving traces of his DNA. He drove to Washington State Game Reserve, near Vancouver Lake, and dumped the body in some bushes, where it was found by a hunter the following day.

Police were appalled to find that the four-year-old had been sodomised and strangled, purplish marks on his wrists and ankles testifying to the fact that he had also been tied up.

Failed abductions

For a few days, the paedophile contented himself by using Lee's underpants as a masturbatory aid; then he sketched out a torture rack, and went to a local lumber yard to buy the materials to build it. A few hours later he had build a wooden rack with attached rope restraints. He wrote in his death diary that he was looking forward to restraining a victim, putting a plastic bag over his head and watching him die.

On Saturday 11 November, he drove to a cinema which was showing a children's film, and followed an eight-year-old boy to the toilet. "You're coming with me," he said, but the boy said assertively that he wasn't and his assertiveness saved his life. Afraid that the child would make a fuss and attract attention, the paedophile left the cinema and went home.

Two days later, having again asked Satan for assistance, he went to a different cinema and accosted a six-year-old boy in the men's toilets, picking him up, punching him and carrying him bodily out of the room. Thankfully the boy continued to scream, despite Dodd saying, "Calm down, son."

There have been various successful kidnappings where passersby have assumed that a distressed child is with their parent, whereas in truth a stranger was abducting them. But in this case the boy managed to scream, "I don't know him. He's trying to hurt me." Cinema staff gave chase as Dodd raced down the street. Fearing that he would be arrested at any moment, he dropped the boy.

But the child's stepfather caught up with the paedophile and marched him back to the cinema, where staff bound his wrists together with a belt and held him against the wall until the police arrived.

Arrested

Dodd was duly arrested and taken to the nearest police station, where detectives were interested to find that he lived near David Douglas Park, where Billy and Cole Neer had been murdered. He also lived near Vancouver Lake, where Lee Iseli's body had been found.

Fearful that he would clam up if asked about the three murders immediately, they began to gently question him about the attempted abduction from the cinema. Relieved that they apparently weren't connecting him to the homicides, Dodd spoke openly about the incident, admitting that he'd planned to molest the boy. He also admitted that he had numerous previous convictions for molestation and attempted kidnapping, but said that he loved children, that he'd never hurt a child.

But he was unable to provide alibis for the times at which the three children died, and when detectives asked to search his room he refused and began to tremble. When they pressed him further, he admitted that they'd find a briefcase containing nude photos of Lee Iseli and cuttings about the Neer brothers, and that he'd murdered all three of them.

He said that he'd had to kill the Neer brothers so that they wouldn't identify him. But the real reason – which he doubtless wanted to hide – was his need to inflict pain. He also minimalised the trauma he'd caused to four-year-old Lee, saying that he'd only tied him up momentarily in order to take photographs of the child in bondage. But marks on Lee's body showed that the child had struggled to escape the ligatures.

Born again

Westley Allan Dodd had always believed in a deity and an afterlife, but told a prison penpal that he'd recently found religion and that God had forgiven him. He said that the Gideons had given him bible study books – he omitted to mention that he'd always owned a bible, and had written in it before and after torturing Lee Iseli to death.

He was more honest about his feelings towards his family, telling his penpal, "I hate my dad and have no feelings for my mom. I'm not even sure where she lives." (She had moved to Minnesota and remarried.) On another occasion he wrote, "I was never molested but was neglected and abused physically, verbally and emotionally."

Perhaps Dodd reflected on his life as he sat in his cell and decided to do one good thing. For he told prison staff that he'd written to the local paper, warning children of how to avoid becoming victims of a paedophile. Called 'When You Meet a Stranger', his lengthy letter stated, "I have never molested or harmed any child that resisted me. Sometimes it took just a 'no', sometimes it took more." He advised children to say no and run away, adding that, if a paedophile bodily picked them up, they should shout and scream.

Sentenced

In June 1990, Dodd was granted a judicial hearing at which he admitted murdering Billy and Cole Neer and Lee Iseli. He said that each of the murders was premeditated, further admitting that he'd planned to rape and kill the child he'd taken from the cinema.

On Thursday 26 July, at Clark County Court, the murdered children's relatives talked openly of their grief whilst Dodd stared expressionlessly at them. They told him that he was sick and cruel and ugly. Dodd then made his own statement, saying, "I should be punished to the full extent of the law as should all sex offenders and murderers . . . I can accept a death sentence and I don't want to see any delays in carrying it out."

The following month, a jury of six men and six women deliberated on whether to give the killer a life sentence or a death penalty. The prosecution argued against leniency, reading out excerpts from Dodd's diary where he outlined the abuses he'd carried out on four-year-old Lee Iseli and made equally heinous plans for future victims. The defence, in turn, said that Dodd only killed children and so wouldn't be a threat if he was given life imprisonment. But Dodd had already admitted that he'd torture and kill further boys if he ever escaped, and that he would enjoy every minute of it. Three days later the jury returned their verdict – the paedophile was to die.

Washington State gives condemned prisoners the option of death by lethal injection or by hanging. The latter is more of a lottery; if the fall doesn't break the prisoner's neck, he or she strangles to death. But Dodd said that he wanted to hang, as it was the way that his youngest victim had died. The paedophile then attended a competency hearing where both a judge and psychiatrist agreed that he was competent to waive future appeals.

Unsurprisingly, the gallows hadn't been used for almost forty years, so prison workers were dispatched to paint the walls, update the trapdoors and buy a new rope.

An unlikely reunion

Later, Dodd gave a television interview, telling a reporter, "I'll go to Heaven. I have doubts, but I'd really like to believe that I would be able to go up to those three little boys and give them a hug."

He remained religious to the end, entering the execution chamber and telling the assembled watchers, "There is hope. There is peace. I found both in the Lord, Jesus Christ. Look to the Lord and you will find peace."

A few minutes into 5 January 1993, the executioner pressed a button and Dodd plunged seven feet, the drop tearing the ligaments in his neck and causing him to lose consciousness. He strangled to death whilst in this state of oblivion and was eventually cremated.

CHAPTER THIRTEEN

JEFFREY RISSLEY

This bisexual paedophile assaulted both girls and boys before murdering a six-year-old girl in 1991.

Early abuse

Jeffrey was born in 1964 and grew up in Benton Harbor, Michigan. He endured a loveless childhood and was repeatedly raped between the ages of nine and twelve. At fifteen, he began to sexually abuse a younger relative and to molest other neighbourhood children. The following year he left school and tried to commit suicide.

He was thrown out of the house and joined the navy in order to have a roof over his head, but they found that he had emotional problems and rejected him. He moved to Arlington, Texas, and bought a small truck, making his living as a travelling handyman. But he remained sexually obsessed with children and often lured them into his vehicle, where he viciously assaulted them.

Arrested for molesting a boy and a girl, he was sent to prison for three months. Upon being paroled, he moved to Iowa and stayed with relatives.

That didn't work out and he supported himself by working as a rent boy, offering his body to older men. Tall, dark and handsome, he also appealed to women and lived off of a female lover until her cash ran out, before moving onto a second woman and then a third.

But his main interest was in young girls, so he hung around the local school and tried making passes. One thirteen-year-old told the police and he was arrested, but he became so distraught that he was admitted to a psychiatric hospital. A psychologist noted that he was a hardcore paedophile who couldn't be rehabilitated, but Rissley charmed some of the other staff and was given an early release.

Further sex crimes

He moved to Missouri and married in 1990, but the union quickly failed. He then went to Michigan and found himself another female lover, but treated her so badly that she threw him out.

In the summer of 1991 he forced a thirteen-year-old girl into his van, raped and sodomised her. That same summer, he performed oral sex on an eleven-year-old girl and raped and sodomised a ten-year-old boy. Before the authorities could track him down, Rissley fled to Iowa and moved in with a gay lover for several weeks. The man was good to him, but Rissley stole his television and pawned it for petrol money before leaving town.

Rootless again, he drove to central Illinois and worked on various farms, helping bring in the harvest. At night, he frequented cafés where children and young teens hung out. He sexually assaulted numerous youngsters of both genders, threatening that he'd return and kill them if they told. Most didn't, afraid that their parents would be angry with them for getting into a stranger's van for lemonade and snacks.

In mid-September 1991 he was driving through Galesburg, Illinois, when he saw a woman standing by her broken-down vehicle. Rissley fixed it, and when the woman realised that he had no place to stay, she offered him a room at her house in return for him doing some DIY. He did this for the next week, and proved so pleasant that she was happy to let him drive her daughter to school.

Rissley drove the child to a cornfield, tied her hands together with rope and raped her in the front seat of his truck. He threatened to kill her if she told anyone, and then drove her to class. The following day he told the girl's mother that he'd secured employment, and she sadly waved him farewell. It was another week before the little girl found the courage to admit to her mother that the handyman had violated her. Meanwhile, he continued his predatory ways.

On 27 September, he drove up in his distinctive small red truck and offered a lift to two girls, aged eight and ten, but they told him that they didn't accept lifts from strangers. When he became angry and insistent, they ran away and told their parents. The parents reported the incident to the police.

Murder

The following night, circa 6:30pm, he was cruising around Spring Valley, Illinois, when he spotted six-year-old Kahla Lansing walking home. She'd been roller-skating with several friends, and was now making the short journey back to her mother before it grew dark. The paedophile lured her into his truck, drove to a convenience store and bought them both cans of lemonade, then drove on to a deserted barn in Jackson County, where he spent the night raping and sodomising her. At daybreak, he wrapped an electric cord around her throat and strangled her to death.

Rissley expected to get away with this crime, but, when Kahla disappeared, passersby said that they'd seen a red truck in the area. The police remembered that, on the previous day, the owner of a red truck had tried to entice two girls into it. This information was made public, and the woman who'd given Rissley accommodation only for him to rape her daughter finally gave the police his name. She also remembered that he'd mentioned that he had a friend in Benton Harbor, Michigan, who would give him bed and board.

Police went to the town and located Rissley's red truck. He was inside, asleep on the couch, when they raided the house at 3am. Taken into custody, he denied everything until 7am, when he drew investigators a map of where to find Kahla's body. The twenty-seven-year-old admitted that he'd raped and sodomised so many children over the years that he'd lost count. He said that children had always 'pressed his buttons', and that he didn't know why.

Trial

Rissley pleaded guilty to murder at his trial in June 1992. On 9 October, the jury recommended the death penalty. He was sent to Death Row at Pontiac Prison, Illinois.

For the next ten years, the paedophile moved closer to his execution date. Then, at the end of 2002, the governor of Illinois, who was about to retire, changed the status of ninety-two prisoners from death sentences to life sentences. One Illinois citizen told the media what many were thinking: "It's lunacy that a killer and serial rapist such as this monster should live because of the whim of a governor."

CHAPTER FOURTEEN

THOMAS SORIA

Having brutally molested girls and boys throughout his adult life, Soria finally committed a premeditated, sadistic murder at the age of thirty-nine.

Early incest

Thomas was born on 27 January 1961, to Jayne and Tom Soria in Sacramento. It was a bad match, and the couple soon divorced. Jayne then remarried, taking on an abused and violent stepson called Ronny Mozingo. The teenage Ronny molested and sodomised Thomas when the latter was only eight years old. Unsurprisingly, Thomas's grades fell at school and he began to regress, terrified of his sadistic stepbrother. Thankfully, the abuse was discovered and Ronny was shipped off to yet another juvenile reformatory, ending up in prison by the time he was eighteen.

With his tormentor locked up, Thomas gradually recovered and began to do better at school. By eighteen he had started university. He still lived at home with his mother and the two were close, often socialising together at a nearby bowling alley. They were more like friends than mother and son.

But Thomas still had problems, and was convinced that some white girls didn't want to date him because he was Hispanic. He also manipulated everyone that he dated, trying to make them dote on him the way that his mother did. Like many abuse survivors he also had health problems, in his case bad migraines and stomach pains.

143

Discovering the body

Shortly after midday on 25 September 1979, the eighteen-year-old drove home from university as usual, and walked into his bedroom to find a terrible scene. His mother lay naked on her back, on the floor, with a towel draped over her face. Her wrists, ankles and neck were tightly bound with wire. She'd been raped and sodomised and hogtied, so that the weight of her legs placed increasing pressure on her neck. Over ten to fifteen minutes she'd slowly strangled to death, as her sadistic murderer watched, revelling in her pain. Jayne had been dead for approximately an hour when Thomas found her – when the police arrived her body was still warm.

The teenager went into shock and afterwards couldn't bear to return to his bedroom, the scene of the crime. He would often become taciturn, and it was difficult for his girlfriend, Francine, to cheer him up. The entire family was shocked when the murderer turned out to be Thomas's sexual tormentor, Ronny Mozingo, seeking revenge for the times when his stepmother Jayne had beaten him. He was sent to jail for life.

Marriage and a Child

The following year, Thomas and Francine married. At first the sex was gentle and romantic, but soon he began requesting sodomy. Sodomised as a child, and having seen his mother after she'd been sodomised, he now seemed desperate to take on the active role. He kept demanding anal sex, despite the fact that she found it painful – proof of his sadism. He also asked her to urinate on him, which suggests that he also had a masochistic side and wanted to be demeaned. Thomas tried to make Francine feel guilty about refusing his increasingly outlandish demands, saying that if she really loved him she'd want to please him in bed. He was also desperate for children, repeatedly stating that he'd like a little girl. In retrospect, he wanted to create his very own sexual slave.

On 9 August 1980, the couple had their first and only child, a son who they called T.J. (Thomas junior). For a while they lived in Nevada, before moving back to Sacramento. Thomas had the family that he claimed he'd wanted, yet was obsessed with sexual thoughts about young girls. When Francine accepted a babysitting job, Thomas molested the six-year-old girl that she was taking care of. He continued to do so again and again. Later, the Sorias moved to Lake Tahoe to make a new start, but Thomas was soon exposing himself to his young female neighbours. Police let him off with a warning and the family relocated again, ending up in California.

Incest

When T.J. turned five, Thomas began to fondle the boy's genitals on a regular basis. He said that he was the only person that loved his son, that Francine had never wanted a child. He made his confused son lick him all over, and then did the same to him. By age six the abuse included sodomy, with Soria telling T.J. that lots of families did this but didn't ever talk about it. The abuse continued for the next ten years.

Abused men and women often become frozen emotionally at the time of their abuse, and Thomas had only been eight when his stepbrother sodomised him. He remained incredibly emotionally immature, and became jealous when T.J. turned fifteen and got himself a girlfriend. Thomas seduced the underage girl and often took her to bed. He could see that T.J. was hurt by it but he was indifferent to his son's feelings, only caring about himself.

By now Francine was working three jobs, and he and T.J. hardly ever saw her. He hoped that she'd stay away for good so that he could indulge his paedophile desires to the full. And she obliged later that same year, leaving the unhappy household. The courts awarded Thomas full custody of T.J. Ironically, it was what the teenager wanted – Francine had often said that she'd never wanted a child, and he believed that Thomas was the only parent who really cared for him.

A second marriage

By now Thomas had tired of having full sex with T.J., though he sometimes requested fellatio if he was feeling depressed. He soon remarried but remained inappropriate, asking T.J. to go to bed with him and his new wife. The confused youth did so. And, when he fell in love with a young, drug-addicted girl his own age, he eventually shared her with his dad.

It was going to take a lot more than a marriage certificate to straighten Thomas Soria out. He soon lost his security guard job after making obscene phone calls to two women, in which he threatened to rape them. He was fined, his jail sentence was commuted to community service and he was placed on parole. He should ideally have received extensive counselling – sex offenders often gravitate from obscene phone calls to indecent exposure and molestation. Indeed, unknown to the authorities, Thomas had already spent years raping his own child.

When his parole ended, he and his second wife left Sacramento to make a new start in Nevada, leaving T.J. and his girlfriend behind to fend for their selves. But, broke and desperate, T.J. passed several bad cheques, got caught and was given a community order. Defeated, he moved to Nevada to live with his dad.

The go-between

Thomas now suggested that T.J. become a counsellor at a local children's club in Nevada, and should bring the prettiest girls to meet him. He also said his son should introduce him as his uncle, rather than his father, perhaps hoping that any abuse victim's testimony would sound confused if they went to the police. He bought lots of toys and games plus a computer, ensuring that the girls could be entertained for hours. Sometimes 'Uncle Tom' would take them into his room and give them money to take off their clothes, warning them that he had cancer and would die early if they told anyone.

Like most paedophiles, Soria was superficially nice to the children he desired, but deep down he hated them and wrote at length in his diary of torturing them to death with a knife. His fantasies swung between the sadistic and the masochistic, and he wrote, "I want to eat their shit. I want them to eat my shit too." He trawled the internet for photographs of children being abused and began to buy child porn.

YOUTHFUL PREY

Premeditated murder

On 19 March 2000, he wrote in his diary that he wanted to "rape a milky white blonde-haired blue-eyed" little girl. Knowing that his second wife was going to be away all day and overnight, he told T.J. to go get him such a child.

Nineteen-year-old T.J. immediately obliged, finding nine-year-old Krystal Steadman playing outside with two neighbourhood girls that he knew well. She had been brought to the apartment complex by her mother Elizabeth, who was visiting her boyfriend. Small and blonde, she fit his father's fantasy. T.J. waited until the other girls went home, and then lured Krystal into his father's apartment – scratches on the youth's side would show that at some stage he'd carried the child against her will.

It's likely that both men abused her at the beginning, for T.J.'s sperm would later be found on her panties. (He denied having anything to do with her sexual assault and murder, saying that he'd introduced her to his father then gone to his own room to masturbate – like many sex abuse victims, he did this compulsively. But he couldn't explain why his DNA was on her underwear.)

Detectives would later ascertain that Thomas Soria had grabbed the nine-year-old and that she fought back, leaving telltale scratches near his rib cage. Carrying her to his bedroom, he covered her mouth with duct tape, using more tape to bind her wrists. Carrying out his brutal fantasies, he inserted a broom handle into her vagina and anus, and tortured her with a knife, cutting her neck and back. He also raped and sodomised her, and beat her about the head, before cutting her throat. She eventually bled to death.

Meanwhile, Krystal's mother Elizabeth had become concerned at her disappearance, and asked the neighbourhood children if they'd seen her. Some of them replied that T.J. had been talking to various children and pointed out his flat. The nineteen-year-old answered the door looking very flushed, and said that he'd seen Krystal riding her bike towards a local caravan park.

Elizabeth Steadman continued her search but, unable to find her daughter, returned to T.J.'s apartment and demanded entry. She searched every room except Thomas Soria's bedroom, as T.J. said that his uncle was sleeping and physically barred her way.

After she'd gone, Thomas called T.J. into the bedroom and showed him Krystal's naked corpse, demanding that he get rid of it. Father and son put the nine-year-old's body into bin bags, then into a box, piling her torn clothing and some duct tape on top. Thomas told his trembling son to throw the wrapped corpse over a cliff near Carson City, and to dispose of the other items in garbage cans elsewhere. Neighbours watched curiously as the teenager struggled out to his vehicle with the heavy box, then drove away.

By now T.J. was so upset that he vomited twice. His terror increased when he saw that the bin bags were leaking blood all over the floor mat. He threw the wrapped body down the mountainside – then he got further spooked when another driver rounded the corner and saw him doing so. Getting back into the vehicle, he found that he had blood on his shirt and hands. The resourceful teenager then put the vehicle through a carwash, but some blood still remained. Meanwhile, back home, Thomas bleached every surface that Krystal had come into contact with.

Desperately worried about her daughter, Elizabeth Steadman called the police and told them that Krystal might have been with T.J. shortly before her abduction. The teenager voluntarily answered the police's questions, saying that he'd spoken to the nine-year-old but that she'd gone off to play on her bike. He claimed that he'd driven to the mountains, parked to admire the view, and then dozed off in the front seat. Suspicious, police took his clothes and found semen stains on his underpants and a spot of blood (later determined to be the victim's) on one of his boots.

Police were still treating Krystal's disappearance as that of a missing person, but realised that they probably had a murder on their hands when they received a phone call from the driver who'd seen T.J. fling something heavy over a cliff. Racing to the area that the woman described, they found Krystal's nude body, completely covered in blood.

They arrested T.J. and charged him with murder, whereupon he refused to say anything.

Autopsy

T.J. was remanded in custody. Everyone assumed that he was guilty of the murder, until the autopsy on Krystal showed that the semen in her body wasn't his, though his semen was on her panties. The fluid in the child's cavities corresponded to a very close relative of T.J.'s, and further tests showed that it belonged to his father. Police checked Thomas Soria's computer, finding that he'd wiped all of his files but had left his warped sexual diary on the hard drive.

Ten days after the murder he was also arrested. T.J. remained in jail. The teenager would later agree to testify at his father's trial in return for being spared the death penalty.

The son's trial

T.J.'s trial began in Nevada on 24 July 2000. The jury heard an impact statement from Elizabeth Steadman, the victim's mother. Her life had been completely devastated by the death of her youngest child and she pleaded for the judge to sentence T.J. to life imprisonment.

The defence spoke about T.J.'s life of sexual and emotional abuse, describing him as a boy who was completely dominated by his father. They suggested that T.J. hadn't known that Krystal was going to die.

The prosecution concurred that T.J. had an appalling childhood, and that was why he was being spared the death penalty. But they added that he was still guilty of luring the nine-year-old to his rapist father's lair, knowing that she would suffer terribly. He had also lied to Krystal's mother, saying that the child wasn't in the apartment, and had physically blocked her way when she'd tried to enter Thomas Soria's bedroom. He was culpable, and the prosecution asked for a life sentence without possibility of parole.

T.J. himself took the stand, apologising to Krystal's friends and family. As usual in these situations, the words sounded hollow and nothing could lessen the family's pain. In summing up, the judge said that T.J. had known that his actions were very wrong and sentenced him to spend the rest of his life in jail.

The father's trial

Thomas Soria's trial began on 25 January 2001. T.J. took the stand, and wept copiously when questioned about his childhood abuse at the hands of his father. The defence countered that Soria's incestuous behaviour didn't necessarily mean that he was a murderer.

In turn, the prosecution read parts of his diary where he wrote about wanting to rape and sodomise little boys and girls, and to rape and stab women that he was attracted to.

Meanwhile, unknown to anyone, Thomas had been pretending to take his antidepressants but had really been storing them up. In the early hours of 28 January he took all of the tablets. The following morning, the prison guards found him dead in bed. (His step-uncle, Douglas Mozingo, who shot twelve people in a bar, killing two of them, also committed suicide in jail.) The only person who mourned for Thomas Soria was his son, T.J., who is destined to die in prison.

CHAPTER FIFTEEN

RICHARD ALLEN DAVIS

This paedophile took twelve-year-old Polly Klaas from her bedroom as she enjoyed a sleepover with friends. His actions were inadvertently responsible for a change to California's sentencing policy.

Early abuse

Richard was born on 2 June 1954 in San Francisco, to Evelyn and Bob Davis. Both alcoholics, they had five children together. Evelyn was a strict disciplinarian who frequently beat the children, before leaving the marriage when Richard was eleven. His dad, a longshoreman, was given custody and moved the family around California before finally settling in a rundown trailer park. It was a frightening existence for the children, as Bob Davis would often have drunken hallucinations and shoot at imaginary objects, and his bad temper ensured he went through another three failed marriages.

All too soon Richard was passing the violence on, setting cats alight and stabbing dogs. He largely raised himself, as his father was away at work all week and he hated all three of his stepmothers. By age twelve he was stealing from mailboxes, and by his early teens he was joyriding. Later he dropped out of high school, an ill-educated youth with ungrammatical speech whose only ambitions were to get high and cause pain.

We're in the army now

At seventeen he joined the military and was posted to Germany. It was a disaster for the hate-filled boy, who loathed authority. He spent most of his time high on drugs or fighting with his fellow squaddies. After a year he stabbed one of them and the army threw him out.

Back home in San Francisco, he was arrested for drunk driving, burglaries and possessing marijuana. He served time in the county jail for one of those burglaries, his probation officer noting that he'd doubtless soon be in the state prison for more serious offences, as he had such a bad attitude and was unwilling to change. By now he was drinking as heavily as his parents had, and his temper was equally volatile.

An early murder?

On 12 October 1973, the teenager attended a party hosted by a young girl who was celebrating being accepted into the navy. He left the party at the end of the evening with everyone else, but then said that he'd forgotten something and had to go back for it. Shortly afterwards he claimed that he'd found the girl dead, and that she'd shot herself.

Seven suicide notes were found at the scene, so the authorities accepted that she'd taken her own life. But those who knew Richard would later speculate that, as he'd hated to see anyone happy, he'd probably held a gun to her head and made her write the notes before murdering her. He later told acquaintances that she'd been his girlfriend, and that he'd virtually walked in on her suicide.

Fatherhood

Richard Davis continued to cause mayhem wherever he went; when he got his latest girlfriend pregnant, he refused to support the baby. When his son was born in 1974, she had to bring him up alone. That same year Richard was caught burgling a school, but was sent to an alcohol treatment centre rather than jail.

At twenty-one he was sent to prison for a further string of robberies, yet the parole board freed him in under a year. By now he was so hated in his adopted hometown of La Honda, south of San Francisco, that the locals threatened to kill him if he didn't leave.

Attempted suicide

He moved to nearby Hayward and attacked a young woman in a car park, pressing a knife to her back and forcing her into his vehicle. He drove for twenty minutes, hitting her when she began to cry. Stopping in a quiet area, he unzipped his trousers and demanded that she fellate him. But she grabbed the knife, cutting her palm, and unlocked the door – fleeing into the road and flagging down a car, which was being driven by a policeman. Davis was swiftly despatched to jail.

He promptly tried to hang himself in prison and was transferred to a psychiatric hospital in Napa, from which he escaped. Breaking into a house, he battered the sleeping female occupant with a poker that he found at the scene. When she sat up, screaming, he ran away. Thankfully, she survived. The following day he stole a gun and tried to carjack another woman but, when she brandished her own pistol, he fled. He returned to La Honda and burgled a neighbour's house, was caught and sent for psychiatric evaluation. Four separate psychiatrists diagnosed him as a sadistic psychopath.

Freed

On 1 June 1976, Davis was given a sentence of one-to-twenty-five years for the attempted rape and various sentences for the other assaults and burglaries, all to run concurrently. Amazingly, he was back on the streets in just six years.

He now took up with drug dealer Susan Edwards, who had abandoned her own family, and from 1982 to 1984 they roamed the Pacific Northwest, burgling homes and businesses and selling drugs. On 30 November 1984 they upped the ante, breaking into a woman's home and pistol-whipping her before forcing her to withdraw her savings from the local bank.

Five months later they were caught. Davis was given sixteen years whilst Edwards got a mere six months. The couple split up and she bigamously married someone else, who was promptly murdered by one of her ex-boyfriends. Enraged at being dumped, Davis helped with the official investigation into her bigamy. As a result, his sentence was halved for good behaviour and he was out on the streets again by 27 June 1993.

CAROL ANNE DAVIS

A new start

Davis moved into a homeless shelter in San Mateo, reporting weekly to his parole officer. He also got a job as a sheet metal worker, a very well-paid trade at which he excelled. This allowed him to buy a white Pinto which he drove around nearby Petaluma, sometimes relaxing in a park there. It was a potential new start.

But residents who looked more closely at the man on the park bench noticed that he had scary eyes, that he was drunken and unkempt, and that he had numerous tattoos all over his arms. In fact, psychopaths often have many more tattoos than the general population. His fantasies were also those of a psychopath.

The murder

In late September 1993 he got permission to visit his sister, who ran a junkyard in Ukiah, and drove through Petaluma on his way back. On the evening of 1 October, he parked in the town and walked around until he passed a Victorian cottage, and heard girlish giggles coming from inside. He peeked inside and saw three young girls.

Entering the house by an open bedroom window, he immediately terrorised twelve-year-old Polly Hannah Klaas, who lived there with her mother and younger sister. Polly was having two of her friends over for the night.

Davis produced his knife and warned the three girls that he'd cut their throats if they made a sound. Unfortunately, they obeyed him. If they'd screamed and run for the door, he may well have fled. He tied their hands with strips of cloth and used hoods that he'd brought with him to cover their eyes, then picked Polly up in his arms and disappeared into the night. Polly's friends soon freed themselves and informed her sleeping mother, so the local police knew within minutes of the abduction. Unfortunately it took time for them to inform forces further afield.

The paedophile left the area and drove for twenty-five miles, till he came to a small wood where he ran his car into a ditch. He must have taken the twelve-year-old into a clearing and removed some of her clothes, for her black sweatshirt and red tights, alongside a makeshift gag and wrist

154

bindings, would later be found strewn around the area. He returned to the roadside and flagged down a passing motorist, terrifying her so much with his aggressive demeanour that she drove on and called the police. They arrived and, finding that Davis smelled of alcohol and had twigs in his hair, questioned him at length about his activities. They observed that he was sweating heavily despite the fact that it was a cool night.

The officers checked and found that the man had no outstanding warrants, so they pulled his Pinto out of the ditch and let him go. If they'd done a background check, they'd have found that he'd served time for abducting and assaulting women. At this stage, according to the paedophile's later testimony, Polly was still alive in the woods.

Davis drove off then doubled back for her, finally parking the car beside an abandoned sawmill near Cloverdale. There, he sexually assaulted and possibly raped her – she'd eventually be found with her skirt rucked up above her waist and her legs spread apart. He strangled her with material made into a ligature before hiding her body beneath a piece of plywood, and covering it with weeds.

Almost two months elapsed before the woman who owned the wooded area found clothing in the clearing which looked like it would fit a twelve-year-old girl. She called the police, who ascertained that Richard Allen Davis had car trouble in the area on the night that Polly Klaas had been abducted. They also found that a palmprint found in Polly's bedroom belonged to Davis, and the two other girls at the sleepover immediately identified him from photographs.

Arrested at his sister's junkyard on 30 November, he continually denied killing the twelve-year-old, stonewalling the increasingly aggressive detectives. Finally, on 4 December, he was questioned by a much less confrontational detective who spoke to him respectfully. "You don't have to be nice to me," Davis said, "I know that I'm a piece of shit." But being treated as a human being must have had some affect, because he admitted the murder and took police to Polly's decomposing corpse.

A vicious lie

But his community spirit was short-lived. At his trial in Santa Clara

County, he cast aspersions on Polly's father's sexuality by saying that she had begged, "Don't do me like my dad." Understandably enraged, Mark Klaas leapt to his feet, shouting, "Burn in hell, Davis." He was escorted from the court by security guards.

Because Polly's body was too decomposed to prove rape, he was charged with her murder plus an 'attempted lewd act on a child'. The defence tried to suggest that it was a robbery gone wrong, but, as Davis had prior convictions for sexually assaulting females, their hypothesis wasn't convincing. On 18 June 1996 he was found guilty of first-degree murder and, on 5 August, was given a death sentence.

By then, California had learned from the mistakes made in Davis's case and had instigated the 'three strikes and you're out' law, whereby someone who offends seriously for the third time is sentenced to life in jail.

Helping other children

Mark Klaas, Polly's father, was also shocked to hear that Davis had frequently been paroled early. Realising that too little was being done for missing and exploited children, he set up KlaasKids (www.klaaskids.com) in Polly's memory, its mission being to focus law enforcement's attention on crimes which have child victims.

Desperate housewives

Meanwhile, Richard Allen Davis remains on Death Row in San Quentin, receiving marriage proposals from lonely women. He enjoys woodwork, has a television in his cell and receives visits from religious penpals. On 23 July 2005, he overdosed on sedatives and had to have his stomach pumped out. Prison officials said that this wasn't a suicide attempt, and that he'd taken the drugs for recreational purposes, though it was unclear who his supplier was.

Widely blamed for the 'three strikes and you're out' policy, he has been beaten up twice by other prisoners. As a result, he now exercises separately from the main population, going out in the yard with sixty-five other inmates who have shown no violent tendencies and are therefore considered unlikely to attack.

CHAPTER SIXTEEN

ARTHUR GARY BISHOP

A former missionary, this prolific paedophile murdered at least
five boys.

A lonely child

Arthur was born in the small town of Hinckley, central Utah, in 1951,
the first child of two devout Mormons. He'd later be described by
his defence team as a lonely, frightened boy. Five years later the couple
had a second son, Douglas. Both boys would grow up to become
remorseless paedophiles.

Arthur wasn't liked at school, being regarded as a nerd. He grew into
a somewhat overweight child with slicked-back hair who none of the
girls fancied. As he matured, he found himself increasingly attracted to
other boys.

Outwardly, he did exactly as his parents required, getting excellent
grades in school and becoming an Eagle Scout. After graduating from
high school he became a teenage missionary, travelling to the Philippines
to promote the doctrines of the Latter Day Saints. But his paedophiliac
urges grew stronger and stronger, and he began to collect child
pornography. Soon, this wasn't enough for him; he obsessively stared at
the crotch of every young boy that he met, and would later fantasise
about what he wanted to do to them.

157

Embezzlement

After his missionary work ended, Bishop went to college and trained as an accountant, graduating with honours – but in 1977 he embezzled over $8,000 from his employer, so that he could enjoy a more lavish lifestyle. He was given five years' probation and ordered to repay the sum, but instead he fled to another part of Salt Lake City and reinvented himself, using the pseudonym Roger Downs. The following year, he was excommunicated from the Mormon Church.

Ironically, in the same time period, he was accepted into the Big Brother program where men mentor boys. He molested several boys during this period, and at least two sets of parents phoned in to make anonymous complaints that their sons had been abused by Bishop. In the same timeframe, his previous record for embezzlement became known to the organisation and he was expelled. Unfortunately, the paedophile who is distanced from one set of victims merely looks for victims elsewhere . . .

The first murder

On 14 October 1979, Bishop glanced out of his Salt Lake City apartment and saw four-year-old Alonzo Daniels playing in the courtyard. He quickly lured the child into his house by promising him sweets. Alonzo's mother checked on her child moments later, but he was gone. The paedophile stripped and molested the little boy, then drowned him in the bath, before taking his body to a remote part of Cedar Fort, Utah County, where he buried it.

The police questioned Bishop twice, as he lived so close to the child's home, but had no especial reason to suspect him of Alonzo's abduction. And, as none of the bodies were found until after Bishop's arrest, they thought that Alonzo might simply have wandered away and died of exposure somewhere.

Animal torture

Bishop felt no remorse at having killed the little boy – but he did have nightmares about the child's parents coming after him, and doubtless

158

wanted to avoid a long spell in jail. As such, he decided to restrict his sadistic urges to hurting animals. At the local kennels he adopted a puppy, took it home and slowly strangled it. A fortnight later he went to another animal shelter and did the exact same thing. Over the ensuing year he brought home more than a score of puppies and killed them all, sometimes drowning or beating them to death. But what he really wanted was to molest and kill another child.

The second murder

Thirteen months after killing the four-year-old Alonzo, Bishop espied eleven-year-old Kim Petersen at the roller-skating rink. He told the boy that he'd like to buy his skates, and Kim later told his dad about the incident. His father replied that the man should come to the house and talk to him. Unfortunately, Bishop met up with the child again later that day, 9 November 1980, and lured him back to his bachelor apartment. There, he made him strip and pose for indecent photographs.

Afterwards he shot Kim in the back, and the boy fell to the floor, paralysed. "I wasn't going to tell," he whispered. In answer, Bishop rolled him onto his stomach and shot him in the head. Afterwards he buried the body at the same remote location where he had buried Alonzo Daniels, then returned to his usual pattern of molesting neighbourhood boys.

The third murder

For the best part of a year, Bishop contented himself with sexually abusing his young friends on days out and on longer camping trips. Then, on 20 October 1981, he saw four-year-old Danny Davis on his own in the toy section of the local supermarket – Danny's grandfather had lost sight of him for a moment, as he waited at the supermarket pharmacy. Bishop told the boy to follow him if he wanted some free toys, and the four-year-old dutifully trailed after the innocuous-looking man. When they reached the car park, Bishop picked the boy up in his arms and ran to his house, a mere half-block away. Back home, he sexually abused then suffocated the child, before burying him at Cedar Fort.

The paedophile was questioned by police about the child's

disappearance, as he lived so close to the supermarket. But, as he had no record of abduction or murder, he wasn't considered a serious suspect.

Brotherly love
After this sexually motivated murder, Arthur Bishop managed to control his homicidal urges for a while, molesting numerous boys but allowing them to live. Sadly, he wasn't the only member of the Bishop family to enjoy raping children. In the first quarter of 1983, his younger brother, Douglas, was arrested for sodomising young boys in Utah County. Found guilty, he was sent to prison where he received death threats.

The fourth murder
On 22 June 1983, Arthur saw little Troy Ward waiting on the pavement for a family friend. It was Troy's sixth birthday, and the man had kindly promised to take the child around the block on his motorbike. Unfortunately, Bishop got to Troy first and lured the boy to his home by promising him an icecream – a witness saw the two walking together, but just assumed that they were father and son.

Once inside the house, the paedophile led the frightened boy to the basement and tied him to a post. He also handcuffed the child's wrists together, and then removed his clothing below the waist. After the sexual abuse, he fatally attacked the boy with a hammer, later disposing of his body in Big Cottonwood Creek.

On another occasion, he took a young boy into the same basement and forced him to strip at gunpoint, before taking photographs of him in obscene poses. He was going to shoot him, then remembered that the child's sister had seen them together and so let him go, hoping that – like most young sex abuse victims – he wouldn't tell. Like most paedophiles, Bishop was very good at manipulating children's fear of their parents, telling them that they'd get into trouble for going home with a stranger or for accepting sweets.

A dangerous guardian
Over three or four years, Bishop had befriended a single mother and had

molested her prepubescent son, whom we'll call Steve. He often took the child camping; Steve was now thirteen, and was often accompanied on these camping trips by his friend of the same age, Graeme Cunningham. They arranged another of these trips to Lake Tahoe for mid-July 1983, a trip that Graeme wouldn't live to enjoy.

The fifth murder

Perhaps Arthur Bishop simply wanted Graeme out of the way so that he could concentrate on Steve. Or perhaps his bloodlust was so strong that he was determined to kill another victim. Whatever his motivation, on 14 July he lured Graeme to his home. There, he persuaded the child to strip and pose for photographs, saying that they were for another man who was blackmailing him.

After sexually molesting the boy, he hit him over the head twice with a hammer and carried the unconscious teenager to the bathroom. As he filled the bath with water, Graeme revived and said that he couldn't move his left arm, but the indifferent paedophile threw him into the tub and held him under until he drowned. Afterwards, he fondled the naked boy and became aroused. When he'd tired of having the corpse in his home, he drove it to Big Cottonwood Creek and tossed it into the water, where it remained hidden under a log.

The final countdown

The following day, whilst the neighbours searched for Graeme, Bishop took Steve to California for their camping trip. But he had killed close to home once too often, and the net was closing in. For when police questioned Graeme's mother about his plans, they found out that he'd been about to go camping with a man in his early thirties called Roger Downs. One policeman remembered that Downs was the alias of Arthur Bishop, whilst another policeman remembered questioning Bishop twice following the disappearance of Alonzo Daniels. They found that he'd also been questioned about the disappearance of Danny Davis.

They ran a background check and found out that Arthur Gary Bishop had a record for embezzlement. And when Steve returned from the camping trip, he told police that Bishop had been sexually abusing him for years.

The police searched Bishop's house and found three hundred and ten Polaroids of naked boys in pornographic poses. Another hundred had been cut from naturist magazines. Detectives begged him to help them find Graeme, though they already feared the worst, but the thirty-two-year-old replied, "It's too late . . . he's dead."

"How do you know?" the detective asked.

"Because I killed him," the paedophile explained.

He soon admitted killing the other four missing boys, saying that he'd gotten a thrill from touching them both before and after death. He giggled during some of his confessions, and mimicked the voices of the young boys as they begged him not to hurt them anymore, pleading for their lives.

Trial

At Bishop's trial, his lawyers contended that he was guilty of manslaughter rather than murder on the grounds of diminished responsibility, and that he had a personality disorder. Rejecting this, the jury found him guilty of five counts of murder. They recommended the death sentence, and he was given the choice of lethal injection or the firing squad. He chose the former, telling a journalist that he wanted to die. "I have messed up this life and I am anxious to get on with what needs to be done in the next one."

Execution

In the three days leading up to his execution, Bishop fasted, prayed and read the Book of Mormon. He told his fellow religious zealots, "I will serve my time in hell." On 9 June 1988, as he was about to be strapped down, he began to tremble and admitted that his nerve had gone. At 12:08am the drugs began to enter his system, and he was pronounced dead at 12:15am. His death brought relief throughout Utah, as he'd told the authorities that, if he was allowed to live, he'd rape and kill again.

CHAPTER SEVENTEEN

RICHARD
MATTHEW CLARK

B rutalised throughout his impoverished childhood, this paedophile finally murdered a seven-year-old girl.

Early beatings

Richard was born on 18 August 1968, to heavy drinker Kathleen Clark. She was married to George Clark and already had two children by him, but Richard was fathered by another man. The Clarks' marriage was deeply unhappy, the adulterous union and its resultant child testing it to the limit. They split up when Richard was sixteen months old. Shortly afterwards, Kathleen found herself a new boyfriend and gave birth to her fourth child, a girl.

This relationship swiftly ended and she took up with yet another man, Bob, who had children of his own. They also had a child together. Bob beat the children, including the pre-school Richard, with a belt. As they grew older, he hit them with an electrical cord and even with a poker, intent on causing maximum pain. The other boys screamed, but Richard would grit his teeth and try not to cry. As a result he became the family scapegoat, his stepfather beating him more often than the others and frequently humiliating him. After these beatings his stepfather would keep him home from school, so that no one could see the marks and report him to the authorities.

The family lived off welfare and moved around the Everett, Washington area, poaching deer and picking berries to supplement their income. Both parents drank every day and took drugs as often as they could.

Suicide attempts

When Richard was fourteen, his drunken and drugged mother was out driving when she hit a bridge. She was killed instantly. Richard went to live with an aunt, but missed his mother and tried to kill himself three times in the following year, by cutting his wrists. After that, he moved from one relative to the next, drinking heavily. Soon he was funding his drinking by stealing cars and selling them. Later still, he gravitated to burglary and was also given a juvenile conviction for assault. Eventually he ended up living in a relative's garage, neglecting himself and his surroundings. Though his more sober relatives were dismayed by his drinking binges, they weren't quite ready to give up on the baby-faced young man.

Abduction

On 28 May 1988, nineteen-year-old Richard Clark saw four-year-old Feather Rahier playing outside her home in Everett – he lived across the alley from her. He grabbed the little girl and raced to his garage home, where he bound her hands in front of her with a sock. She started to cry and he stuffed another sock into her mouth. Fortunately, the child continued to scream through the gag as Clark tried to pull down her underwear. Her family heard her cries and intervened. The paedophile fled, but was caught by two passersby who had heard the commotion. He was arrested and charged with unlawful imprisonment.

Grooming

When Richard Clark was released from prison he continued to cause chaos. He drank heavily, took LSD, cocaine and methamphetamines. He drove without a licence or insurance and spent further time in jail for car theft and burglary. Acquaintances appropriately nicknamed him 'Animal'.

In March 1995, the twenty-six-year-old began grooming his friend Tim's daughter, Roxanne Christine Doll, giving the seven-year-old gifts and sweets. He also bought a puppy, knowing that she loved animals, but Roxanne remained wary of the man and mentioned to schoolmates that she was afraid of him. Roxanne's mother also distrusted Richard Clark, but her father considered him amiable company.

Murder

On Friday 31 March, Richard spent the day drinking then visited Roxanne's parents in the evening at their trailer in Everett. He left but returned around 9pm, entering through Roxanne's bedroom window whilst her mother was at the cinema and her father was asleep on the sofa. Tiptoeing so as not to awaken her eight-year-old brother, who slept in the upper bunkbed, he took the girl from the trailer, leaving her nightdress on top of the dressing table, and carried her to his van. She tried to fight him, leaving a scratch on his chin, but he threw her into the back of the vehicle and tied her up with two socks.

Clark raped the child, causing lacerations and internal haemorrhaging. It's also likely that he sodomised her – her anus was dilated when her corpse was found, and he later told a fellow prisoner that the police had "gotten his DNA from her butt". (In reality, sperm could have drained from her vagina into her anus, as the anal opening can gape as the body decomposes, so he wasn't charged with anal assault.) When he'd finished the rape, Clark stabbed his helpless victim at least seven times in the neck with a small knife, one of the wounds puncturing her jugular. He also stabbed her hands, though detectives couldn't be sure if these were deliberate cuts or wounds that she endured whilst trying to defend herself.

Leaving her body in the van, he went to a friend's house and asked for beer. The friend noticed that he looked nervous. He'd already had a lot to drink, but seemed desperate to get even more drunk. Shortly afterwards, a relative noticed a bloodstain on his shirt and he asked her to wash it for him. He said he'd been out poaching deer, something he often did.

In the early hours of 1 April, he drove Roxanne's body to the forest at nearby East Grand and hid it under a blackberry bush. But as he was wearing shorts, some of the bushes scratched his legs and ankles, leaving telltale marks.

The family friend

Returning to the Doll residence the following day, he comforted her bewildered parents. By now the police and locals were searching anxiously for the missing child. That night, he went out drinking with various acquaintances but was much quieter than usual. Two of them went back to his van with him to do crystal meth, and noticed that the vehicle smelt terrible – doubtless the bodily fluids from his victim were decomposing in the heat.

The following day the police interviewed him as a matter of course, as he'd been in the trailer shortly before Roxanne's disappearance. He said that he hadn't seen her – but later, when they ran his details through the computer, they found out that he'd abducted and sexually assaulted a four-year-old girl seven years before. They arranged for him to take a polygraph test later that same month, which he would fail.

Body found

Meanwhile, on 8 April, two young children were playing in the woods at East Grand when they found Roxanne Doll's naked corpse. Five days later, after bloodstains were found in Richard Clark's van he was arrested. Though his relative had laundered his bloodstained shirt, tests showed that it still bore Roxanne's DNA. A sock in his van showed traces of her saliva, having been used as a gag, and sperm in her vagina was consistent with his genetic profile. He was sent to prison to await trial.

Trial

On 27 February 1997, jury selection finally began in the Everett courtroom. As the trial progressed, the defence said that the state had not proved that the kidnap and murder were premeditated. The prosecution countered that it was proven – Clark had waited until the parents were out or asleep, and had brought a knife, plus socks to bind and gag the victim. He had also attacked another little girl in an incredibly similar way. DNA evidence linked him irrefutably with the child's rape and murder, and his fingerprint had been found outside her bedroom window. He'd even allegedly talked of the rape and subsequent murder to another inmate in jail.

The jury soon returned with their verdict: guilty of kidnap, rape and murder. They immediately went into the penalty phase. The defence now talked about Richard Clark's appalling childhood, but the prosecution pointed out that his siblings had endured an equally horrendous upbringing and hadn't become murderous paedophiles. (This wasn't quite true, as Richard had been the child that his stepfather hated the most.)

But, as an adult, Richard Clark had choices – and he'd chosen to give in to his blood lust. He'd enjoyed a few minutes of pleasure, and for that an innocent little girl had died.

The judge asked him if he'd like to say anything before sentence was passed and, incredibly, Clark blamed the murder on Roxanne's father, who was so upset that he had to leave the courtroom. The jury then sentenced Richard Clark to death. As he left the court he shouted, "See ya, wouldn't wanna be ya." His lawyers soon appealed his death sentence at the Washington State Supreme Court.

Appeal

At the appeal, the defence argued that Clark hadn't had a fair trial because of pre-trial publicity. (They had previously campaigned for a change of venue.) They also complained that his ankles had been shackled in court, making him look like a dangerous man – but the prosecution countered that the jury couldn't see the shackles. Finally, the defence noted that Clark's attack on Feather Rahier shouldn't have been referred to in court, as it prejudiced the jury against him. The court agreed that this testimony shouldn't have been entered in evidence and decided that – though he was still guilty of all charges – the sentencing phase would have to begin again.

A plea bargain

The years passed until, in February 2006, Richard Matthew Clark finally accepted responsibility for killing Roxanne Doll. In exchange, the state dropped its demand for the death penalty. He will now spend his life in jail without the possibility of parole.

PART THREE

WORLDWIDE PAEDOPHILES

CHAPTER EIGHTEEN

MARC DUTROUX

Though the previous chapters have concentrated on British and American paedophiles, the phenomenon is unfortunately widespread. In 1988, Japan was shocked when the mutilation murders perpetrated by paedophile Tsutomu Mizayaki came to light. Mizayaki abducted girls between the ages of four and seven, mutilated and killed them. He also cannibalised some of the victims, roasting then devouring the hands. In an act of sadism, he even dumped the burnt corpse of one female victim in front of her parents' house. Though he later retracted his confession, claiming that the police had forced it out of him, he was sentenced to death in April 1997.

Brazil's Marcelo Costa de Andrade also chalked up a considerable body count, murdering fourteen boys in 1991. This Universal Church of the Kingdom of God devotee – who'd been physically and sexually abused throughout his childhood – strangled and raped preteen boys, believing that he was sending them to heaven.

But Belgium's Marc Dutroux is more notorious than either of the aforementioned men, perhaps because he kept his victims captive in appalling conditions for extended periods. As he preyed on young women as well as girls, he is a situational paedophile rather than a fixated type. He is also Belgium's most hated child killer, a dishonour that should surely be shared with his second wife.

Formative hell

Marc was born on 6 November 1956 in Brussels, to Jeannine and Victor Dutroux who were both teachers. Victor would later say that twenty-year-old Jeannine was already two months pregnant by a previous boyfriend when they met, that he agreed to marry her in order to spare her the disgrace of being an unmarried mother. He would also claim that Jeannine was cold towards Marc and never gave him any love.

The family soon moved to Africa, but Victor's views clashed with those of the school he was teaching at and so the couple returned to Belgium when Marc was four years old. They went on to have four other children, and Victor beat them all severely; neighbours, shocked by their terrified screams, often phoned the police. The couple became well-known to the social services for their loud quarrels, and the cruel things that they would say to their offspring. They told Marc that they'd never wanted him, and that he should go to hell. (Unsurprisingly, Marc wasn't the only Dutroux who became disturbed – in adulthood his brother Serge, a fellow criminal, would commit suicide by hanging himself.)

Marc and his siblings attended the school at which his father taught, yet by age five he was being sent alone on the hour-long train journey. One day his father strode into the classroom where Marc was listening to the lesson and shouted, "You're a good for nothing arsehole!" at the embarrassed boy. Wildly eccentric, Victor told his bemused colleagues that it was possible to learn about a person's sexual responses by studying the hairs on his or her head. He talked a lot about anarchy and tried (and failed) to become a socialist councillor. He took a year's sabbatical in 1967, after which the school declined to renew his contract and he never worked as a teacher again.

Marc was an intelligent child who, forced to largely raise himself, soon became streetwise. He made pocket money by selling toys and comics to his friends. At this stage, he was a likeable boy who feared conflict and ran away at the first sign of a playground fight. As he moved into his teens, he became increasingly obsessed with sex and began to sell pornographic magazines to the other boys.

Abused children often repeatedly draw pretty houses with the sun shining in the background, a visual representation of the calmness and security that is missing in their day-to-day existence. Marc, too, drew houses, but he concentrated on the interiors which were filled with shadowy corners. He was deeply troubled, and eventually switched off his emotional reactions to everyone and everything in order to survive without further pain. He now cared only for himself and his own pleasure – in other words, he was a psychopath.

Sexual abuse

At fourteen, he was seduced by an older paedophile who gave him money and presents. Unpleasant as the sex was, to Marc it was the closest thing to love that he had ever known. He really wanted to have sex with girls, and began to trip them up at the local ice rink, fondling them as he helped them to their feet. This happened so often that the police were called and he was warned off.

The Dutrouxs separated when Marc was fifteen. He stayed with his mother for a year but the relationship remained volatile. At sixteen he fled and lived on the streets. He remained heterosexual but supported himself by offering sexual favours to older men, earning a precarious living as a rent boy. His self-hatred – and his hatred towards society – continued to grow.

A first failed marriage

He married a girl named Francoise when he was nineteen, but soon began to beat and control her. They chose to have two children together but he remained unstable, drifting from job to job. Though he was a competent electrician he preferred to walk on the wild side, supporting himself and his family through drug dealing and stealing cars. By 1983 he'd become increasingly violent and, together with a male accomplice, broke into a woman's house and tortured her repeatedly before stealing the equivalent of £1,000. Their victim was in her seventies.

Dutroux also had various extramarital affairs during his twenties, including one with Michelle Martin, three years his junior, who he met at the local ice rink. She would become his accomplice in various sex crimes and eventually his second wife.

Michelle Martin

Like his parents, Michelle was a teacher. The pretty blonde had low self-esteem and was very shy. She was completely enthralled by the dark good looks of Marc Dutroux, and agreed to live with him and his wife in a *ménage à trois*. Francoise, however, had no intention of sharing the marital bed with another woman and promptly left the marriage, taking the children with her. (The couple divorced when Dutroux was twenty-seven.) By now he'd had his first child with Michelle – they would eventually have three children together, all sons.

Abduction and rape

Unfazed by his failure to establish a *ménage à trois*, Dutroux decided to kidnap young girls and sexually assault them. Michelle witnessed the first abduction. She also stayed in the same room, watching, as he raped the teenager. She even rented the video camera that the couple used to film the rape.

Michelle was also aware of at least four other instances where he raped girls of nineteen and younger, and on two of these occasions she drove the abduction car. Psychiatrists would later say that she'd had an unhappy childhood, which had left her with a passive-aggressive personality.

In February 1986, the couple were arrested for five such abduction-rapes and remanded in custody. It was 1989 before the case came to trial, and Dutroux was sentenced to thirteen and a half years. Michelle was given five. But, rather than spend her time in jail taking stock of her life, she remained devoted to Dutroux, writing him heartfelt love letters. They married whilst they were in prison, though like many professional women she kept her own name.

Michelle was released first, but was joined in April 1992 by her new husband, paroled for good behaviour after serving slightly over six years. He managed to convince a psychiatrist that he was disabled and was given a disability pension. This gave him a legitimate income, and meant that the police would no longer query how he made a living – though in truth he remained an incorrigible criminal, mugging people and dealing in heroin. He and Michelle even tricked his elderly maternal grandmother into giving them her home.

But outwardly he was a respectable family man with a wife, three sons and various dogs. He became a Jehovah's Witness, perhaps following in the footsteps of his father, who also got religion later in life.

House proud

Through his illegal activities, Dutroux gained ownership of seven houses during this period, which doubtless took away the fear he had felt as a homeless teenager. But their main purpose was to give him hiding places from the police, and a secure place to take young victims in future. He constructed a concealed dungeon in the basement of his favourite rundown terraced house in Marcinelle, near the town of Charleroi, the same house where he lived most of the time. The dungeon was hidden behind a massive concrete door and was only five feet high, three feet wide and seven feet long. Michelle, still living in some kind of happy-families dream, painted the back wall a bright yellow. The area had very little ventilation and no natural light, being lit by two lamps.

A tip-off

By now Michelle was busy with their three children, so Dutroux needed an accomplice for further abductions. He asked a friend, saying that they could park the car behind two girls, put their hands around the girls' mouths and drag them into the vehicle. The friend declined and went to the Belgian police, who started a file on Dutroux. Unfazed by this rejection, the psychopath found another criminal partner, twenty-five-year-old Michel Lelievre, a small, comparatively submissive heroin addict. He had no interest in paedophilia, but was keen to do whatever Dutroux wanted as the latter kept him supplied with drugs.

Two victims

On 24 June 1995, Lelievre was driving Dutroux along a highway when they saw eight-year-olds Julie Lejeune and Melissa Russo standing on the flyover, waving at the traffic. Both children were close to home, and had played without incident on that particular bridge before. Dutroux kidnapped them, imprisoning them in his dungeon in Marcinelle where he repeatedly sexually abused them, causing vaginal trauma and abdominal injuries. He also made pornographic videos of some of the rapes. Michelle Martin knew of these appalling acts.

The police enquiry into the girls' disappearance drew a blank so the parents hired a criminal profiler. She said that the kidnapper had almost certainly taken children before as he was obviously confident, having abducted them from such a busy area. She added that he was also likely to be married with children, as he'd been able to get close without scaring the girls away. She said that there were probably only five men in the area who would fit this profile and handed it over to the police, expecting them to act on it. They never did.

Two more victims

By 23 August the sociopath wanted new victims, so drove around with Lelievre until he came to Blakenberg, where he espied An Marchal and Eefje Lambrecks, aged seventeen and nineteen respectively, who were on holiday. The girls were seen leaving a casino to take a tram back to their holiday home, but they never arrived. The two slender teenagers were no match for Dutroux, who by now carried sedatives and date-rape drugs to force down his victims' throats.

Dutroux took them to his Marcinelle residence, but, as eight-year-olds Julie and Melissa were still locked up in the dungeon, he chained the teenagers to his bedstead. They too were sexually abused and videoed – hundreds of these homemade videos would later be found at one of the Dutroux residences. It's likely that he sold copies to equally dissolute acquaintances, though his claims that he kidnapped the girls to pass them on to a vast international paedophile ring appears to have been a self-serving lie. Four of the girls would die in his residence, and two others who survived would testify that they were only ever abused by Dutroux himself.

Dutroux's mother wrote to the gendarmerie, telling them that two girls were being held prisoner in his house, but they failed to act. Apparently the local police were actively investigating Dutroux and there was tension between them and the gendarmerie, with information rarely being shared.

For the next few weeks, Dutroux raped the unfortunate teenagers. Eefje apparently tried to escape twice, once attempting to climb through a skylight. The psychopath beat both teenagers, but finally became overwhelmed by having to control four victims. Deciding to kill the oldest girls, he gave Eefje and An strong sedatives so that they lost consciousness, and then buried them alive.

A monster in a skirt

Towards the end of the year, the police had collected enough evidence to charge Marc Dutroux for his involvement in luxury car thefts. So he would be imprisoned from 6 December 1995 to 20 March 1996.

What happened next was enough to make even hardened detectives cry, for Michelle Martin knew that the little eight-year-old girls were locked in the dungeon, desperate for food and water, but she refused to go in there. Dutroux gave an accomplice, armed robber Bernard Weinstein, money to feed and water the children, but the man eventually lost interest. By the time that Dutroux was released, the girls had starved to death. Martin would later say that she was too frightened to feed the children – but how could a mother of three and a teacher be afraid of two eight-year-old girls? A surviving victim would later describe her accurately as "a monster in a skirt".

Meanwhile, prison had made Marc Dutroux more hate-filled than ever, and he subsequently lured Bernard Weinstein to the house and tortured him by crushing his testicles in a vice, to get him to disclose the hiding place for his savings. Afterwards he drugged Weinstein, and then buried him alive in the garden of one of his houses.

Another kidnap victim

By the third week in May, Dutroux was trawling for victims again, and realised that twelve-year-old Sabine Dardenne (who was small and slight, and so only looked ten) rode to school every morning around 7:20am on her bicycle. Her route took her along a quiet stretch of road heading in the direction of Tournia.

On 28 May 1996, he and Lelievre drove up behind Sabine. Dutroux got out and threw her and the bike into the back of his van, making the two-hour journey back to his main residence, where he chained her to a bunkbed. The next day he took photographs of her without her clothes. On the third day she was imprisoned in the cellar where eight-year-old Melissa and Julie had died, only brought into the main part of the house whenever he wanted to sexually assault her. After a few days of this she began to haemorrhage, but his only response was to give her a disposable nappy to staunch the flow of blood.

There was also ongoing emotional cruelty when he said that her parents had refused to pay him a ransom, and that they no longer wanted her. He would eat steak and chocolate whilst she subsisted on sour milk and mouldy bread. Dutroux was the ultimate control freak, choosing when she could wash, what she could read or listen to on the radio, even cutting her hair for her.

After a few weeks, Sabine was so damaged inside that Dutroux had to stop assaulting her. He went trawling for another victim and, on the evening of 9 August, saw Laetitia Delhez, aged fourteen, walking through Bertrix. She had gone to the public baths there with a group of friends, but was menstruating so she hadn't wanted to go swimming. Bored, she'd decided to walk home.

Another kidnap victim

Once Dutroux and his accomplice Lelievre had got Laetitia into the van, they forced her to take drugs and drove her to the same house where he was holding Sabine. The teenager would remain drugged for the next two days, during which he sexually assaulted her (having first given her the contraceptive pill). Neighbours had seen him carrying the drugged girl into the house and had asked what had happened, but he'd told them it was one of his sons, who had taken ill. Chillingly, he was desperately trying to have a daughter with Michelle Martin, as a way of 'growing' his own victim. He'd heard that older sperm often produced a girl child, and so was masturbating into a bag then artificially inseminating her at a later date.

Dutroux introduced Laetitia to twelve-year-old Sabine, who had by now been captive in the house for seventy-seven days. He put both girls down in the cellar so that they were sharing the same limited air supply.

But two witnesses had seen (and heard) Dutroux's ancient Renault Traffic, with its faulty exhaust, being driven by Lelievre in the moments before Laetitia was kidnapped. One witness, a student, could even recall part of the number plate, and it led the police to known sex offender Marc Dutroux.

On 13 August, Dutroux was arrested. A police officer searched the house, including the cellar, but didn't find the area – well-hidden behind a concrete door and a pull-out shelving unit – where the two girls were fast asleep.

Fortunately, Lelievre was also arrested, and confessed that the girls had been taken to the house. The police told Dutroux that they knew the full story, and on 15 August he admitted that Laetitia was hidden in the dungeon, as was Sabine.

Police took Dutroux back to the cellar, where he revealed the hidden dungeon. The girls were released and taken to the police station to be reunited with their traumatised parents. The authorities then began to dig up the garden of another of Dutroux's houses, located in Sars-la-Buissiere, finding the bodies of Julie, Melissa and Bernard Weinstein. Dutroux, his wife and Lelievre were remanded in custody.

The following month, on 3 September, they found the bodies of An and Eefje in the garden of Bernard Weinstein's chalet in Jumet.

Escape

Dutroux continued to be a thorn in the authorities' side, complaining about the conditions that he was being kept in. In truth, his surroundings were luxurious compared to those that he'd kept his victims in. But like all psychopaths, he only thought of himself.

178

Late in 1997, whilst in a court building to consult his case file, he beat up two policemen and escaped, taking one of their guns with him. He stole a car and drove wildly to the nearest woods, with the police in hot pursuit. Fortunately, he was discovered there by a forest warden and returned to prison within hours.

A suspected cover-up

Meanwhile, the people of Belgium were coming to the conclusion that there were paedophiles in high places; that certain authorities had known of Marc Dutroux's criminal activities; that there had been a cover-up. Why, they asked, hadn't Dutroux been in handcuffs when escorted to the court? It also transpired that a member of the gendarmerie had heard that the house was to be searched, and had asked to be the one to carry it out. He'd been made to take a locksmith along with him.

The locksmith had insisted they go down to the cellar, where they'd found vaginal lubricant – an odd thing to be kept in a basement. They'd also heard children's voices and cries. The locksmith had called out to them, but the gendarme had shouted, "Silence!" and the children's voices had stopped. The officer said that the sounds were coming from outside, but the locksmith wasn't convinced and wanted to go on searching. After the gendarme had said, "Just who is the policeman around here?" they'd both left the house.

Judge Jean Marc Connerotte, who'd worked tirelessly to uncover the truth, had been sacked from the case because he'd had a bowl of pasta with the victims' families as part of a fund-raising dinner. The authorities said that this meant he was getting too close and had lost his impartiality.

Three hundred thousand Belgians took to the streets to demand answers, and to honour the dead children. As a result, twenty-nine paedophiles were eventually arrested, including several policemen. A parliamentary enquiry found that there had been no corruption but said that the structure of the police had to change.

Trial

Marc Dutroux's trial finally began on 1 March 2004 in Arlon, the capital of the Belgian province of Luxembourg. Three hundred police were drafted in for security, and the defendants had to give their testimony from behind bulletproof glass.

The jury wept when they heard about the conditions that the children had been kept in, and what they'd gone through. Yet they were still capable of gross stupidity, with one juror asking Laetitia how Dutroux could have raped her whilst she was menstruating. This juror clearly had no idea of how a sex offender operates. Indeed, Dutroux had continued to rape Sabine whilst she haemorrhaged.

Michelle Martin told the survivors, "I know I did wrong," but understandably they chose not to forgive her. She could have chosen to free the first captives and go to the police.

Sentences

The trial lasted four months, after which Marc Dutroux was given a life sentence for the teenagers' murder, rape and kidnap, as the death penalty has been abolished throughout the European Union. (No one has ever been tried for the murders of Melissa and Julie, because of uncertainty as to who was responsible. Dutroux said that Julie was dead when he got out of prison, and that Melissa died two days later in his arms.) His wife got thirty years for conspiracy to kidnap, whilst the van driver, Michel Lelievre, got twenty-five years for kidnapping. Another man who Dutroux had implicated got five years for trafficking in prostitutes, albeit women rather than children.

Sadly, life doesn't necessarily mean life in the case of Marc Dutroux, for after thirty years his sentence will come up for review. By then he will be in his late seventies – but paedophiles of this age tend to retain their libidos and frequently reoffend. He has already written dozens of sexually explicit love letters to a fifteen-year-old schoolgirl who got in touch after seeing him on television, having decided that the media had exaggerated his crimes.

CHAPTER NINETEEN

JAVED IQBAL

An increasingly deranged paedophile, Iqbal murdered a hundred boys during a five-month period in his native Pakistan.

Failed marriages

Virtually nothing has been made known about Iqbal's formative years – though, by the time he became a serial killer in his mid-forties, he had two failed marriages behind him and was the father of two children. He lived in a rundown flat in Lahore with four teenage servants – this was quite common in this deeply impoverished area, where boys desperate for accommodation were willing to give sexual favours in return.

Javed had been raised on the Koran, which forbids homosexuality, yet he had numerous male lovers. He later claimed that a group of them beat him up, and that he was so badly injured that his shocked mother died of a broken heart. That said, he lied constantly about almost everything and the press couldn't even be sure about his job – he sometimes claimed to be a social worker, but at other times said he was a journalist.

Rent boys

In June 1998, Iqbal was arrested for using two rent boys, impoverished brothers who had fourteen other siblings. He denied sodomising both boys and was immediately granted bail. He went on to molest other male children, but feared that they would tell and that the authorities would catch up with him. Determined not to leave behind any witnesses, in the summer of 1999 he began to kill. Others were aware of his murderous actions – his four servants would later be tried as his accomplices.

Many of the boys that Iqbal targeted were living on the streets, so he knew that no one would report them missing. The homicides all followed the same cruel pattern: he would persuade a boy to accompany him to his house, where he would give him food or drink laced with a sedative and would ask the boy about his life, taking a sadistic pleasure in the invariably sad account.

During these prolonged interviews, the drugs would begin to take affect and the boy would belatedly realise that he was in danger. When he was too weak to resist, Iqbal would rape him before slowly strangling him with a chain. He kept many of the children's garments as murder trophies, storing them in bin bags in his lounge.

At first, Iqbal disposed of the bodies by dismembering them, liquidising the pieces in a vat of acid and dumping the liquid in a nearby sewer. But neighbours complained of the stench, so he began to use the Ravi river instead.

After killing fifty boys he decided to photograph subsequent victims, asking each child to strip to the waist and pose for the camera. Some smiled shyly whilst others looked apprehensive, perhaps sensing that he meant them harm.

The slaughter continued, with victims as young as nine years old, the eldest in their early teens. All too soon, the flat in Ravi Road held eighty-five pairs of deceased boys' shoes.

In November, after he'd raped and dismembered his hundredth victim, the paedophile wrote to the police confessing his many crimes. They threw the letter in the wastepaper basket. Iqbal then wrote to the Pakistani press, telling them that he planned to drown himself in the Ravi river. Journalists visited the flat and found blood all over the walls and floor, and a vat of acid outside the house containing a boy's bones.

An implausible tale

The police thought that the killer had gone on the run as he didn't return to his flat, so they were amazed when he handed himself in to the local newspaper office, saying that he hated society and that he'd killed one hundred boys. Duly arrested, he seemed to exult in the media attention, giggling wildly and examining press photographs of himself.

But later he changed his story, saying that he hadn't killed the boys but had merely pretended to in order to show the world the impoverished children's plight. Only twenty-five of them had been reported missing, and he told the police that they must be living elsewhere under assumed names.

However, he found it impossible to explain away the skeletonised remains of Ijaz, which had been found in the acid vat. Ijaz and his younger brother, Riaz, had met up with the paedophile in November 1999; Ijaz had accompanied him home to give him a massage, and was never seen alive again. He was the killer's ninety-seventh victim. Iqbal's four servants were also arrested for the same hundred crimes.

One hundred strangulations

In March 2000, Javed Iqbal was sentenced to the unnecessarily melodramatic punishment of being strangled one hundred times, then cut into one hundred pieces and dissolved in acid. One of his accomplices, Sajid, who had just turned twenty, was dealt the same tariff whilst the teenage servants got twenty years each. But mental health authorities, convinced that Iqbal was mentally ill, were disturbed by the sentence and demanded that it be examined by a religious court. Others refuted the sentence on religious grounds, as cutting the killer's corpse into pieces would constitute the desecration of a body – disallowed under Islamic law.

Death in custody

On 8 October 2001, three days before the religious court's ruling, both Iqbal and Sajid were found dead in adjacent cells, with bruises visible on their bodies (some new, some partially healed) and blood around their noses and mouths. The police said that they had strangled themselves the previous night with their own bed-sheets in a suicide pact.

CHAPTER TWENTY

CLIFFORD ROBERT OLSON

O riginally a thief and petty criminal, Olson went on to murder at least eleven children and eventually found that he enjoyed the killing more than the sexual assaults.

Early psychopathology

Clifford was born on 1 January 1940, to Leona and Clifford Olson in Vancouver, British Columbia. The couple, who were devout Roman Catholics, went on to have two more sons and a daughter in quick succession. Leona worked in a fish-canning factory and Clifford senior delivered milk. The family soon moved to the Vancouver suburb of Richmond, where Mr Olson worked as a bingo caller. He would later be investigated for bingo-related fraud and, on another occasion, found guilty of a breach of the peace. The Olsons were simple people who worked long hours and couldn't spend much time with their children. But none of their other offspring showed the criminality that Clifford junior did. Some neighbours thought that he was just boisterous and that he'd unfairly been labelled the black sheep of the family, getting blamed for things that he hadn't done.

Clifford had a slightly below average IQ, which doubtless contributed to his lifelong inferiority complex. He couldn't write grammatically and his spelling was poor, though he could copy other people's work and sign his name. His teachers noted that he was always desperate for attention, even the negative attention that he got when he misbehaved.

He persuaded them to put him into the remedial class where the work was easier, and they noted that he liked to play dumb rather than strive.

In the playground, he proved to be a bully and a pathological liar who stole from the other children. They feared and hated him, and he spent his breaktimes alone. At nights and weekends he got his revenge on society by tormenting the neighbourhood cats and dogs, and it was rumoured that he suffocated two pet rabbits to death.

At ten, he started to play truant on a regular basis and was soon stealing from younger children. Noticing that he was a pretty good streetfighter, someone took him along to the local junior boxing club where he showed enviable talent. He even took part in an out-of-town tournament, where he embarrassed his fellow boxers by stealing repeatedly from the local store. Too unreliable to turn up for the regular training sessions, he soon dropped out and spent his time stealing from neighbourhood orchards and businesses. His sister adored him and believed that he was being victimised, but everyone else thought that he was bad news.

At sixteen he left school and briefly took a job at the local racetrack, but was sacked for stealing a cheque from his employer, forging the man's name and cashing it. That summer he also broke into a garage for kicks and stole a few dollars. Later still, he stole from a local engineering firm; once again the break-in earned him very little money, but he was hooked on the illicit thrill.

Becoming bisexual

At seventeen, he was sent to a reformatory for nine months on a breaking and entering charge. The curly-haired, good-looking youth was attractive to many of the other boys and was soon having sex with them. (He may well have been raped, a common occurrence in reformatories and prison, but no one except Olson knows what actually happened. He was only five foot seven and would have been easily overpowered by taller teens.) Until this imprisonment he had been strictly heterosexual, but now he had become sexually attracted to young males.

Olson soon escaped from the reformatory, whereupon the police interviewed his parents. His mother described him as an easily-led coward, whilst his father said, "I hope they get him before he does something really bad. He's done bad enough now."

The desperado gave himself up when approached by a policeman with a tracker dog – he was terrified of the animal – and was sentenced to an additional three months. But as he'd committed an armed robbery and had stolen property during his time on the run, he was given another two years. Later in his sentence he was paroled, but was sent back to the reformatory when further burglaries came to light.

As he moved into adulthood, his criminal exploits included obtaining money by false pretences and possession of a firearm. In the summer of 1961, he was sent to the Saskatchewan Penitentiary at Alberta – from which he promptly escaped, being adept at opening handcuffs and locks.

For the next few years, Olson was in and out of jail. He continued to break out, though he was always recaptured within the week. During one escape, in 1968, he held up a Vancouver supermarket at gunpoint, for which he was sentenced to nine years. Despite his poor literacy, he became a would-be jailhouse lawyer and wrote numerous letters of complaint to the authorities.

Rape

In August 1972 he was paroled, but violated his probation the following March and was sent back to the British Columbia Penitentiary in New Westminster. The following year he raped a seventeen-year-old male inmate, his first known sexual assault, and was moved to the prison's maximum security unit, designed to house the most dangerous prisoners. There, in 1976, he offered his services as an informant, giving the authorities details of his fellow prisoners' past crimes.

Word soon got round that he was a snitch and he received death threats, so he asked to be moved to Saskatchewan for his own protection. But details of his informant status had preceded him and, half an hour after he arrived, he was stabbed seven times by a group of prisoners and had to be rushed to hospital. Olson made a full recovery, after which he was moved around the prison to keep him from further violence. Never one to waste an opportunity, he persuaded the authorities to give him $3,500 compensation.

That same year he was put in a cell with paedophile Gary Francis Marcoux, who had sexually abused and murdered a seven-year-old girl in Mission. Olson asked Marcoux to write down all of the gory details for their mutual delectation. The paedophile obliged. He admitted to raping and sexually mutilating the child, strangling her, and hanging her nude body from a tree. Olson apparently took sexual pleasure from this description, before passing the information on to the authorities. He later testified against Marcoux in court, and the letters he'd written to Olson about the murder were used to convict him of the crime.

Hearing about Marcoux's sexual abuse of various young girls aroused Olson, and he incorporated it into his fantasies. From now on, he would be sexually interested in children and would go on to molest dozens of them.

Sexual assaults

In August 1978, whilst out on licence, Olson was arrested for sexually assaulting a seven-year-old girl in Nova Scotia. On the drive to the police station he talked the police into taking him back to his hotel, so that he could explain to his friends where he had gone, but instead escaped out of a hotel window. He was never charged with this offence, but was almost immediately put back behind bars for theft. A warder with psychiatric training noted that he was a braggart, a petty criminal with delusions of grandeur, and a pathological liar. He was also highly manipulative.

The paedophile was released again in January 1980, but by the following month he'd picked up a teenage boy who was hitchhiking. Olson drove him to a hotel, violently buggered him, stole his possessions and left. He had given the boy a false name, so it was some time before he was identified.

Free

In June 1980, Olson was released again on mandatory supervision. He was drinking at a popular local pub when he got talking to a forty-year-old divorcee called Joan. She found him physically attractive and good company, and let him move in with her after only three days. Olson was soon spending her $43,000 divorce settlement on alcohol and drugs, offering both to the bored thirteen- and fourteen-year-olds who he approached in shopping malls.

Foolishly, Joan let herself become pregnant by him in August of that year. By now she knew that he had an extensive prison record, but she was religious and believed that he was completely reformed. She was disabused of this when they were asked to leave their fundamentalist church, after Olson was discovered sexually interfering with several of the congregation's children. But no charges were filed, so the paedophile remained free to assault other juveniles. In the same timeframe he sodomised a boy in a sauna, but again no charges were brought.

Pregnancy brings out the worst in many violent men (they are emotionally still children themselves, and can't cope with the cessation of sex or with responsibility), and Clifford Olson was no exception. Before long he was beating Joan up. But in public they pretended that they had a good marriage, and became regulars at another gospel church. Olson could quote biblical chapter and verse, and told various acquaintances that "Jesus Christ and preaching the word of God" were very important to him.

Unable to connect with humans, he may have genuinely desired a supernatural bond. Deep down, he was very lonely. Adults soon saw through his posturing, so he turned to children for company and validation, again and again. He'd hang out with them for hours at local shopping malls, boasting of the fictitious business that he owned. He even got business cards made up, bearing his own name and Joan's, though he refused to pay for them. Some of these children were impressed by his fast talking and sought out his friendship. But when he'd been drinking heavily, his dark side surfaced and he felt the urge to rape and kill . . .

Another sexual assault
On 10 November 1980, he lured a fourteen-year-old Vancouver Island

boy to a Richmond motel with an offer of construction work. Realising belatedly that he was alone with a paedophile, the boy tried to leave the room, but Olson barred his way and knocked him to the ground. He violently buggered the teenager, fleeing the scene before his bleeding victim could raise the alarm. It would be a year before the police tracked him down.

Olson had let the boy live, yet the following week he would kill and go on killing. Later, even he wouldn't be sure why he murdered some children after raping them, yet spared others.

Christine Weller's murder

On 17 November 1980, he stopped twelve-year-old Christine Weller as she cycled past his apartment, on her way home from a shopping mall in Surrey. He offered her an evening job and drove her to Richmond, plying her with drink en route. In the early hours of the following day, he stripped her and probably raped her, before stabbing her ten times in the chest and stomach, his knife penetrating her heart and liver. In an act of overkill, he also strangled her with a belt.

Unfortunately, her parents had assumed she was staying with a friend, so she wasn't reported missing until 25 November – by which time the trail had gone cold. Her mutilated body was found on 25 December. Richmond police considered Olson as a suspect because he lived so close to the child, but they thought that another two men looked even better for the homicide and concentrated on them.

Joan would never suspect her partner of such acts, as he secretly destroyed his clothes after each murder, replacing them with identical garments. And he buried the children's personal effects near the bodies, rather than bringing them home as masturbatory souvenirs.

Rape

The New Year saw Olson in predatory mode again. He picked up a sixteen-year-old girl at Squamish on 2 January 1981, with the offer of employment in nearby Whistler. He gave her alcohol as he drove, then parked and raped her, buggered her and carried out a further act of gross indecency. He also beat her with his fists, leaving many bruises on her face, and causing her to fear for her life.

She went to the police the following day and picked him out of a selection of four hundred photographs, after which he was arrested by Squamish detectives and kept in custody for three months. But the courts decided not to proceed with the charges, possibly because the girl had previously been made to work as a child prostitute by a ruthless pimp, and was considered an unreliable witness. The paedophile was again set free, and probably began to feel invincible.

Fatherhood

On 10 April 1981, Joan gave birth to the couple's son. (Various reports say that he was named Clifford Olson III, but Olson said in later missives from jail that they'd named the baby Stephen.) He brought several acquaintances from their church back to see the baby and seemed very proud. But a crying baby reminds a damaged man of his own unmet childhood needs, so within days Olson went in search of prey . . .

Colleen Daignault's murder

On 16 April, he approached thirteen-year-old Colleen Daignault in South Surrey as she waited at a bus stop. The shy, petite teenager was on her way home from a friend's house. She refused a lift from the smiling family man but he was persistent, explaining that they were near-neighbours and showing her his business card. Colleen had to catch two buses to get home, yet Olson was promising to take her to her door. She was too young to realise that the person who refuses to hear "no" is trying to control you. She got into his car and accepted a coke, unaware that it was laced with drugs.

The paedophile drove her to a nearby forest and pulled her from the car, then ripped the clothes from her body and raped her. She crawled away from him, still heavily drugged, but he walked up behind and battered her to death with a hammer before covering her with branches. Her remains were eventually identified through dental charts.

Unfortunately, the Royal Canadian Mounted Police treated her case as that of a teenage runaway; as her parents had split up, they theorised that she'd gone in search of her mother. Relatives begged them to take her disappearance seriously, but they failed to investigate and the trail grew cold.

Daryn Johnsrude's murder

Five days later, Olson was two blocks away from his home in Coquitlam when he saw sixteen-year-old Daryn Todd Johnsrude, returning from a shopping mall. Daryn lived with his father but had flown to Vancouver to visit his mother, who'd paid for the flight as a birthday gift. Olson offered the boy casual work and drove him to Deroche, where he stripped him and battered him repeatedly about the head with a hammer. His body was found the following month, lying beside a dyke.

Marriage

On 14 May, Joan had a bridal shower with her female friends on the eve of her wedding to Clifford. He offered to babysit for her friends' children and promptly sent them all to the shops, with the exception of the child that he was most attracted to – a girl aged five. He immediately sexually assaulted her and warned her not to tell anyone.

But she found the courage to tell her mother the following day, and Olson was subsequently interviewed by the police. Dressed in a powder blue suit with gold accessories, he looked and sounded supremely confident as he denied any wrongdoing. Police let him go, aware that there were no witnesses and the child was too young to testify.

Happy families

Work-shy and a spendthrift, Olson soon ran out of money and had to move his family to a rundown Coquitlam housing complex, occupied by single mothers and other welfare recipients His parents were caretakers of an apartment block around the corner. Olson told his neighbours that he owned the block and that he could evict them if they didn't do as he said. He monopolised their teenage daughters, trying to persuade the cutest, slimmest girls to come for a ride in his latest rented car. He liked to rent a different vehicle every day, though he sometimes defaulted on his bills and his wife had to bail him out.

But consensual sex in cars wasn't what Olson really wanted. He preferred to rape and kill . . .

Sandra Wolfsteiner's murder

On 19 May, sixteen-year-old Sandra Wolfsteiner left the house that she shared with her sister in Langley, Surrey, to take her boyfriend a packed lunch. He worked in a car repair shop on the Frasier Highway, and she was walking there when Olson offered her a lift. He also offered her a job cleaning windows and drove her towards the supposed work venue – but he turned into dense bushes off Chilliwack Lake Road, where he battered a hammer repeatedly into her head, stripped and murdered her. She was reported missing by her boyfriend the following day.

As always happens in such missing persons cases, various people reported seeing her at a variety of locations, leading to the mistaken belief that she was a runaway. (Bones belonging to a girl of Sandra's age were eventually located, though the flesh had been eaten by animals. Olson admitted killing her for kicks and stealing the few dollars that she had in her pocket. He'd driven her to a cashline and thought that she'd withdrawn a hundred dollars, money he wanted to spend on drink.)

A lucky escape

On 26 May, he was trawling for another victim when he spotted a small blonde teenager standing outside a café in Coquitlam. She was a mere block away from where he'd picked up one of his previous victims, Daryn Johnsrude. He spoke to the girl, who explained that she was fifteen and looking for part-time work.

Olson told her that he owned a construction company and wanted someone to wash windows and do odd jobs. He said that she could start right away, and that he was en route to a construction site in a nearby town.

The girl got into the car and Olson started driving, stopping briefly to open two beers. He drank freely as he drove whilst she sipped her drink more cautiously. When he parked to open more beers, he gave her four chloral hydrate tablets, telling her that they would mask the smell of beer on her breath and make her more acceptable as an employee to his business partner. He knew that they would make her drowsy in ten to fifteen minutes, then virtually knock her out.

The teenager took three of the pills then felt uneasy, and hid the fourth inside the back pocket of her jeans. As a paralysis crept over her body and limbs, Olson started touching her. Seconds later, he lost control of the station wagon and crashed.

Amazingly, the sociopath kept control of the situation, holding on to the near-comatose girl and summoning a taxi. Fortunately, a concerned receptionist phoned the police. Olson fled the scene and threw away his bloodstained T-shirt, but was caught and arrested. Chillingly, he was carrying a large knife. He had decided to stab some victims, and to bludgeon or strangle others in the hope that, if the authorities found the bodies, they wouldn't realise that just one man was responsible for the homicides.

The police ran Clifford Robert Olson's details through their system and found that he'd previously been charged with several sexual assaults. On one occasion he'd offered work to a fourteen-year-old boy, driven him to a quiet location and buggered him. But the Crown had decided not to proceed with the case, as there was a problem with a later photo-lineup identification.

Olson had also offered a fifteen-year-old girl a job, driven her to a motel room, raped and buggered her. He'd promised to drive her home afterwards, but had pulled over and violently assaulted her again. She'd only escaped by running into the ladies' room in a petrol station and locking herself in until he'd gone. She was convinced that he was about to kill her – and she was probably right. Again, the charges had been dropped as the authorities didn't believe that the girl would make a good witness. Comparatively few rape cases actually make it to court.

Now a veteran Mountie called Daryll Kettles interviewed Olson, and became convinced that he was the killer of Daryn Johnsrude. But his superiors were not persuaded, and Clifford Olson was let out on bail.

Ada Court's murder

On 21 June, Olson was leaving his house when he looked across the lane and saw thirteen-year-old Ada Court leaving her brother's residence. The popular schoolgirl had been babysitting for her two little nieces, something she did all the time. He offered her a lift and she accepted – she probably knew him, his wife and son by sight. Like his previous victims she was drugged, stripped, probably violated and bludgeoned to death. Her skull and upper jawbone were eventually found near Weaver Lake in Agassiz.

Simon Partington's murder

On 2 July, the paedophile was driving towards a casual construction job in Surrey when he spotted nine-year-old Simon Partington, who was cycling back from a friend's house a mere two blocks away from home. Olson stopped the car, got out and talked to the boy – passersby saw the child talking to a well-built man who looked to be in his thirties. (Olson looked younger than his actual years.) When there was no one in sight, he bundled the boy into his car, abandoning the nine-year-old's prized new bicycle. The paedophile drove the child to a quiet part of Richmond, where he stripped and strangled him.

Simon's deeply religious parents were convinced that he was still alive and community prayers were said for him. Two hundred officers searched for the missing child, to no avail.

The one that got away

Thankfully, Olson's next attempt at murder was a failure. On 6 July he offered two sixteen-year-old girls a job. Later, he sent one of them home, saying that there was only enough work for one teenager. He plied the remaining girl with drink and, when she refused to take the pills that he offered, bundled her into the backseat of his car. He tried to rape her, but she became so hysterical that he dumped her onto the road. She flagged down another vehicle to report the attempted rape, and Olson was arrested. But because the girl had been drinking heavily the charges against him were dropped.

Judy Kozma's murder

Three days later he was driving around New Westminster with a teenage boy whom he'd befriended, when he saw fourteen-year-old Judy Kozma, a talented gymnast, en route to a friend's house in Richmond. He gave her a lift and tried to ply her with alcohol as he drove. She indicated to the older teenager that she didn't want any rum, so he gave her cola instead and told her to pretend that it was laced with spirit. He knew that Olson, like many heavy drinkers, became angry if his friends didn't match him drink for drink.

Judy realised that Olson was trouble, and whispered to his friend that she didn't want to be left alone with him. But Olson became aggressive and dropped the boy off at a shopping mall.

He quickly drove Judy to Weaver Lake. She may have jumped out of the car and he may have deliberately run her over, for when he later returned the Ford Escort to the rental company the front had two dents in it. When she was incapacitated, he stripped her and stabbed her nineteen times, mutilating her so badly that heavy decomposition set in and her body took days to identify.

On 13 July, four days after Judy had been abducted, the manageress of the building where she had lived with her parents was woken by a phone call in which a young girl moaned and whispered unintelligibly. She thought that it sounded like the missing Judy, whose parents had only just moved into the building and who didn't yet have a telephone. Suddenly the line went dead, and, though the manager phoned the police, they were unable to trace the call.

Journalists later suggested that this was indeed Judy Kozma, perhaps phoning in a drugged state from a motel room. But by now – if the police had their dates right – Olson was on holiday with his new wife and baby son in California. (Somehow, he got past the US border monitoring system despite his extensive criminal record.)

What's more likely is that he taped Judy's cries in the few moments leading up to her death, and played the tape down the phone to the manageress, whose number he'd taken from Judy's address book. He'd have used the session as a masturbatory aid.

Raymond King's murder

By the third week in July, the paedophile was back in Canada and offering to act as an informant for the local police. He wanted a hundred dollars for each burglar's name that he gave them. They accepted, as he knew many other criminals and also because it would make it easier for them to keep an eye on him.

But their surveillance methods must have been weak, because on 23 July, Olson offered work to sixteen-year-old Raymond King, who was cycling to the local job centre in New Westminster in the hope of finding a summer job. He drove the boy to a remote location and tortured him by driving a three and a half inch nail into his head. He stripped the teenager and battered a rock into his head until he lost consciousness, before rolling him down an embankment. (His naked body was found on the embankment near Agassiz the following month.)

Possessed of a streetwise intelligence, Clifford Olson continued to rent a different vehicle every few days, making it less likely that the murders would be connected to a single killer. His wife lied to one rental company to save the Olsons the rental fee, saying that the vehicle he'd been given was unsafe so they wouldn't be paying the bill.

Sigrun Arnd's murder

The paedophile claimed another victim in July, offering a lift to a German tourist, Sigrun Arnd, whom he met in the same pub in which he'd first met Joan, his wife. He drove the eighteen-year-old to Richmond, where passersby saw them sitting beside a dyke and thought that they were enjoying a summer picnic. When the coast was clear, he stripped her and battered her to death with a hammer, before throwing her body into a water-logged ditch and piling peat on top.

Terri Lynn Carson's murder

Incredibly, Olson struck for a third time that same month. On 27 July, he approached fifteen-year-old Terri Lynn Carson at a shopping mall in Surrey and offered her a holiday job, which she gladly accepted. He drove her to Chilliwack near Agassiz, giving her lemonade which he'd

196

secretly laced with chloral hydrate. When she was near-comatose from the drug, he violated, stripped and strangled her, leaving her body near the Fraser river. After throwing some of her possessions into the water, he burned her clothes. Her distraught mother reported her missing the following day but the police believed that she was a runaway, as she and her mother had had a massive argument the previous week.

That same month, he plied his male teenage friend with drugs and alcohol and violently raped him. The boy was able to stagger away when the drugs wore off, but was so traumatised that he later attempted suicide.

Louise Chartrand's murder

At the end of the month, the prolific paedophile killed again. Early in the evening of 30 July, he offered a lift to seventeen-year-old Louise Chartrand, who was petite and looked much younger than her actual years. Louise had set off from Maple Ridge to hitchhike to work, something she did on a regular basis. One man gave her a lift part of the way, and then Olson picked her up. He drove her to Whistler Mountain, nine miles away, where he cut her clothes from her body with his knife, shredding her blouse and cutting her trousers at the crotch. Detectives believe that he violated her before battering her repeatedly about the head with a hammer, fracturing her skull. Dumping her body in a gravel pit, he casually left the scene.

Surveillance

As body after body was found – all from Olson's neighbourhood, all of children who were the age that he was most attracted to – police realised that they had to put a more formal round-the-clock surveillance on the paedophile.

In early to mid August, they watched as he entered an old folks' home and two residential homes. After he'd left, the police approached the owners and found that Olson had stolen large sums of money from the premises.

On 12 August he went to Vancouver Island, picked up two young female hitchhikers and began to ply them with drink. Suddenly he ordered one of the women out of the car. Terrified that he was about to abduct, rape and kill the other, the police closed in on him.

Seeing them approach, Olson put his foot down on the accelerator and raced away, but had to stop when he reached the Royal Canadian Mounted Police roadblock. They arrested him and charged him with drunk driving. To their surprise, he submitted without a fight. They searched his car and found an address book with one of the murdered children's names, Judy Kozma, in it.

Determined to keep Olson off the streets until they could investigate further, the police charged him with the burglaries that they had witnessed. He appeared in court and was remanded in custody.

Admission

Detectives kept looking into Clifford Olson's background, but his wife refused to be interviewed and took refuge at her parents' house. And his father's main worry was that the scandal might cost him his caretaking job.

Olson had always denied that he'd murdered anyone, but this time he was shaken by the fact that he'd been under surveillance. Over the next few days he talked with various investigators, and eventually admitted to murdering Christine Weller, Colleen Daignault, Daryn Johnsrude, Sandra Wolfsteiner, Ada Court, Simon Partington, Judy Kozma, Raymond King, Sigrun Arnd, Terri Lynn Carson and Louise Chartrand. He added that he'd give them the location of one of the bodies for free – but that they'd have to pay his wife $10,000 for the next body. When she'd received the payment, he'd give them details of where to find another corpse and so on, up to a total of $100,000.

The law is an ass

Bizarrely, the government, reluctantly supported by the police, now agreed to pay Joan Olson this money in instalments – arguing that it would prevent the police having to work overtime. They also rationalised that Joan could use the money to relocate so she wouldn't have to become a welfare recipient.

She begged her husband to tell them everything, so that the children would have "a Christian burial" and their son could have a new start in another part of the country. According to Olson, she said that they would eventually be reunited in heaven. The authorities now offered the paedophile a total of $70,000 to locate seven bodies, as they'd already found four of his victims. The other $30,000 was for showing them to locations where evidence would be found.

Day trips

A visibly aroused Olson was soon taking detectives to the children's bodies, found unburied on mountainsides and in forests, or hidden in ditches. He was handcuffed to a police officer and guarded by a police dog during these days out, talking openly about the murders whilst detectives, forced to hide their revulsion, recorded his every word. But he refused to admit that he'd raped the children, as he knew that this would result in a longer time in prison. Instead, he said that he'd gotten off on the killing, that this alone had given him a sexual charge.

However, this contrasted with his treatment of the youngsters whom he'd abused but allowed to live – they had all been raped or sodomised. And why had he stripped each victim if the bludgeoning or stabbing was all that turned him on?

Olson loved being the centre of attention during these jaunts, smoking cigars and demanding steak dinners whenever detectives stopped for a break. He tried to act just like one of the boys.

Though shocked by the state of the corpses that they uncovered – most of the females had been extensively mutilated – detectives treated the paedophile courteously so that they could continue to locate the children's remains.

Trial

On 11 January 1982, Clifford Robert Olson was tried on ten counts of first-degree murder. (He wasn't tried for Sandra Wolfsteiner's homicide, because only a few bones – almost certainly hers – had been found, so the body couldn't be formally identified.) Incredibly, he pleaded not guilty on all counts. But when his taped confession was played in court, he changed his plea to guilty and also admitted Sandra's murder, bringing the total to eleven.

The judge then sentenced him to eleven life sentences, which unfortunately had to be served concurrently rather than consecutively due to Canada's liberal sentencing policy. Execution wasn't an option, as the country had repealed the death penalty in 1976. Chillingly, this meant that the sex killer of eleven children would automatically be considered for parole in twenty-five years, though the judge added the recommendation that he never be freed.

Another day out

That November, Olson claimed responsibility for two additional murders, saying that he'd killed another two girls in 1980, that they were both aged approximately sixteen, and that one was buried near Chilliwack, the other on Vancouver Island. He also said that he'd take detectives to the bodies if he could be moved to a prison closer to his wife and child. They flew him to Ontario, where he visited Joan – who had been sending him homemade cookies – then refused to help the authorities. He was returned to Kingston Penitentiary.

A difficult prisoner

Olson had caused mayhem all of his life, and saw no reason to change his ways now that he was in prison. He filed a court action against a prison officer, claiming that the man had prevented him from joining the Book of the Month club. The action was dismissed, whereupon he filed another action alleging that he'd been denied free sleeping tablets. He filed a total of thirty such frivolous claims. (William Begg, profiled in *Sadistic Killers*, has caused similar mayhem in the Scottish legal system, petitioning for everything from greater computer access to gay pornography.)

Eventually the authorities fought back, and a federal judge decreed that Olson couldn't file any more lawsuits without the court's permission.

Determined to remain notorious, he claimed responsibility for some of the Green River murders, despite the fact that he'd been incarcerated when they took place. (The Green River Killer was eventually caught and identified as Gary Ridgeway, a man from a repressed religious background who was both fascinated and repulsed by prostitutes.)

Blood money

Some of the families of the victims now tried to get the money back from Joan Olson, arguing justifiably that Olson had benefited from his crimes – some of the money had been used to buy a television for his cell, and a newspaper subscription. Joan had by now distanced herself from her husband, and said that she'd told her son that Daddy was a "very bad man" who would spend the rest of his life in prison. She added that she'd done nothing wrong and considered herself a good person. The families lost their case.

Self-portrait

Throughout the rest of the eighties and early nineties, Olson remained incarcerated in Kingston Penitentiary, spending twenty-three hours a day in a specially constructed stone-and-steel cell. This had a glass wall in front of the bars to prevent other prisoners throwing scalding water over him. He was one of Kingston's most hated prisoners, as both an informant and a sexually motivated child killer, both types regarded in jail as the lowest of the low.

Still self-obsessed, he began to write his autobiography, *Clifford Olson: Portrait of a Serial Killer*, a poorly-spelt, ungrammatical attempt at aggrandising his destructive life. The book included lists of his favourite colours, pop groups, foods and films, the sort of trivia that preteen girls want to know about their pop idols. He also stated that religion was very important to him, and that he liked "a good Christian woman". (But it appears that he settled for a lawless Christian man, as he later entered into a gay marriage with a fellow prisoner.)

Handle with care

In 1997 his case came up for review, but parole was denied. The psychiatrist who interviewed him noted that Olson saw himself as an intelligent career criminal and VIP, rather than a sub-literate killing machine who had spent most of his adult life in jail.

Determined to curry favour with the authorities, he offered to show them where further bodies were buried, saying that they were six feet under, but again, he failed to locate them. The authorities later dismissed this as a false confession and a plea for attention – Olson hadn't buried his eleven known victims, merely dumped them, so why would he suddenly change his *modus operandi* and dig such deep graves?

That same year, he was transferred within the maximum security prison at Sainte Anne des Plaines, Quebec, to their Special Handling Unit. There he entered a rehabilitation programme, and appeared to be making progress. But in 2003 he told his psychologist that he was no longer interested and dropped out. He remained housed with other very dangerous prisoners in a special section of the jail.

Parole denied

In August 2006, Olson became eligible for parole and attended a four-day hearing in Saint Anne des Plaines, claiming that he had killed up to one hundred and sixty-eight children. The families of the victims wept as they gave their victim-impact statements, and the judge had to order a recess in order to compose himself, but Olson remained impassive throughout. Realising that these statements were oral pornography for the paedophile, some of the families refused to talk about their pain.

Unsurprisingly, the parole board determined that Clifford Robert Olson was still a very dangerous individual and turned down his application. Determined to exert some control, he refused to leave his cell to hear the verdict, saying that he knew their summary would be "retarded". By then he was in his mid-sixties, and the Canadian taxpayer had been supporting him for almost his entire life.

Olson loves to think of himself as a celebrity and may well enjoy many more such days in the judicial spotlight, as, unless he requests otherwise, his case will be automatically reviewed every two years.

CHAPTER TWENTY ONE

GORDON STEWART NORTHCOTT

Police incompetence was blamed when Belgium's Marc Dutroux, Pakistan's Javed Iqbal and British Columbia's Clifford Olson got away with repeated acts of murder. But in the following case, which spans America and Canada, the authorities acted as soon as they found that there was a sadistic paedophile in their midst.

Early abuse

Gordon was born to Sarah Louise and Cyrus George Northcott (both generally known by their middle names) in 1908 in Canada. He was the couple's second child, as they already had a daughter named Winnifred. The extended family later moved to America and the Northcotts settled on a poultry ranch in Wineville, near Riverside, California.

Gordon was repeatedly beaten by his father and was overindulged by his more timidly protective mother. It was the classic recipe for creating a serial killer.

When Gordon was ten, his father allegedly sodomised him. Other family members proved equally violent, and one of his paternal uncles was sent to San Quentin after being found guilty of murder. He would eventually die in jail.

Gordon began to fantasise about having sex with boys, something which clashed with his family's religiosity. As he moved into early adulthood, these daydreams became increasingly sadistic, involving beatings which cumulated in his victims' death. By his late teens he was stronger than his sixty-year-old father, and the tables turned as the older man became afraid of him. Becoming the lord of the manor, Northcott was able to do as he pleased.

He began to hire young boys who were travelling in search of work as casual labour on the ranch. They were at first lulled into a false sense of security by his baby face and articulate speech. Only later did they realise that he had the pitiless eyes of a sociopath. For as soon as he knew that no one was aware of the boys' location, he raped them and turned them into rent boys, lending them out to wealthy local paedophiles. When the men tired of the boys – something which didn't take long, as jaded paedophiles are always in search of fresh flesh – Gordon Northcott tortured and murdered them.

By age nineteen Gordon was acting *in loco parentis* for his fifteen-year-old nephew, Sanford Clark. The latter would later claim that the Northcott family had kidnapped him from his home in Saskatchewan, Canada, and kept him prisoner at the American ranch – but it's likely that he invented this story to distance himself from the murders he witnessed whilst living there.

Known victims

Some time in late 1927 or early 1928, Gordon Northcott raped and tortured a Mexican teenager in his employ, before decapitating him with an axe. (His body was found near La Puente in February 1928, though at this stage police had no idea who the killer was.) Both Louise Northcott and Sanford Clark witnessed this homicide, and George Northcott knew about it.

In April 1928 Gordon struck again, persuading his mother to murder a young boy called Walter Collins. She would later serve life imprisonment for this.

In May, he raped, tortured and killed twelve-year-old Lewis Winslow and his ten-year-old brother Nelson. Their bodies, and that of Walter, were never found as Northcott had dissolved their flesh in quicklime, brought to the ranch by his father. A toenail belonging to one of the ten-year-olds was the only clue that would remain on the grisly ranch.

The paedophile would have continued getting away with murder if he hadn't been incredibly arrogant. A neighbour had seen him flogging fifteen-year-old Sanford and had sworn at him, ordering him to stop. But instead of putting away his whip, an enraged Northcott went to the police and said that his neighbour had used profane language in front of his teenage relative. He also lied, saying that Sanford was training for the priesthood and had been horrified to hear such profanity. Police talked to the neighbour, who said that he'd heard screams coming from the Northcotts' ranch and that they should investigate.

In a similar timeframe, Sanford's older sister had travelled from Canada to visit him and was horrified to see how badly he was being treated. Back in British Columbia, she told their parents that he was being abused and they in turn complained to the immigration authorities.

They took Sanford Clark into custody and began to question him about his experiences. Realising that he was about to be exposed, Gordon Northcott dug up the remaining body parts and buried them in the desert, then fled north to Canada with his mother and sister.

Haltingly, Sanford began to tell of the depravity that had taken place at the Wineville ranch. He was promised immunity if he'd testify against the Northcotts, whereupon he admitted that he'd seen four boys being sodomised and murdered. One boy had been making the death rattle, and Gordon had made him stuff the boy's mouth with mud. He took detectives back to the ranch and they found that Gordon Northcott, his mother and his sister had fled back to their native Canada. George Northcott remained and admitted that he'd known of the murders, but said that he was terrified of his son.

Sanford pointed out makeshift graves in the bloodsoaked soil, and detectives found that they contained fragments of human fingers and ankle bone. They also found the bloodstained axe that had been used to chop up some of the corpses.

Arrest

For two months Gordon Northcott and his mother evaded detection, despite a nationwide hunt in Canada. When they were caught, in British

Columbia and Calgary respectively, they were extradited back to California to face various murder charges. Gordon's sister Winnifred remained missing for some time, and it was feared that he had murdered her, but she was eventually found unharmed.

On the understanding that she'd serve a life sentence rather than face the death penalty, Louise Northcott pleaded guilty to the murder of Walter Collins. When her son heard this, he was enraged and pretended that he'd committed the murder.

At his trial, he said that he'd killed up to twenty boys, but it was impossible to know if this number was accurate as he was desperate for notoriety. He fired his attorneys and represented himself, questioning his nephew about the final noises that some of his youthful victims had made. He continually referred to a large photograph showing one of his decapitated victims, knowing that the jury would have to look at it. It was yet another form of sadism, and a way for him to relive the murders again.

He boasted to the media that he'd go down in history as one of the region's most prolific killers, that he'd never be forgotten. He promised to show the authorities the bodies of his other victims, taking them to various remote locations, but then laughed and said that he couldn't remember where they were. On other occasions he suggested that he was innocent, that someone else had murdered the boys, and that his nephew and niece had made the stories up.

He was sentenced to hang and sent to San Quentin's Death Row. There, he gave the prison's Warden Duffy full details of the torture, sodomy and fatal bludgeoning that he'd inflicted on the boys. The man was disgusted at these acts of almost unbelievable cruelty, but it was clear that Northcott was enjoying recounting them.

Christine Collins, whose son Walter had died at the Northcott ranch, begged an audience with the killer to find out exactly what had happened to her beloved child. Northcott kept her waiting for several hours before telling her he'd had nothing to do with the murder of the little boy.

Meanwhile, Wineville was becoming known throughout America as the home of the child torture murders, and the locals were so upset that they petitioned to have the town's name changed to Mira Loma, which it has been known by ever since.

Death becomes him

On 2 October 1930, the twenty-two-year-old was taken from his cell to face the hangman. He collapsed and begged to be blindfolded, explaining that he couldn't bear to see the gallows. The guards blindfolded him and half-carried him towards the noose. "Don't, don't," he whispered over and over, perhaps echoing the last pleas of his victims. He screamed, "A prayer! Please say a prayer for me!" as the trap was sprung. But there was obviously nobody listening, for the rope failed to break his neck and it took eleven minutes for him to strangle to death.

CHAPTER TWENTY TWO

FEMALE PAEDOPHILES

Female paedophiles are much rarer than their male counterparts, with some experts estimating that they comprise only three percent of sex offenders, whilst others believe that it's as high as thirteen percent. As most women find it easy to gain private access to children – either by having their own or by babysitting for other people – they rarely abduct or murder the objects of their desire.

But there's an occasional exception to every rule. Rose West, convicted of ten murders committed in tandem with her late husband Fred, was undoubtedly a paedophile, as she sexually abused her stepdaughter Anne-Marie and was later found to have indecent photographs of various young children. Imprisoned for life, she has now abandoned her grown-up offspring, telling them that she could never be a mother to them.

Rose was repeatedly sexually abused as a child by her father, and then rescued by Fred West, who is believed to have been molested by his mother. Rose was much younger than Fred and this age gap is also notable in the following case, where a woman helped kill a teenage girl after repeatedly raping her.

JANEEN SNYDER

Janeen started off as the victim of a paedophile. When she ran away at age thirteen, she was seduced by thirty-seven-year-old Michael Thornton and moved in with him. He soon got her a part-time job as

208

a stripper in Las Vegas, whilst he concentrated on running a string of beauty parlours. But Thornton was more beast than beauty, and he was soon bringing home underage girls and persuading Janeen to have sex with them whilst he watched. He also had intercourse with the girls.

At first these sessions were consensual, though they were still statutory rape as the girls were under sixteen. But over time, they became more coercive and, sometime in 2000, whilst living in San Bernardino County, California, they kidnapped a girl in nearby Fontana, repeatedly sexually assaulting, torturing and holding her against her will for a month.

They eventually let her go and she went to the police, after which the pair were charged with lewd acts and false imprisonment with violence. But as there were no corroborating witnesses the case was dropped. (Fred and Rose West were treated with similar leniency when they kidnapped their first shared victim, Caroline Roberts, who was interviewed for *Couples Who Kill*. They too went on to murder future sexual abuse victims rather than leaving witnesses.)

Abduction

On 4 April 2001, Michael and Janeen struck up a conversation with petite sixteen-year-old Michelle Curran shortly after 7am, as she walked to school in Las Vegas, Nevada. She'd had an argument with her sister and was still upset. Thornton would later say that the teenager was hitchhiking to see a friend, and that they offered her a lift.

The couple checked out of their local hotel room and went on the road with Michelle, whom they'd drugged with methamphetamine. Michael Thornton, who had an obsession with photography, took a Polaroid of both females in his Chevrolet, with Janeen at the wheel and Michelle putting on her seat belt. Janeen looks tense whilst Michelle's features, part hidden behind dark sunglasses, are inscrutable. Unfortunately Michelle often played truant, so the authorities weren't surprised when she didn't arrive in class, though her mother reported her missing late that night.

By 6 April, the couple had driven the teenager to Thornton's mother's house in Mesa, Arizona, which was vacant. They stayed there until the

11th, beating and sexually assaulting her. On the 12th, they checked into a hotel near their home in Fontana, California, where again she was repeatedly raped and sexually assaulted. An unidentified man or woman took Polaroids of the couple and their victim during some of these acts.

One of their friends was joining in a foursome when a drugged Michelle became so dehydrated that she lost consciousness. The couple revived her with water, continuing their drug-taking and sexual assaults for another two days before going on the road again. Eventually the trio ended up in a hotel near Rubidoux, California.

Murder

On 17 April, they took the teenager to a nearby ranch, broke in and ate a hasty meal. The couple also ransacked the place for cash. Then, tiring of their victim, they took her around the back to the stables and prepared to execute her.

By sheer chance, the owner of the ranch returned at this very moment and overheard Thornton giving Snyder orders. A shot rang out, and then Janeen appeared at the stables door. The woman phoned the local deputy, who arrived in time to see Michael Thornton driving rapidly away with Janeen Snyder in the passenger seat. He gave chase and, after a mad dash through red lights and over lawns, managed to trap their Chevrolet in a dead-end street.

The pair were charged with breaking and entering and were sent to an LA detention centre, pending further investigation. Their car was searched and found to contain bloodstained duct tape, a ski mask, guns, rope, handcuffs and dildos. They also found the missing teenager's purse and her ID card.

Back at the ranch, police found a large pool of blood on the stable floor, but their search failed to unearth the body of Michelle Curran. It was on the premises, but they didn't discover it.

On 22 April, the unfortunate ranch owner found the girl's decomposing corpse in a horse trailer at the stables. Abrasions on her wrists and ankles showed that she'd been tightly bound, whilst cuts on her arms and legs indicated that she'd been tortured with a knife. Her vagina was also badly swollen and showed signs of having been penetrated by a foreign object. (Impotent men and angry women often penetrate their victims with such objects.) A nylon tie remained around her right wrist and she had been shot in the head.

The couple were now charged with murder, torture, kidnapping, rape and sexual assault. In court, Thornton's defence team said that Snyder was the killer, that she'd tired of having the teenager as her sex slave and had put a bullet through her forehead. Witnesses said that both Thornton and Snyder toted guns, but deciding whodunnit proved complex as the murder weapon hadn't been found. The trial lasted for five long months, during which time the jury heard graphic details of the couple's sexual exploitation of underage girls.

On 30 March 2006, the jury deliberated for seven hours, then found both defendants guilty of all charges. On 10 July they recommended that they both be put to death. In September, a judge confirmed death sentences for both defendants. Unless this is subsequently overturned, they will eventually be executed by lethal injection.

Sadly, women are often culpable of helping paedophile males. One Costa Rican child – now living in a children's home – spoke to the makers of the BBC documentary series *This World* of how her mother would tie her up and let male paedophiles abuse her. She had been repeatedly sexually assaulted from the age of five. There have even been instances of lovelorn single female parents offering their children to their boyfriends, to stop them walking out.

FEMALE PAEDOPHILES WHO BABYSIT

Nineteen-year-old Tanya French from Hatfield, Hertfordshire was recommended in 2004 as a babysitter to a family who had a newborn daughter. She was soon childminding on a regular basis, alongside her boyfriend, Alan Webster, who was twice her age.

Webster came to the attention of international law enforcers when he downloaded seven thousand images of young children being abused. They tipped off local detectives, who raided his home and found numerous paedophiliac images, including indecent photographs of the child that he and Tanya were currently babysitting, a twelve-week-old girl. Further investigation showed that he'd raped the infant four times. Detectives visited the baby's mother, who'd had no idea that the couple were abusing her child.

Tanya French admitted one rape and four indecent assaults whilst her boyfriend admitted four charges of rape and five indecent assaults. Both admitted making indecent images of children. They had made videos in which Tanya fed the baby with a bottle whilst Webster sexually assaulted the child.

Alan Webster was sentenced to life imprisonment with the stipulation that he serve a minimum of six years, but this was later increased by two years by the Court of Appeal. Prosecutors had hoped that he'd get a tariff of eighteen years. Tanya French was given five years. The family of the baby who was raped said that they were appalled that she could be released in as little as two and a half years, and that she was as guilty as her boyfriend – especially as she'd admitted that she looked forward to the babysitting sessions. But the court said that she was comparatively young and had been corrupted by Webster, hence the lesser sentence.

Sent to Bristol's Eastwood Park women's prison, French pretended that she'd committed a non-sexual crime. But when details of her conviction became known, she received death threats and was terrorised by some of the other prisoners when she joined them at mealtimes. Eventually she had to eat all of her meals alone in her cell.

CHAPTER TWENTY THREE

TEENAGE PAEDOPHILES

Though the stereotype of the paedophile is that of a dirty old man, a third of child molesters are teenage boys. As the following cases from America and Britain show, they are often lonely and disturbed individuals who feel compelled to act out their homicidal fantasies.

SAM MANZIE

Torn between the conflicting demands of his childhood religion and his homosexuality, fifteen-year-old Sam Manzie went on to abduct and kill an eleven-year-old boy.

A lonely child

Sam was born in 1982 to Dolores and Nick Manzie. The couple, who already had a daughter, lived in New Jersey. Nick was a deeply devout Catholic, and so Sam was sent to a religious school and to church. Teachers at his school in Jackson Township noted that he was a very sad little boy who often fought with other children and found it difficult to make friends. He began to have vague memories of being frightened – and possibly sexually abused – whilst at kindergarten, started having nightmares and was clearly disturbed.

By age eight, he was wishing that he'd been born a girl. He started fires and put the family's kittens behind the cushions, hoping that someone would sit on them – both fire-setting and cruelty to animals are two of the warning signs that a boy may grow up to become a killer, though many abused children grow out of these destructive behaviours.

At age eleven, Sam began to desire other boys but repressed his desires, as his religion said that homosexuality was a mortal sin. But at summer camp that year, he touched the anus of an eight-year-old boy and made the boy touch his penis. Shortly afterwards, his fantasies became homicidal – now he wanted to kill a younger child.

At thirteen he molested a three-year-old boy he was babysitting, and once again got away with it. By now, he was hanging around the boys' toilets at school, hoping that another teenager would initiate a sexual encounter with him. Picking up on this, some of the other pupils started calling him 'Manzie Pansy'. Deeply ashamed of these feelings, he increasingly avoided his parents and spent hour after hour in his room – though, in a rare moment of honesty, he admitted to his father that he wanted to kill himself, and that no one understood him. Sadly, he was right.

Then, for a short time, he stabilised when he got a computer with an internet connection installed in his bedroom. Soon he was logging on to gay chatrooms, no longer feeling alienated and alone. He set up a website in which he talked about his favourite pop group, the Smashing Pumpkins, and wrote about the importance of friendship. He also admitted that he liked hiding from people and confusing them.

If only Sam Manzie had been able to wait a few more years, he'd have been old enough to leave home and explore his adult sexuality. Instead, he met an older paedophile online . . .

Seduced

By age fourteen Sam had decided he was bisexual, so he was happy to be chatted up by a forty-three-year-old called Steve Simmons. Steve had grown up with a drunken, violent father and an overprotective mother. He was now in a long-term relationship with a fifty-nine-year-old man, though his strongest sexual attraction was to teenage boys. Within a week of meeting online, Sam gave Steve his home number and the two chatted for hours, night after night, about homosexuality.

They arranged to meet at a shopping mall on 10 August 1996, and then they went to the cinema, where they touched each other. Afterwards they kissed in the nearby woods, moving on to Steve's immaculately maintained house on Long Island. There they got into the hot tub, before going to bed with Steve's older lover. But Sam ignored the fifty-nine-year-old, who soon left the house in a jealous rage. Fourteen-year-old Sam had sex twice with forty-three-year-old Steve, and would later tell police that he thoroughly enjoyed it. Meanwhile, Sam's parents were frantic about his disappearance and feared that he was dead.

The following day, Sam went home and confided in his mother that he was bisexual. His suspicious father began to say a rosary every morning, praying that his son wasn't gay. Finding that he was making numerous expensive calls to Long Island, they forbade him to use the phone and his relationship with Simmons petered out for a while. Still confused about his own sexuality, Sam met a teenage girl online and was soon referring to her as his girlfriend.

But she lived far away, whereas Steve Simmons was accessible and eager for further sexual encounters. Soon the two were meeting at motels for the afternoon, where they engaged in mutual masturbation and oral sex. Sam admitted that he fantasised about molesting very young children, and Steve lied in saying that he'd had sexual knowledge of a ten-year-old boy.

Psychiatric help

By spring 1997, Sam was so confused that he wrote to a teacher offering to fellate him. The school told his parents that he needed counselling. Ashamed, Sam subsequently began to play truant and lost a lot of weight. As he was six feet tall he looked lanky and strange. Becoming jealous of other gay teenagers' online friendships, he hacked into their computers and destroyed their files. His mood deteriorated further on 1 June, when his grandmother died – disturbed children are much more likely to kill after the death of a beloved relative. He began to throw things at his parents and kicked large holes in his bedroom wall. Finally, his father called the police, who took him to a private psychiatric hospital. The next day he was released.

Later, he had more substantial counselling and his mood improved somewhat. He was given medication for depression and encouraged to talk about whatever was troubling him. It seems that he mentioned having sex with an older man, and that a nurse passed this information on to his parents who called the police. In August 1997 the authorities began to investigate Simmons, interviewing Sam at length.

At first the teenager co-operated with the enquiry, as he'd fallen out with Simmons and was trying to bond with his online girlfriend. He told police officers about the consensual sex encounters that he'd had with the older man, and showed them photographs that Simmons had taken in which he, Sam, posed in lewd half-naked poses. The police ran Steve Simmons's name through their computer and found that he had earlier arrests for child molestation and sodomy.

The police now asked Sam to call Steve, to get him to say something incriminating on the phone. It was a cruel thing to do, as Sam still had very few friends and must have had residual feelings for his first lover. Worse, Steve was incredibly supportive during the phone call, reminding Sam that he was a bright teenager with a good future ahead of him if he could only find a direction. He said that he still liked Sam – and Sam admitted that he missed Steve.

Afterwards, the police were elated. (Steve had also told Sam that he had a "cute butt", so they had further proof of inappropriate contact between the middle-aged man and the teenager.) But Sam Manzie felt increasingly guilty and torn. Later, he phoned Steve and warned him that the police were closing in. Later still, he destroyed the recording equipment that the police had set up in his room. He became so upset that the social services and the judiciary became involved, and his mother pleaded for them to commit him to a psychiatric institution. But the authorities decided that Sam should go home with his parents, and that the entire family needed to calm down.

YOUTHFUL PREY

The murder

On the afternoon of Saturday 27 September 1997, Sam's parents were out and he was in his bedroom alone – possibly contemplating suicide – when the doorbell rang. He answered to find eleven-year-old Eddie Werner selling candy to make money for a school project. Sam at first said that he didn't want to buy anything, but he felt strong stirrings of desire as he watched Eddie walk away. So he called the boy back and invited him inside. Eddie was reluctant but Sam was persuasive, so the eleven-year-old relented. As soon as he was inside, Sam locked the door. Sensing danger, Eddie began to cry, but the remorseless teenager carried him upstairs to his bedroom. He'd already decided to kill the younger boy.

Eddie continued to sob as Sam stripped him and performed oral sex on him. He didn't have a clue what the older boy was doing and became deeply distressed. Unable to stand the crying, Manzie threw Eddie to the floor and wrapped a cord around his neck, squeezing it tighter and tighter. The eleven-year-old struggled valiantly but was no match for the exceptionally tall teenager.

Sam kept tightening the cord for so long that he went into a fugue state. When he next focused on his alarm clock, an entire forty minutes had elapsed. Wanting a memento of his first kill, the paedophile found his instamatic camera and took a photograph of the dead boy lying on the floor. Then he bundled the body into a suitcase which he hid in the backyard.

That night, Sam stayed in his room as usual. His mother knocked on his door and asked if he wanted something to eat, but he replied that he wasn't hungry. He remained in his bedroom until he was sure that the household was asleep, then tiptoed to the yard, retrieved the suitcase and walked to the adjacent woods with it. Dumping Eddie's corpse in a stream, he returned home.

When Eddie didn't come home for his evening meal, his concerned parents phoned the police who made door-to-door enquiries. Most neighbours were helpful and co-operative, but when they talked to Sam Manzie he accused them of picking on him, becoming defensive and

217

rude. He chainsmoked nervously as he admitted being home when Eddie had called.

Body found

On the Monday, police found Eddie's corpse in a wooded area close to the Manzie house. Checking out possible suspects in the neighbourhood, they found that Sam had a history of violence and so took him into custody for further questioning. His mother accompanied him. Mother and son talked together, and she asked Sam if he'd killed the younger boy. He said that he had, telling her where to find Eddie's possessions and the horrifying photograph.

A life sentence

Arrested and charged, Sam was soon diagnosed as bipolar and prescribed several different tranquilisers. He decided to plead guilty rather than go to trial. He was subsequently sentenced to seventy years and ordered to serve sixty before becoming eligible for parole. (Later this was reduced to a minimum of thirty years.)

Steve Simmons's trial

The authorities now tried to persuade young paedophile Sam Manzie to testify against middle-aged paedophile Steve Simmons. But Sam refused. The judge sentenced Manzie to an additional six months in jail for contempt of court, but this was subsequently waived.

The jury heard how Simmons had first seduced Sam when he was only fourteen, though Sam had been an eager partner. Hearing of one of the sex acts between Sam and Steve, Nick Manzie punched the wall. Simmons said that Nick had verbally abused his son and that only he had provided companionship to the lonely boy. He was sentenced to five years.

Sam Manzie then took the stand to make a victim-impact statement, in which he described his love for Steve and said that he'd seen him as a role model. He added that he'd never regretted the relationship.

ERIC SMITH

A lonely thirteen-year-old with developmental problems, Eric Smith murdered a four-year-old boy in his native New York.

Early trauma

Eric's mother, Tammy, took anti-epilepsy medication whilst she was expecting him, so he may have been damaged in the womb. Born in 1980, he was later adopted by her new husband, Ted Smith.

By age two he was showing developmental problems, banging his head repeatedly on the floor. He also had a bad speech defect. He'd later say that his home life was difficult – and in court there was testimony that his older sister had been sexually abused by a male relative.

From his first days at school, Eric was bullied mercilessly because of his freckled complexion and bright red hair. He was also kept back a year because he was failing academically. He became increasingly distraught and isolated, cycling around town alone for hour after hour.

Eric told his adoptive father that he was sometimes overwhelmed with rage, and asked what to do about it. His father suggested he get himself a punch bag, whereupon Eric went outside and hit a tree, skinning his knuckles and bloodying his palms.

At thirteen, Eric attended a daily entertainment program at a local park. But by now his thoughts were permanently dark, a potent mix of fear and anger. The other children had told him that he was worthless, leaving him full of hate.

Murder

On 2 August 1993, four-year-old Derrick Robie's mother prepared to take him to the park in Savona, New York, as usual. But her younger child was distraught, so the four-year-old said that he'd make the journey alone. As he was almost five and the park was only a block away, she agreed.

But within moments, Eric waylaid the younger boy – who he knew by sight – and suggested they take a shortcut across the field. He hid his bike in the bushes and took Derrick to a wooded area, where he picked the younger boy up and strangled him until he lost consciousness. He also dropped a twenty-six-pound rock on the boy, using it to batter him again and again. Finally, he sodomised him with a stick in a sexually sadistic attack.

His rage not yet satiated, the teenager smashed up the food in Derrick's lunchbox and threw red lemonade all over him, then posed the corpse so that the child's sneakers were positioned next to his hands. Derrick's lifeless body was found by searchers later that same day.

That night, Smith spent several hours at his neighbour's house – he spent lots of time there and they were supportive of the lonely teenager. But this time he talked endlessly about the murder, and it remained his main topic of conversation for the next two nights. He casually asked them, "What would happen if a kid did it?" and they replied that he'd be in need of psychiatric help. He also asked about DNA evidence and how it worked.

Eric relived the killing for the next four days. Keen to talk about it with others, he then went to the local police station. There, he asked if he could be of assistance in solving the crime. The police asked if he'd seen Derrick and he said no. But then he changed his story, describing what the child had been wearing and even mentioning that he'd been carrying a picnic lunch.

"You think I killed him," he said to the police officers, then asked for a break. When his adoptive father brought him a glass of lemonade, the teenager threw it onto the police station floor and became distraught.

The following day he confessed to the murder. When his mother asked him why he'd done it, he repeatedly said, "I don't know," and wept.

Convicted

Smith's guilt was a foregone conclusion, so the judge had only to determine how culpable he was. The defence noted that the anti-epileptic medication (Tridione) that his mother had taken could cause birth defects, and suggested that this explained the teenager's developmental delays which led to his frustration and anger. Their psychiatrist diagnosed Intermittent Explosive Disorder. But Smith had kept his anger under wraps until he'd taken Derrick to an isolated place, which suggested premeditation. As the prosecution put it, "He did a bad thing."

In 1994, Smith was found guilty of murder in the second degree and given the maximum sentence, nine years to life. At the time he showed no emotion and didn't express any remorse.

He spent the remainder of his juvenile years in Brookwood Juvenile Detention Centre, where he received extensive counselling. During these years he admitted that hurting Derrick Robie had given him pleasure, and that it felt good not to be on the receiving end of the abuse.

As he matured, he realised how his painful childhood had left him with uncontrollable anger, and how he'd chosen to victimise someone else as a short-lived means of feeling good. When he turned twenty-one, he was transferred to Clinton Correctional Facility in New York, a maximum security prison. He has said that, when he is released, he wants to conduct research into why children kill.

In June 2004, Eric Smith became eligible for parole. Derrick's parents, who have a surviving twelve-year-old son, were terrified that he would be let out, but, in this instance, his application was denied.

MICHAEL HAMER

Mercilessly bullied at school in England, fourteen-year-old Michael Hamer murdered an eleven-year-old pupil who'd never done him any harm.

A lonely childhood

Michael was born to Julie Hamer in May 1991, by which time his father, policeman Philip Brimelow, had already left the relationship. Six months later, Philip wed another woman and went on to have two children with her. He also had two children from a previous marriage. Michael grew up believing that he was the least favoured child, the one that his father didn't like.

At primary school, the teachers found him to be developmentally slow. He was immature and the other children picked on him. He was devastated at age twelve, during a rare visit from his father, to hear the man admitting, "I have no feelings for Michael at all."

By the time he moved to secondary school, St Gabriel's Roman Catholic High in Bury, Michael was so unhappy that he virtually stopped eating. At lunchtimes he had no option, for bullies regularly stole his dinner money. They also mocked and hit him, so he often pretended to be ill in order to avoid school. As he matured he suffered from increasingly bad acne, which made him want to retreat further from the world. With the violence inside him growing, he took to stabbing a knife into the walls of his home.

In order to cope, Michael retreated into a fantasy world where he was a powerful schoolteacher rather than a helpless student. He made up timetables and a school register, using the names of his fellow pupils. In real life, *they* dominated *him* – but in his dreams, he was in charge.

He began to fantasise about having sex with other boys, though this conflicted with his school's religion. Over time, the fantasies became progressively sadistic and were more about causing pain than having sex.

When he found the courage to tell his teachers about the bullying, the bullies were enraged and warned him that he was a "dead man walking". Hamer now determined to make someone else feel equally afraid. When he saw eleven-year-old Joe Geeling in the hallway at school, he thought he'd found the perfect victim. Joe suffered from cystic fibrosis, which, Michael hoped, would make it difficult for him to fight back.

A cunning plan

For three weeks in February 2006, the fourteen-year-old planned how to abduct the younger boy, writing one note admitting that he was attracted to him, then discarding it and writing two others. Finally, on the day of the murder, 1 March, he wrote another letter, purporting to be from the school's head teacher, saying that Joe should go home with his new mentor, Hamer, to fetch some books.

Sensibly, Joe showed the note to his teacher, who said that it was a fake and to take it to the deputy head. But Hamer saw Joe outside the deputy's office and shooed him away. Two teachers saw the boys together and asked Joe if he had seen the deputy. Hamer stared intimidatingly at the eleven-year-old who said, "Yes." At this stage, the fire alarm went off and everyone was sent outside.

The afternoon passed normally, and Joe left with his friends to begin the walk home. But he doubled back, telling them that he was going to the shop. Sometime after this he met up with Hamer, and followed him to the older boy's semi-detached home.

Michael Hamer took the eleven-year-old upstairs and made a pass at him. But Joe rebuffed his advances, and an enraged Hamer battered him ten times with a frying pan, hitting him so hard that the pan broke. He then fetched two knives and stabbed Joe in the face, neck and body. The eleven-year-old put out his hand at one stage to ward off another blow, sustaining a cut to his thumb.

The fourteen-year-old dragged the dying boy downstairs, then stabbed him in the buttock post-mortem. He put Joe's corpse into a wheelie bin and pushed it to Whitehead Park, half a mile away. There, he hid the body in a gully and covered it with leaves, dirt and discarded furniture.

Afterwards, whilst walking home, he phoned his mother at the call centre where she worked. He said that he was on his mobile because their home phone wasn't working. She called him back and said, "Where the hell have you been?" He replied, "Just over to the park." He sounded completely normal, something that police were later able to verify as the call centre recorded the conversation.

Hurrying home with the empty wheelie bin, he cleaned Joe's blood from the landing carpet. When his mother arrived, he told her that the remaining stains were from a broken red biro. He went on to do his homework, based on the Ten Commandments, had a bath and then went to bed.

The following day his mother dropped him off at school as usual. At 10:45am, Joe's body was discovered with the note from Hamer, now heavily bloodstained, in his pocket. Police went to the school and, at

11:45am, arrested Hamer, who was in the middle of his religious instruction class. He denied everything until 10:30pm, when he spoke to a psychiatrist and confessed, admitting that he'd wanted to make someone else feel as lonely and frightened as himself.

Like most killers, he was keen to hide the sexual aspect of the crime, initially saying that Joe had gone to his house to charge up his mobile phone. But he eventually admitted that he'd wanted to have sex with the youngster, and had become enraged when Joe refused. Asked if there was a special reason why Joe had been victimised, he replied, "It could have been anyone." But psychiatrists were convinced that eleven-year-old Joe's cystic fibrosis made him appear an easy target for the older boy.

Sentence

After pleading guilty at Manchester Crown Court, Michael Hamer – by now aged fifteen – was given a life sentence and told that he'd serve a minimum of twelve years. Mr Justice McCombe told him, "You took away Joe's life and damaged the lives of all who loved him. At the same time, you did a terrible damage to yourself." The sentence was later increased to a minimum of fifteen years.

JOHN WILLIAMS

The aforementioned paedophile murders all took place recently, but the following case from 1965 illustrates that teenage paedophiles aren't a new phenomenon.

Home alone

Eighteen-year-old John Williams lived in Wellington Drive, Dagenham, on the east London/Essex borders, with his family. On 23 September 1965, he had the house to himself and lured his neighbour, eight-year-old Catherine Duncan, into his bedroom. He stripped her and eventually strangled her, then forced her body into a drawer.

Police and local people soon mounted a huge search for the child and John joined in, appearing as concerned as the others. The following week he was best man at his brother's wedding, and showed no apparent signs of distress.

For the next twelve days, the girl's corpse remained in its unlikely hiding place before the police discovered it. Confronted, Williams said that he'd killed the child because she kept knocking on the door to speak to his mother and had irritated him. This didn't explain why the body was naked, so he added that he'd stripped it so that it would fit in the drawer.

Later he changed his story, telling detectives that he'd run the child over with his scooter and accidentally killed her. He knew that he'd get into trouble for riding on the pavement, so he had picked her up and hidden her in the house.

No one believed the teenage paedophile's self-serving stories. He was convicted of murder and sentenced to life imprisonment.

UNSOLVED

Teenage killers are usually caught comparatively quickly, as they tend to lack a vehicle to transport the body and may not have the physical strength to carry it any distance. They are also more likely to have behaved impulsively, leaving themselves no alibi. But occasionally a teenage paedophile does get away with a brutal sex murder, as in the following Welsh case.

Twelve-year-old Muriel Drinkwater – nicknamed 'the Nightingale', because of her lovely singing voice – was ambushed as she walked home through Penllergaer Woods near Swansea, on 27 June 1946. Her killer hit her about the head, raped her and then shot her twice, one of the bullets piercing her heart. At one stage he ejaculated on her dress. Police found her bloodspattered body and the murder weapon, a US Colt 45 service pistol. As this was a farming community, most men in the locale would have been *au fait* with a variety of weapons and would have had access to the guns which were circulating at the time of the murder, immediately after the Second World War.

But the police were convinced that the killer was young, though they didn't give their reasons for stating this. They interviewed twenty thousand men of various ages in the neighbourhood, without success.

Recently, South Wales Police reopened the case, though they have stressed that – despite reports on various websites and a populist television programme – this was not in response to visions of the murder reported by a so-called psychic. Officers said that they have retained the bullets and murder weapon and that the latter may still contain traces of the killer's DNA, lodged in the grips of the gun. They have also extracted DNA from the semen on Muriel's clothing, though it doesn't match that of any offender currently on the database.

They added that, if the killer was a youth in 1946, he will now be in his late seventies or early eighties and is probably convinced that he's gotten away with it. They are hoping that the re-opened investigation and new DNA evidence will give him sleepless nights. They also plan to carry out further DNA testing in case any of the killer's close relatives are on the offender database.

PART FOUR

NEUTRALISING
PAEDOPHILES

CHAPTER TWENTY FOUR

TREATMENT OPTIONS

There are currently one hundred and ten thousand convicted paedophiles in the UK, most of who groom their victims rather than killing them. The majority of them have been offending for six years or more before they are convicted for the first time. In eighty-five percent of cases they molest the child in its own home, or in a caregiving environment such as a babysitter's house or scouting group. Over the decades, the judicial system has experimented with various forms of punishment and post-prison monitoring and will doubtless continue to do so. Below are the recently-piloted and current schemes available in the UK.

Sex Offenders Register

In 1997 the government introduced the Sex Offenders Register, essentially a database of offenders' names, addresses, photographs, risk assessment and *modus operandi*. Some remain on the register for life, whilst others are given shorter notification periods depending on the seriousness of their crimes.

Offenders have to report their new address within three days of moving house. They also have to confirm annually that their details haven't changed. Failure to do so can result in imprisonment of up to five years.

The database can be accessed by police and by some members of the probation service. So, if a five-year-old girl is lured to a shady corner of a park and assaulted by a man pretending to have lost his own child, the police can quickly determine if any other known sex offender in the area has used a similar ruse on girls of this age.

Ninety-seven percent of sex offenders currently register, but the recidivism rate is high. Roy Whiting was on the Sex Offenders Register for his previous abduction and sexual assault of a little girl when he murdered Sarah Payne.

Multi Agency Public Protection Panels

Commonly abbreviated to MAPPPs, these panels are part of the Multi Agency Protection Arrangements system which was put in place by the Criminal Justice and Courts Service Act 2000. These panels, comprising members of the police, probation and prison services in England and Wales, are responsible for managing paedophiles – and other dangerous offenders – in the community.

MAPPPs devise risk-management plans which can involve placing an offender in a probation hostel, putting a civil order in place to prevent him having contact with children, and warning any members of the public with children whom he attempts to befriend.

Befriending schemes

Several years ago, the Home Office funded a pilot scheme called Circles of Support and Accountability, whereby four to six trained volunteers befriended a paedophile after his release from prison. Volunteers helped the former prisoner with practical problems such as finding accommodation and employment, as well as with emotional issues such as loneliness. This scheme was piloted by the Wolvercote Centre which closed in 2002.

Stop It Now! campaign

The Lucy Faithfull Foundation, a child protection charity operating in the UK and Ireland, specialises in safeguarding children from sexual abuse. (The foundation ran the aforementioned Wolvercote Centre.) They assess and treat offenders and victims, and work with the family courts and criminal justice system. They also run the Stop It Now!

campaign, whereby people worried that they might abuse a child, or who have already abused a child, can phone for help. The friends and families of actual and potential abusers can also call in with their concerns. The national freephone helpline number is 0808 1000 900.

Chemical castration

Drugs which tamp down a paedophile's sex drive have been prescribed for the past twenty years. They include Leuprorelin, which switches off the production of testosterone. (It's also used to treat prostate cancer.) Cyproterone, which opposes the action of testosterone rather than stopping its production, is also used. Some psychotherapists prescribe Prozac to paedophiles, as it dampens down their libido and makes it easier for them to concentrate on conversation-based therapy.

Chemical castration, usually in the form of pills, is currently used in America (being compulsory in Texas and several other states), France, Germany, Sweden and Denmark. Side effects include heart problems and osteoporosis, so many paedophiles stop taking the medication because it makes them feel unwell.

Therapists who oppose this treatment note that it doesn't change the rage that a paedophile may be feeling, and that this rage may cause him to penetrate his victims with blunt objects or other penis substitutes.

Naming and shaming

A scheme in which parents can find out the identities of local paedophiles superficially sounds like a good idea – but in practice, it has caused mayhem. When *The News of the World* (who, in fairness, warned their readers against resorting to vigilantism) named and shamed various child molesters, several innocent men were beaten up due to mistaken identity, and sex offenders who were being carefully monitored by the police fled their known addresses and went to ground. A paediatrician had her offices smashed up by vandals who thought that the words 'paedophile' and 'paediatrician' were synonymous. Small wonder that MP Colin Pickthall commented that the campaign to name and shame would appeal to "the rabble-rouser, the violent and the just plain thick".

Sarah's Law

The News of the World has also campaigned for a law named after victim Sarah Payne, murdered in 2003 by known paedophile Roy Whiting. Sarah's Law proposed that parents should be given controlled access to information about convicted child sex offenders in their area.

Sarah's mother said that she'd never have let her daughter play outside if she'd known that there was a convicted paedophile in the area – but Roy Whiting had actually travelled several miles from his home to the field where he abducted the six-year-old. Knowing his home address would have made no difference to the outcome of this tragic case. Many of the British paedophiles profiled in this book carried out their murderous assaults quite a few miles from their residences, including Leslie Bailey, Raymond Morris, Howard Hughes and Brian Field.

The idea behind Sarah's Law came from Megan's Law, currently part of the judicial system in the United States. Megan's Law came into being after paedophile Jesse Timmendequas murdered the daughter of his new neighbours, Megan Nicole Kankas, on 29 July 1994, having previously served nine years for the sex assault and murder of another girl. Timmendequas raped, tortured and strangled seven-year-old Megan after luring her into the New Jersey house that he shared with two other paedophiles. Eighty-nine days later Megan's Law was introduced, to allow parents to know about convicted sex offenders in their area.

One such registered sex offender, based in Texas, whom I'll call Thomas Bell, wrote to me in 2004, suggesting that some of the individuals on the database weren't a danger to the public, but that their pariah status might make them increasingly antisocial. He outlined his own case, as someone who had been charged with (but not convicted of) exposing himself to a child.

Thomas said that, due to a large malformation on the left frontal lobe of his brain, he suffers from severe seizure disorder and often does things that he later has no memory of. Acrimoniously divorced with a six-year-old daughter, he was in a long-term relationship with a supportive girlfriend.

One night he had overnight supervision of his daughter, a common occurrence. The following day his ex-wife told the police that he'd exposed his genitals to the little girl. He was arrested for 'indecency by exposure', and told the police that he had no memory of the incident – but that, if his daughter said that he had done it, then he assumed that he must have done it. The case was given deferred adjudication status for five years. If, at the end of this period, there have been no further incidents, there will not be a conviction and the case will be closed – but he will stay on the Sex Offenders Register for another decade.

Thomas said that the public makes no distinction between a sexual predator and an alleged sexual offender such as himself, and that the register makes everyone look duplicitous by referring to offender's aliases. His 'aliases' were simply versions of his name – Thom, Tom and Tommy. He was also concerned that someone such as himself was using up a long-term place in compulsory group therapy, when many of the predators subsequently added to the register – over twenty-eight thousand of them in Texas – couldn't get a place.

British controls

Meanwhile, back in Britain, the government continues to make minor changes to the law. In June 2007, then Home Secretary John Reid announced new controls on paedophiles, including chemical castration and compulsory lie detector tests. He also said that single mothers could give their new boyfriends' names to the police, and, if any of them had convictions for child molestation, they would be told. Tempering this, mothers who used the information to encourage vigilantism could end up in court. (In February 2008 trials of this scheme began in Cambridgeshire, Hampshire, Cleveland and Warwickshire.)

In autumn 2007, Home Secretary Jacqui Smith opened a new behavioural analysis unit which forms part of the Child Exploitation & Online Protection Service. It will analyse more than one thousand hours of interviews with convicted paedophiles in a bid to understand how they operate, and so help prevent further crimes.

A capital solution

So what kind of punishment do the professionals advocate? I asked former detective Dick Kirby – who served with the Metropolitan Police, the Serious Crime Squad and the Flying Squad, from 1967 to 1993 – for his views.

"I have no doubt now, nor have I ever possessed any doubt, that paedophiles who kill should be executed," says Kirby who has written four hardhitting books – *Villains, You're Nicked!, The Real Sweeney* and *Rough Justice* – about arresting everyone from international gangs and armed robbers to child predators. "The vast majority of Britons want the death penalty reintroduced; it is purely the lack of gumption on behalf of the government, who are terrified of criticism. Far better to leave things as they are and when the next tragedy occurs, to roll out the usual platitudes, call for an enquiry and at the end of it to murmur, 'Lessons have been learnt' – when, of course, they haven't."

So what penalty would he advocate for paedophiles who kill if execution isn't an option? "Incarcerate them forever, with no option of parole."

Kirby has seen at first hand just how manipulative paedophiles can be. He comments: "No-one who is not actively engaged in hunting down paedophiles – i.e. the police – has any idea as to how deviant and manipulative they are. They can evoke tears at the drop of a hat, they can control, absolutely. There is no cure for them. They can and they will pretend that they're cured and the soppy social workers will beam with pleasure and congratulate themselves (as well as the pervert, naturally) on a job well-done. Then, with everybody happy, they can go out and re-offend."

He has also seen how their offending tears families apart. "Nearly forty years ago, I arrested a sixty-four-year-old car park attendant who admitted three charges of gross indecency, another three charges of indecent assault on boys under the age of fourteen and asked for four other cases to be taken into consideration. With the usual manipulative cunning of paedophiles, he sought to put the blame on the boys, saying they had instigated the offences. I discouraged this argument fairly rapidly and he pleaded guilty, his solicitor making much of the fact that he had no previous convictions; for that, read 'never been caught, before'. He was placed on probation for two years. There was a knock-on effect, as well. Two of the victims, both brothers, admitted to their father that they regarded the drooling old pervert as their 'friend' and had enjoyed what he'd done to them. Dad hit the roof (hit one of the boys, as well) and stormed out of the house. Half-an-hour later, having cooled down, he returned to find his wife and the two boys gone."

Kirby recounts a chilling tale about a well-travelled paedophile in his latest book, *Villains*. A member of the public phoned the Metropolitan Police to say that they'd seen a man dragging a girl from a car into a block of flats. A PC who was in the area hastened to the building, and heard a child's scream. He kicked down the door to find the naked ten-year-old tied to a bed, with a middle-aged paedophile, Jimmy Munson, advancing upon her with a gag in his hands. Arrested, he admitted to abducting and raping two other girls in England, one in France, two in Holland and three in Vietnam. Given a lengthy sentence, he eventually died of natural causes in prison.

Arresting paedophiles

Clearly, the law enforcement system needs to arrest paedophiles early in their offending careers and give them lengthy custodial sentences, so that they can't molest further victims. For that, we need specially-trained police officers and judges who understand what paedophiles are really like.

In autumn 2007, I interviewed former detective Ray Gardner (a pseudonym to protect his identity), who spent thirty-two years as an undercover officer in the police force and became an expert on child sex abusers, hosting international seminars about paedophilia.

So how did his professional interest start? Ray explains: "In 1987, together with two other officers, we were tasked with setting up a nationwide school for undercover officers. This ensured that every undercover officer had the same training and would work in the same way. This meant that undercover officers from Scotland could be employed to work in London or anywhere else in the country and vice versa.

"In 1987 I was asked to infiltrate an active paedophile who was a teacher at a well-known private school. I was the first undercover officer to play the role of a paedophile. I successfully infiltrated the teacher and he was subsequently charged. I found this operation the most disturbing role I had ever undertaken.

"At one stage I had to sit with him in a hotel bedroom whilst he masturbated watching child pornography. Not only that, I had to show to him that I was enjoying it as much as him, by making sexual comments whilst watching the video. While I was watching the videos and looking at the victims' faces, all I could see was the faces of my own two children when they were that age. After one meeting with the paedophile I was physically sick. I realised that if an undercover officer were to try to infiltrate paedophiles he would need extra tuition before undertaking any such operation. I then started a school for undercover officers who wished to enter into this field. It was five years before I had my first applicant.

"During the time that I was infiltrating paedophiles, I read many books on the subject, but found that the persons in the books were completely different to the ones that I had met. I then realised that the persons in the book were speaking to police officers, prison officers, barristers, social workers or authors and manipulating them to tell them what they wanted to hear. The social worker wanted to hear that after speaking to the paedophile he realised the error of his ways and showed genuine remorse. The same applies to lawyers and police. In all of the books that I read, they showed remorse and wanted to be cured. I have heard some of them say, 'Why can't you cut my testicles off?' The truth of the matter is that they know that no authority would be allowed to commit an act of GBH even with consent.

"The paedophiles that I met in my role as a fellow paedophile were completely different. None of these showed any remorse and in fact did not believe that they were committing any offence. They felt that they were sexually educating their victims. None of them wanted to be cured.

"I was instructed by them what to do if I were to be arrested. I would firstly deny everything; after all, my accuser will be a child and may not be believed. Secondly, if it did go to court the child would be cross-examined by a trained barrister. If there was overwhelming evidence against me, then I should break down and admit my guilt and ask if I could apologise personally to the victim for ruining his life.

"They said that I should act suicidal and swear that this would never happen again. They said that if I did this I would have a better chance of getting a lesser sentence because I would be showing that I am no longer a threat to society. They did mention that I should state that I was abused as a child. In fact I found that most of the paedophiles who I met *had* been abused as a child, but they did not say that they were abused, they spoke about their first sexual experience."

So was there a common denominator, apart from their unhealthy desire for children, amongst the seductive paedophiles that he encountered? Ray says that there was not. "They came from educated, illiterate, affluent and poor backgrounds. Some were married with children, the majority single. I found that whatever age that they were first abused was the age group that they now preferred."

He adds that, "Paedophiles are the greatest groomers of people that you will ever meet. I especially include adults in this category. They will groom all social workers, police, lawyers, etc. They will always try to portray themselves as victims of society."

(Interestingly, Thomas Bell, who got in touch with me about his experience of being on the Sex Offenders Register in Texas, portrayed himself as a victim of his own ill health and possibly of his vindictive ex-wife.)

Unfortunately, seductive paedophiles are prolific offenders. "On average, every paedophile will abuse two hundred different victims in his lifetime. If you guestimate that one hundred of these victims will go on to be abusers, that will give you some idea of the extent of the problem."

Ray also has personal experience of victimhood. "I myself was abused on three separate occasions by separate paedophiles when I was a child. None of these were reported. I did not know how to report them, or indeed what to report. They did no permanent damage to me and it did not effect my adolescent years. I believe that if you were to ask any man if he had been abused in some form or another, I would be surprised if

YOUTHFUL PREY

at least fifty percent did not admit that they had suffered some non-reported abuse."

As to who they victimise, Ray found that girls were more likely to be victims within the family circle, being abused by their father, uncle or older brother. But he also found that there were far more male victims than female, as it's easy for men to have apparently innocent access to boys in public toilets, parks and swimming baths.

The paedophiles he pretended to befriend were all male. "I have not personally encountered any female paedophiles and it is obvious from records that they are in a minority. I personally believe that the reason for this is because it is a natural reaction to believe that any woman showing an interest in a young girl or boy is merely displaying her natural maternal instincts."

Whether the abuse is by a male or female perpetrator, victims can take many years to report the molestation: "I have found that in many cases where a father has abused his daughters, they have not reported the matter until they have children of their own and they are fearful that their father will abuse their child. That is the reason why many historic abuse cases are reported."

It's obvious that paedophiles can be incredibly manipulative, so does he think that therapeutic clinics can stop seductive paedophiles from re-offending?

"I think that such clinics are well-intentioned and trying very hard to reduce the amount of abuse which their clients perpetrate. They teach the paedophiles how to control their urges. I don't wish to criticise any person for trying to cure paedophiles or to help them to control their urges, but I must repeat that I have never found a paedophile that wants to be cured. They are highly manipulative individuals who love to play mind games with you. I do not believe that you can cure someone who does not want to be cured. I believe that the only way that we can protect the public from these people is to isolate them from the public. I do not believe that the legal system treats paedophile offences as seriously as it should."

He adds, "The theft of a child's innocence, in my opinion, is far more

237

serious than the theft of two million pounds from a train, and should be sentenced accordingly."

So was he resultantly wary of befriending schemes? "I think that paedophiles thrive on any attention from well-meaning groups. The fact that people with no background knowledge of paedophilia could think that they could possibly influence them is absurd. The paedophile would manipulate these people to such an extent that they would use them in any subsequent trial for their defence."

What about drugs to tamp down the paedophile's sex drive? "Chemical or any other form of castration does not work. It only takes away their ability to have sexual intercourse with their victims, it does not stop their urges or their ability to abuse their victims with implements and then kill them after they have satisfied their lust."

Ray is aware that there's no foolproof way of protecting a child from a seductive paedophile. "If you labour the point of the dangers lurking all around the child, you take the risk of taking the child's innocence away yourself. The fact of the matter is that a seductive paedophile will always be able to groom their victims, but for that they need access. The best thing a parent can do is to be more vigilant with the people who have access to their children."

Homicidal paedophiles are harder to avoid. "I believe that if a paedophile wants to take your child, you will not be able to stop him. The problem is that parents of abducted children feel that they are responsible, rather than the evil actions of the perpetrator, who should take one hundred percent responsibility."

He's also wary of schemes which give the public information about a paedophile's whereabouts. "I really think that under the present structure of Megan's or Sarah's Law it would be counterproductive to make the addresses of local paedophiles available to parents in the area. I agree with the fundamental principle that parents should be allowed to protect their children, and that should be a priority over the welfare of paedophiles. In practice it would result in all of the paedophiles being assaulted or worse, and then having to be rehoused in another area. At the same time another paedophile would move into the vacated area."

We discuss a recent Somerset case where an elder in the Jehovah's Witness Church, who had been sexually molesting children for eighteen years – and whose youngest victim was an eighteen-month-old baby – was given a three-year community rehabilitation order after promising to go into therapy. (He was later jailed following a public outcry.) Does such a naïve sentence encourage other paedophiles to offend? Or are most sufficiently arrogant that they don't believe they'll ever be caught?

"All paedophiles will use every advantage they can find to show that they are either victims, undergoing therapy or in a state of remorse. The sad thing is that there are judges who believe what they hear. They genuinely believe that they are giving them another chance to mend their ways, rather than a golden opportunity to be released into the public to offend again. There are many people who state that a child giving evidence about an abuse is tantamount to that child being abused again. It is even worse if the child's evidence is not believed and the paedophile walks free. I know many cases where paedophiles will obtain occupations which give them easier access to children such as Scout leaders, teachers etc. In some cases they are vastly overqualified and can easily obtain employment for more money, but prefer to have an occupation which gives them legitimate access to children. Also, as a custodian of children, they would be less likely to be suspected or accused."

Ray notes that all offences investigated by the police are as a result of a complaint by a victim or witness. "Very seldom are there any proactive investigations. If you look for paedophiles you will find them. If you do not look, then statistically you will not find them and you will not have a paedophile problem in your area."

Being pro-active

Whether we give paedophiles therapy, chemical castration, life imprisonment or death sentences, it's still a case of closing the stable door after the horse has bolted. So how can we protect children from such predators in the first place? The final chapter offers advice from safety experts and child protection organisations.

CHAPTER TWENTY FIVE

PROTECTING CHILDREN

O nly a naïve writer would suggest that the children in this book could have escaped their homicidal killers. Safety experts suggest that children go about in groups of three – but Sarah Payne was with three of her siblings when she was snatched by Roy Whiting. Other British paedophiles – including Leslie Bailey, Raymond Morris and Brian Field – abducted some of their victims at lightning speed. Most of the American child killers profiled here similarly employed a grab-and-go approach.

But such homicidal paedophiles are in the minority, responsible for killing an average of six to eight children a year in Britain. (Contrast this with the eighty children a year murdered by their own parents and caregivers – and the one child a day murdered by its parents in America – and it's clear that most youngsters are more at risk in their own homes than they are on the streets.) Statistically, children are more likely to encounter a *seductive* paedophile who will groom them for months before beginning the sexual abuse. Alert parents can often spot these predators and refuse to allow them access to their family unit.

Self-belief

Paedophiles – like any other criminal type – prefer an easy target, so they look for the unloved, unpopular, bullied or neglected child who will be grateful for their attention. They also hone in on the child who is desperate to please. They may start by giving the child sweets or violent comics, suggesting, "Your mum would be angry that I gave you this, so let's make it our secret." Later the secret becomes pornography, or alcopops, and escalates to sexual abuse.

Children are less vulnerable to such manipulation if they have been brought up to believe in themselves. They should be taught that they own their own bodies, so they shouldn't be made to kiss their grandmother or hug their uncle if they don't want to. They should also be told that no one has the right to touch their vagina or penis, even through their clothes.

They should be taught the real words for body parts. The child who states, "If you touch my penis again, I'll tell," is far more likely to be taken seriously by a paedophile than the child who pleads, "Don't tickle my front bottom." (Suggesting that they won't tell this time – even if they later break that promise – is a good way to ensure that the paedophile doesn't panic and resort to violence.)

Children should know that they are allowed to withdraw consent at any time from another person's touches. Paedophiles sometimes start off by tickling, hugging or stroking a child, and the child understandably consents to, or even encourages, this. They then escalate to, say, naked tickling or genital stroking, knowing that it's difficult for the victim to say no.

A child should also be told not to touch anyone else's penis or vagina, and not to take off their clothes or let anyone take pictures of them naked. As one American paedophile said, "Parents . . . don't tell their children about sexual stuff. I used that to my advantage by teaching the child myself."

Well-meaning parents often balk at talking about such sexual matters for fear that they'll frighten or confuse their children. But Ken Wooden, who runs a child protection programme in America, notes that this isn't the case. "Remember, even very young children know that some things can be dangerous: moving cars, electrical outlets, and so forth. If fear exists, it is almost always diminished when prevention strategies are provided."

Michael Hames, the detective who headed Scotland Yard's Obscene Publications Squad for many years, has estimated that one adult in sixty is a paedophile. Here are just some of the guises that they use to get close to children.

The live-in paedophile

It's not unusual for a man to romance a single mother with a young child and act in *loco parentis*, only molesting the child when he or she reaches their preferred age. The child may then cling to the mother in a desperate attempt not to be left alone with the abuser – but busy mothers often assume that the child is simply at a 'difficult' developmental stage.

The man often tells his victim that if he or she discloses the abuse they will split up the family and be taken into care. Other paedophiles threaten to kill the child or the mother. Yet others rely on the child's previous love for them, or their need to please.

Even if the child dares to divulge the abuse, it's not unknown for the mother to refute the allegations. The paedophile will have spent years gaining her trust and her love, and it's difficult for her to acknowledge that this was all a lie.

Signs of sexual abuse include the victim washing excessively (or, conversely, a sudden refusal to wash in the hope that their lack of hygiene will repel their abuser), wearing layers of clothes even in hot weather, sleeplessness, and withdrawal from the rest of the family. Many abuse victims complain of frequent headaches and stomach pains. They may also have difficulty concentrating, become argumentative or start getting into trouble at school. Children who are being raped or sodomised may have difficulty in walking or sitting down – though many paedophiles confine their activities to mutual masturbation and/or oral sex.

Louise, who tells her story in the sociological text *Child Prostitution in Britain*, was sexually abused from age eight by a male family member. She assumed that all families did this, and didn't realise that the man's behaviour was wrong until she was thirteen. She then told her mother, who didn't believe her. Louise was so upset that she ran away from home and lived on the streets. Ironically, numerous social work agencies returned her to her deeply religious family, refusing to believe that a supposed pillar of the community would repeatedly sexually assault her. Yet convicted paedophiles include everyone from policemen to magistrates.

Rather than ignoring their child's silent pleas for help, parents should remember that eighty-five percent of child sex victims are abused in their own home, or that of a trusted caregiver such as a babysitter. In a San Francisco study in 1981, a tenth of the molested children were found to have been abused by strangers, a third by their fathers and the remainder by stepfathers.

The family friend

The family friend is similar to the live-in paedophile, the main difference being that he doesn't have a sexual relationship with the children's mother. Instead, he's a platonic friend who increasingly takes the children on day trips or even on holiday. The child is put into an impossible position – if he complains that he no longer wants to go on such trips, his parents often accuse him of being ungrateful. They assume that he would tell them if he was being sexually abused. But paedophiles often encourage children – especially boys – to smoke or drink, behaviour that the child knows his parents would disapprove of. He's desperate to keep this 'bad' behaviour secret, something on which the paedophile relies.

Moreover, children often love the family friend – who listens to all of their problems and gives freely of his time – and don't want to get him into trouble. They put up with the sexual abuse in order to maintain their confidant.

The neighbourhood entertainer

Paedophiles often use recreational ploys to lure children to their work premises or home. Dean Corll installed a snooker table in the back room of his candy factory and regularly invited boys to play games there. Profiled in one of this author's previous books, *Couples Who Kill*, he became one of the worst torture-murderers of children in American history.

243

The American paedophile Thomas Soria kept a playroom of girl's dolls and computer games, whilst Canadian Clifford Olson offered his victims highly paid after-school jobs. (Both are profiled in this book.)

Closer to home, Ray Eustace, a single man in his mid-thirties, owned a minicab firm in London in the 1970s. A remorseless child abuser, he installed a Space Invaders machine in his premises and encouraged young boys to play it for free. When he'd won their trust, he'd take them away on go-carting weekends and would share a hotel room with them, encouraging them to wrestle naked together. He repeatedly sodomised one vulnerable boy from the age of fourteen.

Word reached the police that he was sexually abusing these boys, and they called eight of them in with their parents for questioning. But, because their mothers and fathers were present, all of the teenagers denied that Eustace had touched them at all inappropriately. Fortunately, when one boy was questioned later without his foster mother being present, he admitted that Eustace had buggered him regularly for the past two years. Ironically, the foster mother refused to believe this disclosure and told the police that Eustace was a very nice man. (Paedophiles usually seem to be nice men, as this allows them to ingratiate themselves with both parents and children. Seeming to be nice is not necessarily proof of good intent.) At the Old Bailey, Ray Eustace pleaded guilty to abusing the aforementioned teenager for two years and was merely fined £300.

Middlesex-based cartoonist Charles O'Rourke used his artistic talent to impress children and their parents. (He had created the Charlie character for BBC Television.) He abused children over a twenty-year period and his youngest known victim was an eight-year-old neighbour, who he abused until the boy was sixteen. Found guilty at Isleworth Crown Court, he was sent to prison for four years.

The employer

Many of the paedophiles described in this chapter employed children on a part-time basis. As employers, they had power over their charges and could groom them at length.

One such paedophile, Wladimir Dektereff, ran a restaurant in Harrogate, North Yorkshire, in the 1980s, and used young girls as waitresses. He made increasing sexual advances towards a thirteen-year-old and raped her when she was fifteen. He also indecently assaulted another teenager in the kitchen when they were alone together. His youngest victim was ten years old.

Dektereff fled to Portugal with his partner to avoid rape charges, but was arrested in October 2007 when he returned to the UK for a visit. Now in his mid-seventies, he admitted to nineteen indecent assaults and one rape, all of which took place between 1982 and 1985.

As usual, the defence made him out to be the victim, noting that he'd had a drink problem and financial difficulties at the time of the assaults. He was jailed for seven years.

The teacher

Sadly, the number of male teachers has declined in recent years as entirely innocent men fear that they'll be suspected of paedophilia. This robs boys of positive role models and the educational system of good science and maths teachers, areas where men often specialise. Male teachers also encourage competitiveness in the classroom and many boys thrive on this competition, as opposed to the non-competitive/continuous assessment programmes that female teachers are more likely to implement, which are more suited to girls' psychology.

That said, schools – particularly primary schools – are magnets for the paedophile, who often changes jobs as soon as he realises that he is under suspicion. That way, he doesn't have the shame of being sacked or arrested on his record, and he can go to a new school with a clean slate.

But some paedophiles remain with the same educational establishment for many years. From 1969 to 1977, Robin Peverett, then headmaster of Dulwich College Preparatory School in Kent, sexually abused an unknown number of female pupils and one male pupil. A complaint about his behaviour was lodged with the school in 1975, but staff did not act on it.

In adulthood, one such survivor, Jo Evans, found the courage to report the paedophile to the police. She told of how he would undress her below the waist, put her over his knee and violently rub her buttocks, all the while warning her that he was thinking of telling her parents about her poor scholastic performance. The abuse started when she was aged ten and ended when she moved to secondary school at twelve. Jo haltingly told her family of the abuse, but the headmaster was a family friend and they believed his version of events, that he'd been physically disciplining her. They were perturbed by this, as they hadn't given permission for her to receive corporal punishment, but he was allowed to continue socialising with the family.

After Jo went to the police, more than a dozen other female survivors came forward to report almost identical sexual abuse by this man, who ironically had an OBE for services to education. Peverett now faced imprisonment of up to a decade. But he plea-bargained that he'd enter a guilty plea to avoid a prison term. He was given an eighteen-month suspended sentence and placed on the Sex Offenders Register for ten years.

Jo Evans wrote a short book, *An Invisible Child*, delineating how badly the abuse had affected her childhood confidence and her adult relationships. She and seven other abuse survivors subsequently brought a case against Dulwich College Preparatory School for failing in its duty of care, and were awarded compensation payments in an out-of-court settlement totalling over £200,000.

The child care worker

Children's homes, filled with lonely, vulnerable youngsters, are the ideal setting for opportunistic paedophiles. (They are also beloved by pimps, who hang around the gates and start grooming girls as young as ten, using them as prostitutes when they run away or leave care.)

Michael Hames, former head of the Obscene Publications Squad, has written that "the child-care system has been thoroughly infiltrated at all levels by abusers. They have protected each other by subtle processes of misinformation, by the creation of doubt about the credibility of their victims, and by steady reassurances that all is well. Blatant and arrogant denial, even in the face of incriminating evidence, is a reaction native to the mentality of the paedophile, and it gets more of them off the hook than might be imagined."

Throughout the 1960's, paedophile Edward Paisnel visited the Haut de la Garenne care home in Jersey, bringing the children toys and dressing up as Father Christmas. But he sexually abused them mercilessly, whilst threatening to kill them if they told. He was given a thirty-year jail sentence in 1971 and died in 1994. In February 2008, the skull of a child was found in a bricked-up cellar at the former orphanage, leading to speculation that the place was targeted by a murderous paedophile ring. Over a hundred former Haut de la Garenne residents subsequently phoned the authorities to report being flogged and raped there.

Similar widespread abuses have only recently been reported, as victims of the care system watch their children grow up and are vividly reminded of their own abuse.

The children's club master

Paedophiles gravitate to youth clubs, where they can legitimately organise sports and games with children or take them on camping and fishing trips. Though Thomas Hamilton was suspected of inappropriate behaviour with boys and quickly drummed out of the Scouts, he merely set up private boys' clubs – where he partially undressed, spanked and photographed his young victims. Rumours of his unhealthy sexual preferences abounded, yet some of the parents he spent time with were convinced that his motives were pure.

T.J. Soria became a children's club counsellor so that he could lure little girls to the apartment that he shared with his paedophile father. And Arthur Bishop became a mentor in America's Big Brother programme, so that he had easy access to boys.

Parents withdraw their children from such clubs when they disclose that they've been sexually abused, but often don't report the abuse to anyone in authority, leaving the paedophile free to molest other boys and girls.

The clergyman

Detective Chief Inspector Bob McLachlan, who has headed the Paedophile Unit at Scotland Yard, has written that, "The most brutal and sadistic offenders were religious figures, fathers and men of high social status in paedophile rings." And Ray Wyre, a former probation officer who ran the Gracewell Clinic, which successfully treated paedophiles for many years, told *Achilles Heel* magazine, "I've worked with more born-again Christian abusers than any other. The religious sex offender is the bane of my life."

Many of the homicidal paedophiles in this volume were deeply religious, and this is equally true of seductive paedophiles. There have been numerous instances of faith teachers, priests and vicars abusing the children in their care – and many of these cases are only now coming to light.

From 1971 to 1978, ordained priest William Manahan sexually abused boys aged twelve and under at Buckfast Abbey Catholic Prep School in Devon. In 2007, aged eighty, the former teacher pleaded guilty to eight counts of sexual abuse and was jailed for fifteen months.

Such men often project the blame onto the child. One son of the manse told three sets of parents that he was taking their children camping. But he set the tent up in his own parents' back garden, telling the three boys to take out their penises and play with themselves. One of the boys refused and later told his parents, whereupon the man was charged. His supposed defence was that the boys had started it – and his sister said that it was the parents' fault for allowing their sons to go on the camping trip.

The Church often covers for these men. A priest called John Geoghan abused boys over a thirty-year period, his religious work bringing him into contact with children who were often from broken homes and especially vulnerable. He'd befriend them then sexually assault them when he'd won their trust. Geoghan often abused children who were around ten years old, tucking them into bed then sexually molesting them whilst whispering prayers.

Whenever the Catholic Church heard of a complaint against him they'd simply move him to another parish where, of course, he'd offend again.

He was finally ousted from the priesthood in 1998, and charged in 2002 with indecent assault and battery on a ten-year-old boy in a swimming pool. The Church now faced compensation claims from numerous victims (they eventually paid out £6,000,000), and were belatedly forced to look at the other questionable priests whom they'd been surreptitiously moving from parish to parish. As a result, three hundred and twenty-five priests were either dismissed or resigned.

Geoghan went to a prison near Boston in 2002. In August 2003 he was strangled by fellow prisoner Joseph Druce, a thirty-seven-year-old in prison for murder and armed robbery. The priest was taken to hospital but died of his injuries. Several of his victims later spoke out via their lawyers, saying they would rather have had him rot in jail.

Another religious zealot who abused children for most of his adult life was bible study teacher Geoffrey Schaub, who raped and molested children in New York and Miami throughout the seventies and eighties, occasionally being caught and convicted. By 2005 he was the assistant pastor at a Presbyterian church in Oviedo, Florida, and babysitting a seven-year-old child whom he allegedly raped. When police tried to arrest him, he aimed a flare gun at them and a sheriff's deputy shot him dead.

Though these men (and occasionally women) believe that they will be judged in an afterlife by a supernatural being, they admit that the pleasure they gain from sexually abusing children far outweighs the risks of any possible Judgement Day.

The online predator

The internet is a wonderful educational and social resource – but, like all public access media, it can cause problems for the unwary. Paedophiles love to join children's chatrooms, and will pretend to be the same age and gender as the child that they are communicating with.

Lesbian paedophile Kelly Trueman, twenty-three, posed as a sixteen-year-old boy on the internet and began an online relationship with various young females, eventually befriending and indecently assaulting a twelve-year-old girl. She was found guilty of eight counts of indecent assault by a Derby court in February 2004.

In 2002, Stan Mallon, the acting head of the Ulster-Scots Agency, befriended a fourteen-year-old girl online and arranged to meet her for sex in a Chicago hotel room. (He was stopping over in Chicago on his way to a White House reception.) The religious father-of-five would later claim that he was hallucinating whilst sending the emails to the child which solicited sex. But the girl was really an undercover FBI agent trying to trap paedophiles, and sixty-two-year-old Mallon was arrested in America and jailed for twenty-one months.

During an American police sting, one man who infiltrated a child's chatroom – and arrived at her home in the belief that they were about to have sex – was a rabbi. Another man who sent sexually explicit photographs of himself to a twelve-year-old girl, and wrote about how he'd massage her when they met, was a former Catholic priest.

Parents should explain calmly to their children that people online may not be what they seem, and that they should never disclose personal details – such as their full name, address or school – to another chatroom member. They should also avoid sending digital photographs of themselves to anyone that they meet on the internet, and should never open an attachment – some paedophiles email attachments containing photos of their genitalia to children that they've met online. And if they want to meet someone that they've only previously communicated with via the internet, they must take an adult with them and meet in a public place.

The stranger in the park

Child Lures Prevention in America – run by former reporter Ken Wooden – explores the ways that paedophiles lure children away from safety. The most common one is for the man to pretend he's lost his dog and ask the child to help locate it. As Ken says, "There's no lost puppy – that lure has killed numerous children in the twentieth century."

He also describes the authoritarian lure, where the paedophile pretends to be an important person whom the child must obey without question. "Ted Bundy told one child that he was with the fire department and that she had to come with him because her house was on fire." Wooden has also shown that children are susceptible to people who pretend to have media connections. Approached by adults who said that they were from a TV agency and had recording equipment in their van, dozens of children trustingly entered the vehicle.

In reality, the homicidal stranger in the park is in the minority of paedophiles – as has been previously noted, numerous British child predators groom their victims, whilst approximately seven every year will go on to kill.

Trust your intuition

Gavin de Becker, a world-renowned expert on predicting violent behaviour, believes that we should trust our gut instincts about the new babysitter, over-friendly neighbour or anyone else who we instinctively feel may have ulterior motives towards children. But he stresses that fear and worry are entirely different, and that the latter is often self-defeating. "Worry is the fear that we manufacture: it is a choice. Conversely, true fear is involuntary; it will come and get our attention if necessary."

He tells parents to make sure that they choose the people who enter their family lives, rather than being chosen by them. (The same advice holds true for a lost child – it's far safer for the child to approach a maternal-looking woman and admit that they are lost rather than to wait to be picked up, possibly by an opportunistic paedophile.)

He counsels parents to be wary of anyone who rushes the friendship process, or who seems overly interested in their children. But he strikes a balanced note. "Each new person that presents himself in your child's life (and yours) could be the best thing that ever happened – or the worst. He could contribute humour, joy, friendship, even heroism to your family – or he could contribute pain and regret. Parents who appreciate that these are the stakes make more careful choices."

Wisconsin's Assistant Attorney General, Gregory Posner-Weber, who specialises in prosecuting paedophiles, also stresses the importance of open family communications. He notes that, "The safest child is the child who knows that he can bring his problems and concerns to parents and adult caregivers without reproach or retaliation." Young children blame themselves for everything, and we must work to allay their fears.

The legal system, schools and social services must take paedophilia seriously, as should concerned individuals. As Robert M, Holmes writes in his landmark book *Sex Crimes*, "The victimisation of children has grown to such pandemic proportions . . . that each citizen should be vitally concerned with the ramifications of such acts. Children must not be viewed as objects to be used, abused and discarded like broken toys. They are indeed the future of our society and we, as concerned adults, must protect them from those who would do them harm."

APPENDIX

USEFUL INFORMATION

www.childline.org.uk A website aimed at supporting children. Any child who needs to talk in confidence can call their freephone helpline on 0800 1111.

www.childluresprevention.com An American project offering online and general safety tips for parents.

www.kidsmart.org.uk An internet safety programme for young people, parents and schools.

www.millysfund.org.uk Promotes personal safety amongst children. Originally set up by the family of teenage murder victim Milly Dowler, this is now run by the Suzy Lamplugh Trust.

www.napac.org.uk This is the website for the National Association of People Abused in Childhood. Their freephone helpline – 0800 085 3330 – is for any adult who was abused, physically, sexually or emotionally, as a child. Or write to them at NAPAC, 42 Curtain Road, London EC2A 3NH.

www.stopitnow.org.uk A project of the Lucy Faithfull Foundation, aimed at preventing child sexual abuse. Telephone their freephone helpline on 0808 1000 900 if you fear that you will abuse or have already abused a child, or know of another family member or friend who you suspect is behaving inappropriately with a child.

RECOMMENDED READING

Protecting the Gift by Gavin de Becker
Subtitled *Keeping Children and Teenagers Safe*, this book tells parents how to screen babysitters and recognise the warning signs of sexual abuse.

The Family Friend by Matt Lowe
The author charts his years of sexual abuse at the hands of a family friend, and his determination to overcome the resultant adulthood depression.

SELECT BIBLIOGRAPHY

Barer, Burl *Broken Doll* Pinnacle Books, 2004

Barrett, David *Child Prostitution in Britain* Children's Society, 1997

Bidinotto, Robert James *Freed To Kill* Safe Streets Coalition, 1996

Bright, David *Catching Monsters* John Blake Publishing, 2003

Dardenne, Sabine *I Choose To Live* Virago, 2005

de Becker, Gavin *Protecting the Gift* Dell Publishing, 1999

Evans, Jo *An Invisible Child* Book Guild Ltd, 2005

Ferry, Jon and Inwood, Damien *The Olson Murders* Cameo Books, 1982

Furneaux, Rupert *Famous Criminal Cases 6* Odhams Press, 1960

Gerrard, Nicci *Soham: A Story of Our Times* Short Books, 2004

Hames, Michael *The Dirty Squad* Little, Brown & Co, 2000

Hawkes, Harry *Murder on the A34* John Long Ltd, 1970

Holmes, Ronald M. *Sex Crimes* Sage Publications, 1991

King, Gary C. *Driven To Kill* Pinnacle Books, 1993

Kirby, Dick *Villains* Robinson, 2008

Linedecker, Clifford L. *Thrill Killers* Futura Publications, 1987

Long, Bob and McLachlan, Bob *The Hunt for Britain's Paedophiles* Hodder & Stoughton, 2002

Lowe, Matt *The Family Friend* Ebury Press, 2007

Lucas, Norman *The Child Killers* Arthur Barker Ltd, 1970

Molloy, Pat *Not the Moors Murders* Gomer, 1988

Moore, Pete *The Forensics Handbook* Eye Books, 2004

North, Mick *Dunblane: Never Forget* Mainstream Publishing, 2000

O'Brien, Bill *Killing for Pleasure* John Blake Publishing, 2001

Oliver, Ted and Smith, Ramsay *Lambs to the Slaughter* Warner Books, 1993

Pantziarka, Pan *Lone Wolf* Virgin Books, 2000

Payne, Sara *A Mother's Story* Hodder & Stoughton, 2004

Pryor, Douglas W. *Unspeakable Acts: Why Men Sexually Abuse Children* New York University Press, 1996

Rose, Jonathan *Innocents: How Justice Failed Stefan Kiszko and Lesley Molseed* Fourth Estate, 1997

Scott, Robert *Like Father, Like Son* Pinnacle Books, 2002

Smyth, Frank, Hall, Allan and Black, Ray *Real Life Crime Scene Investigations: Forensic Science Case Files* Abbeydale Press, 2006

Wynn, Douglas *Settings for Slaughter* Chivers Press, 1990

Yates, Nathan *Beyond Evil* John Blake Publishing, 2005

MAGAZINES AND NEWSPAPERS
Ronald Castree case:

Jenkins, Russell 'Justice at Last as DNA Traps Girl's Murderer 32 Years on' *The Times*, 13 November 2007

Roy Whiting case:

McVeigh, Karen and McDougall, Dan 'Hidden History of Sex Assaults' *The Scotsman*, 13 December 2001

Mills, Phil 'Life and Times of a Serial Defiler' www.thisisalbion.co.uk

'Shy Loner Who Hid Monster Within' *Yorkshire Post*, 12 December 2001

Armstrong, Jeremy 'My Terror in Cell 336' *Daily Mirror*, 15 January 2007

General:

Laurence, Jeremy (Health Editor) 'How Do You Deal with Sex Offenders, and Does Chemical Castration Work?' *The Independent*, 14 June 2007

Cordery, Jack and Shevills, Jerry 'All Wyred Up' *Achilles Heel*, Issue 13, summer 1992

FILMOGRAPHY

Sally Jesse Raphael: 'Help, My Child Is Missing', produced 1996, broadcast on ITV2 in June 2004

Real Crime: 'Mr Nice Guy' (Brian Field), produced by Granada and broadcast on ITV1 in June 2002.

Real Crime: 'The Perverted World of Marc Dutroux', produced by Granada and broadcast on ITV1 in May 2007.

The Investigation (film about the police's early failure to bring Clifford Olson to trial), produced by Investigative (Voice Inc) for Canadian Television Fund and broadcast on BBC1 in July 2003

The Protectors (two-part series about sex offenders and their probation officers), produced by A Film of Record for the BBC and broadcast on BBC1 in May 2004